The Bible Speaks Today
Series editors: Alec Motyer (OT)
John Stott (NT)
Derek Tidball (Bible Themes)

The Message of
Prayer

D0370026

The Bible Speaks Today: Bible Themes series

The Message of Prayer

Approaching the Throne of Grace

Tim Chester

InterVarsity Press

InterVarsity Press
P.O. Box 1400, Downers Grove, IL 60515-1426
World Wide Web: www.ivpress.com
E-mail: mail@ivpress.com

Inter-Varsity Press
38 De Montfort Street, Leicester LE1 7GP, England
World Wide Web: www.ivpbooks.com
E-mail: ivp@uccf.org.uk

InterVarsity Press® is the book-publishing division of InterVarsity Christian Fellowship/USA®, a student movement active on campus at hundreds of universities, colleges and schools of nursing in the United States of America, and a member movement of the International Fellowship of Evangelical Students. For information about local and regional activities, write Public Relations Dept., InterVarsity Christian Fellowship/USA, 6400 Schroeder Rd., P.O. Box 7895, Madison, WI 53707-7895.

Inter-Varsity Press is the book-publishing division of the Universities and Colleges Christian Fellowship (formerly the Inter-Varsity Fellowship), a student movement linking Christian Unions in universities and colleges throughout the United Kingdom and the Republic of Ireland, and a member movement of the International Fellowship of Evangelical Students. For information about local and national activities write to UCCF, 38 De Montfort Street, Leicester LE1 7GP, England.

USA ISBN 0-8308-2408-1
UK ISBN 0-85111-406-7

Printed in the United States of America

British Library Cataloguing in Publication Data

A catalogue record for this book is available from the British Library.

Library of Congress Cataloging-in-Publication Data has been requested.

P	18	17	16	15	14	13	12	11	10	9	8	7	6	5	4	3	2	1
Y	17	16	15	14	13	12	11	10	09	08	07	06	05	04	03

Contents

General preface

THE BIBLE SPEAKS TODAY describes three series of expositions, based on the books of the Old and New Testaments, and on Bible themes that run through the whole of Scripture. Each series is characterized by a threefold ideal:

- to expound the biblical text with accuracy
- to relate it to contemporary life, and
- to be readable.

These books are, therefore, not 'commentaries', for the commentary seeks rather to elucidate the text than to apply it, and tends to be a work rather of reference than of literature. Nor, on the other hand, do they contain the kinds of 'sermons' that attempt to be contemporary and readable without taking Scripture seriously enough.

The contributors to The Bible Speaks Today series are all united in their convictions that God still speaks through what he has spoken, and that nothing is more necessary for the life, health and growth of Christians than that they should hear what the Spirit is saying to them through his ancient – yet ever modern – Word.

ALEC MOTYER
JOHN STOTT
DEREK TIDBALL
Series editors

Preface

There are already many books on prayer. What, then, is the rationale for another one? The answer is, as one church leader suggested to me, 'when it comes to prayer we have not paid enough attention to the Bible'. He went on, 'we have a whole tradition of prayer with helps and guides which are not necessarily informed by Scripture'. This book is driven by the conviction that we need to reform not only our thinking and behaviour in the light of God's Word but also our praying.

This book is not about my experience of prayer. I am not an exemplary prayer. I once heard the story of a noted Christian writer and academic who was asked by a publishing company to write a book on prayer. He demurred, suggesting five people whom he considered would be better suited for the task. The publishing company said all five had already been asked but had declined! The great Dr Martyn Lloyd-Jones wrote, 'I have never presumed to produce a book on prayer, or even a booklet.'[1] So I had better get my confessions in early: I cannot claim to be a great prayer warrior; I find prayer difficult. As the Scottish preacher Alexander Whyte said, 'If you want to humble a man ask him about his prayer life.'

Instead, in keeping with The Bible Speaks Today series, this treatment of prayer consists of a number of expositions of God's Word. The Bible not only teaches us *about* prayer; it gives us many examples *of* prayer. It is not only God's Word to us but it also teaches how we should respond to that Word. Those Bible prayers form a Spirit-inspired response to the Spirit-inspired Word of God. If prayer is the language of faith, then it should reflect the language of Scripture.

My aim has been a treatment of prayer in which the Bible sets the agenda. Many books on prayer are based on the author's experience. Others respond to the questions we ask about prayer: Does God

---

[1] Lloyd-Jones, *Preaching and Preachers*, p. 169.

change his mind? What about unanswered prayer? and so on. This book will touch upon such questions. But primarily I have wanted the Bible to dictate the focus, for its concerns and interests are often different from ours. It is this contrast that leads at times to polemical elements in the book.

The expositions that follow focus to a greater or lesser extent on the subject of prayer, so much that could have been said on each passage has been omitted. I say to a greater or lesser extent because an understanding of prayer is bound up with a wider understanding of God and the gospel. There is an ancient maxim: *lex orandi est lex credendi et agendi* (the rule of prayer is the rule of belief and of action). If you cannot pray it, then you should not believe it or do it. The reverse, however, is also true: 'one's prayers and one's concept of prayer can rise no higher than one's concept of God'.[2] As I have studied the subject the conviction has grown that the best way to teach prayer is not to teach about prayer per se but to teach the doctrine of God. Eugene Peterson says:

> The reason that we who pray need a theologian at our side is that most of the difficulties of prayer are of our own making, the making of well meaning friends or the lies of the Devil ... We get more interested in ourselves than in God. We get absorbed in what is or is not happening in us ... Prayer has primarily to do with God, not us ... And the theologian's task is to train our thinking, our imagination, our understanding to begin with God not ourselves.[3]

It seems appropriate to take this opportunity to acknowledge the different prayer partners I have had over the years: Paul Sadler and Andrew Smith, Adam Court, John Miller, Rob Spink, Mark Hodgkinson, Stephen Timmis and my wife, Helen. The discipline of praying with them has not only enriched me but has been a major factor in my growth as a Christian. I suspect that I have often used phrases and ideas that originated with others. I trust they will forgive me and be encouraged that their teaching was not in vain. Thanks belong to those who have commented on various drafts, especially Ken Armstrong, Lyssa Bode, Richard Chester, Stephen Timmis and David White, as well as Derek Tidball, the series editor, and Colin Duriez and Philip Duce from IVP. The book is dedicated to Staines Baptist Fellowship with whom I have learnt so much about prayer and who have supported me in far more ways than I suspect they realize.

[2] Peskett, 'Prayer in the Old Testament', p. 28.
[3] E. H. Peterson, *Living the Message*, p. 252.

Abbreviations

AB	The Anchor Bible
AV	The Authorized (King James) Version of the Bible, 1611
BAGD	Walter Bauer, *A Greek-English Lexicon of the New Testament and Other Early Christian Literature*, tr. and augmented by William F. Arndt and F. Wilbur Gingrich, 2nd ed. (University of Chicago Press, 1979)
BNTC	Black's New Testament Commentaries
BST	The Bible Speaks Today
CD	Karl Barth, *Church Dogmatics*
CGTC	The Cambridge Greek Testament Commentary
DJG	*Dictionary of Jesus and the Gospels*, ed. Joel B. Green, Scot McKnight and I. Howard Marshall (IVP, 1992)
DLNT	*Dictionary of the Later New Testament and its Developments*, ed. Ralph P. Martin and Peter H. Davids (IVP, 1997)
DPL	*Dictionary of Paul and his Letters*, ed. Gerald F. Hawthorne, Ralph P. Martin and Daniel G. Reid (IVP, 1993)
EBC	Expositor's Bible Commentary
ESV	English Standard Version
ET	English Translation
GNB	Good News Bible
IBC	Interpretation Bible Commentary
ICC	International Critical Commentary
JSOTSup	Journal for the Study of the Old Testament: Supplement Series
LXX	The Old Testament in Greek according to the Septuagint, third century BC
NCB	New Century Bible (Commentary)
NDBT	*New Dictionary of Biblical Theology*, ed. T. D. Alexander and Brian S. Rosner (IVP, 2000)

NDT   *New Dictionary of Theology*, ed. Sinclair B. Ferguson
          and David F. Wright (IVP, 1988)
NIBC   New International Biblical Commentary
NICNT   New International Commentary on the New
          Testament
NICOT   New International Commentary on the Old
          Testament
NIDNTT *New International Dictionary of New Testament
          Theology*, ed. Colin Brown, 4 vols. (Paternoster,
          1975–78)
NIGTC   New International Greek Testament Commentary
NIV   New International Version of the Bible
NIVAC   The NIV Application Commentary
NRSV   New Revised Standard Version of the Bible (1995)
NTCS   New Testament Commentary Series
NTL   New Testament Library
OTL   Old Testament Library
par.   parallel passage
TDNT   *Theological Dictionary of the New Testament*, ed.
          G. Kittel and G. Friedrich, tr. G. W. Bromiley, 10
          vols. (Eerdmans, 1964–76)
TNTC   Tyndale New Testament Commentary
TOTC   Tyndale Old Testament Commentary
TynB   *Tyndale Bulletin*
WBC   Word Biblical Commentary

Bibliography

Anderson, Hugh, *The Gospel of Mark*, NCB (Eerdmans/Marshall, Morgan & Scott, 1976).

Arnold, Clinton E., *Powers of Darkness* (IVP, 1992).

Baelz, Peter, *Prayer and Providence* (SCM, 1968).

Baldwin, Joyce G., *Daniel*, TOTC (IVP, 1978).

Balentine, Samuel E., *Prayer in the Hebrew Bible: The Drama of Divine-Human Dialogue* (Fortress, 1993).

Barclay, William, *The Plain Man Looks at the Lord's Prayer* (Fontana, 1964).

Barnett, Paul, *The Servant King: Reading Mark Today* (Aquila, 1991).

Barr, James, ' "Abba, Father" and the Familiarity of Jesus' Speech', *Theology* 91.714 (May 1988), pp. 173–179.

Barrett, C. K., *The Gospel According to St John*, 2nd ed. (SPCK, 1978).

Barth, Karl, *Church Dogmatics* III/3, ed. G. W. Bromiley and T. F. Torrance (T. & T. Clark, 1960).

—— *Dogmatics in Outline*, tr. G. T. Thomson (SCM, 1949).

—— *Prayer and Preaching* (SCM, 1964).

Barth, Markus, *Ephesians: Introduction, Translation and Commentary*, vols. 1, 2, AB (Doubleday, 1974).

—— *The Broken Wall: A Study of the Epistles to the Ephesians* (Collins, 1959).

Bauckham, Richard, *Jude, 2 Peter*, WBC (Word, 1983).

—— 'Prayer in the Book of Revelation', in Longenecker, *Into God's Presence*, pp. 252–271.

Beasley-Murray, George R., *John*, WBC (Word, 1987).

Bennett, Arthur, *The Valley of Vision: A Collection of Puritan Prayer and Devotions* (Banner of Truth, 1975).

Berkhof, Hendrik, *Christ and the Powers* (Herald, 1962).

Berkouwer, G. C., *The Person of Christ* (Eerdmans, 1954).

Bewes, Richard, *Talking about Prayer* (Christian Focus, 2000).

Bigg, Charles, *Epistles of St Peter and St Jude*, ICC (T. & T. Clark, 1902).

Blocher, Henri, *Evil and the Cross: Christian Thought and the Problem of Evil*, tr. David G. Preston (IVP, 1994).

—— *In the Beginning: The Opening Chapters of Genesis* (IVP, 1984).

Bloesch, D. G., 'Prayer', in Elwell, *Evangelical Dictionary of Theology*, pp. 866–868.

Bock, Darrell L., *Luke*, NIVAC (Zondervan, 1996).

—— *Luke*, NTCS (IVP, 1994).

Bolt, Peter, and Mark Thompson (eds.), *The Gospel to the Nations: Perspectives on Paul's Mission* (Apollos, 2000).

Bonhoeffer, Dietrich, *Letters and Papers from Prison*, 3rd ed. (SCM, 1971).

—— *Life Together*, tr. John W. Doberstein (SCM, 1954).

—— *The Cost of Discipleship*, tr. R. H. Fuller and Irmgard Booth (SCM, 1959).

—— *The Psalms: Prayer Book of the Bible*, tr. Isabel Mary (SLG, 1982).

Bradshaw, Timothy, *Praying as Believing: The Lord's Prayer and the Christian Doctrine of God* (Regent's Park College/Smyth & Helwys, 1998).

Bray, Gerald, *The Personal God: Is the Classical Understanding of God Tenable?* (Paternoster, 1998).

Brown, Raymond, *The Message of Hebrews*, BST (IVP, 1982).

Bruce, F. F., *Romans*, TNTC, rev. ed. (IVP, 1985).

—— *The Epistle of the Hebrews*, NICNT (Eerdmans, 1964).

—— *The Epistles to the Colossians, to Philemon and to the Ephesians*, NICNT (Eerdmans, 1984).

Brueggemann, Walter, *First and Second Samuel*, IBC (John Knox, 1990).

—— *Genesis*, IBC (John Knox, 1982).

—— *Praying the Psalms* (Saint Mary's Press, 1993).

—— *The Message of the Psalms: A Theological Commentary* (Augsburg, 1984).

—— *Theology of the Old Testament: Testimony, Dispute, Advocacy* (Fortress, 1997).

Brunner, Emil, *The Christian Doctrine of the Church, Faith and the Consummation, Dogmatics*, tr. David Cairns, vol. 3 (Lutterworth, 1962).

Buchanan, James, *The Holy Spirit* (1843; repr. Banner of Truth, 1966).

Caird, C. B., *Principalities and Powers* (Clarendon, 1956).

Calvin, John, *A Harmony of the Gospels*, tr. A. W. Morrison, vols. 1, 3 (St Andrew, 1972).

—— *Commentary on the Book of Psalms*, tr. James Anderson, 5 vols. (Calvin Translation Society, 1845–49).

—— *Genesis*, tr. John King, 2 vols. (Banner of Truth, 1965).

—— *Hebrews and First and Second Peter*, tr. William B. Johnston (St Andrew, 1963).

—— *Isaiah* (A. P. & A., undated).

—— *Romans and Thessalonians*, tr. Ross Mackenzie (St Andrew, 1961).

—— *The Epistles of James and Jude*, tr. A. W. Morrison (St Andrew, 1972).

—— *The Gospel According to St John 11–21 and the First Epistle of John*, tr. T. H. L. Parker (St Andrew, 1961).

—— *The Institutes of the Christian Religion*, tr. F. L. Battles, ed. J. T. McNeill, vols. 20, 21, Library of Christian Classics (Westminster/SCM, 1961).

Carson, D. A., *A Call to Spiritual Reformation: Priorities from Paul and his Prayers* (Baker/IVP, 1992).

—— *For the Love of God*, vol. 1 (Crossway, 1998).

—— 'Learning to Pray', in Carson, *Teach us to Pray*, pp. 13–18.

—— *Jesus and his Friends: His Farewell Message and Prayer in John 14 to 17* (Baker, 1980/IVP, 1986).

—— *Matthew*, vol. 8, EBC (Zondervan, 1984).

—— 'Paul's Mission and Prayer', in Bolt and Thompson, *Gospel to the Nations*, pp. 175–184.

—— *The Gospel According to John* (IVP/Eerdmans, 1991).

—— *The Sermon on the Mount: An Evangelical Exposition of Matthew 5–7* (Baker, 1978).

—— (ed.), *Biblical Interpretation and the Church* (Paternoster/WEF, 1984).

—— (ed.), *Teach us to Pray: Prayer in the Bible and the World* (Baker/Paternoster, 1990).

Chester, Tim (ed.), *Justice, Mercy and Humility: Integral Mission and the Poor* (Paternoster, 2002).

Childs, Brevard S., *Biblical Theology of the Old and New Testaments* (SCM, 1992).

—— *Introduction to the Old Testament as Scripture* (SCM, 1979).

Cho, Paul Y., *Prayer: Key to Revival* (Word, 1984).

Clines, David J. A., *Job 1 – 20*, WBC (Word, 1989).

—— 'The Image of God in Man', *TynB* 19 (1968), pp. 53–103.

—— 'The Psalms and the King', *On the Way to the Postmodern:*

Old Testament Essays 1967–1998, JSOTSup 292.2 (Sheffield Academic Press, 1998), pp. 687–700.

———— 'Universal Dominion in Psalm 2?' *On the Way to the Postmodern: Old Testament Essays 1967–1998*, JSOTSup 292.2 (Sheffield Academic Press, 1998), pp. 701–707.

Clowney, Edmund P., 'A Biblical Theology of Prayer', in Carson, *Teach us to Pray*, pp. 136–173.

———— 'Prayer, Theology of', *NDT*, pp. 526–527.

Coggan, Donald, *The Prayers of the New Testament* (Hodder & Stoughton, 1967).

Conzelmann, Hans, *An Outline of the Theology of the New Testament*, tr. John Bowden, NTL (SCM, 1969).

———— *The Theology of St Luke*, tr. Geoffrey Boswell (SCM, 1960).

Cotton, Ian, *The Hallelujah Revolution: The Rise of the New Christians* (Little, Brown, 1995).

Craddock, Fred B., *Luke*, IBC (John Knox, 1990).

Craigie, Peter C., *Psalms 1–50*, WBC (Word, 1983).

Cranfield, C. E. B., *I & II Peter and Jude: Introduction and Commentary*, Torch Bible Commentaries (SCM, 1960).

———— *The Epistle to the Romans*, vol. 1, ICC (T. & T. Clark, 1975).

———— *The Gospel According to St Mark*, CGTC (Cambridge, rev. ed. 1977).

Cullmann, Oscar, *Prayers in the New Testament*, tr. J. C. B. Mohr (SCM, 1995).

Dabney, Robert L., 'Prayer Reasonable', *Discussions: Evangelical and Theological*, vol. 1 (1890; repr. Banner of Truth, 1967), pp. 670–675.

Davids, Peter H., *The Epistle of James*, NIGTC (Eerdmans, 1982).

Davies, W. D., and Dale C. Allison, *The Gospel According to Saint Matthew*, vol. 1, ICC (T. & T. Clark: 1988).

Davis, Dale Ralph, *1 Samuel: Looking on the Heart* (Baker, 1988/ Christian Focus, 2000).

Dillard, Raymond B., and Tremper Longmann III, *An Introduction to the Old Testament* (IVP/Apollos, 1995).

Dostoyevsky, Fyodor, *The Brothers Karamazov*, tr. David Magarshack (Penguin, 1958).

Dunn, James D. G., *Jesus and the Spirit* (SCM, 1975).

———— 'Prayer', *DJG*, pp. 617–625.

———— *Romans 1 – 8*, WBC (Word, 1988).

———— *The Epistles to the Colossians and Philemon*, NIGTC (Eerdmans/Paternoster, 1996).

Dunn, Ronald, *Don't Just Stand There ... Pray Something!* (Scripture Press, 1991).

Ellingworth, Paul, *The Epistle to the Hebrews*, NIGTC (Eerdmans/Paternoster, 1993).

Elliott, Charles, *Praying the Kingdom: Towards a Political Spirituality* (DLT, 1985).

Elwell, Walter A. (ed.), *Evangelical Dictionary of Theology* (Baker/Marshall Pickering, 1984).

Fee, Gordon D., *1 and 2 Timothy, Titus*, NIBC (Hendrickson, rev. ed. 1988).

Fensham, F. Charles, *The Books of Ezra and Nehemiah*, NICOT (Eerdmans, 1982).

Fenton, J. C., *Saint Matthew*, Pelican Gospel Commentaries (Pelican, 1963).

Ferguson, Sinclair B., *John Owen on the Christian Life* (Banner of Truth, 1987).

—— *Let's Study Mark* (Banner of Truth, 1999).

Forsyth, P. T., *The Soul of Prayer* (1916; repr. Independent, 1949).

Foster, Richard, *Celebration of Discipline* (Hodder & Stoughton, 1988).

—— *Prayer: Finding the Heart's True Home* (Hodder & Stoughton, 1992).

—— *The Celebration of Discipline: The Path to Spiritual Growth* (Harper & Row, 1978/Hodder & Stoughton, 1980).

Frame, John M., *The Doctrine of God* (P. & R., 2002).

France, R. T., *Matthew*, TNTC (IVP, 1985).

Gathercole, Simon, 'The New Testament and Openness Theism', in Gray and Sinkinson, *Reconstructing Theology*, pp. 49–80.

Godet, Frederic Louis, *Commentary on Luke* (ET Kregel, 1981).

Goldingay, John E., *Daniel*, WBC (Word, 1989).

—— 'The Logic of Intercession', *Theology* 101.802 (July/August 1998), pp. 262–270.

Gooding, David, *An Unshakable Kingdom: The Letter to the Hebrews for Today* (IVP, 1989).

Goodwin, Thomas, *The Return of Prayers* (1893; repr. Baker, 1979).

Goold, William H. (ed.), *The Works of John Owen*, vols. 4, 8 (Banner of Truth, 1967).

Gordon, Robert P., *I & II Samuel: A Commentary*, Library of Biblical Interpretation (Zondervan, 1986).

Gordon, S. D., *Quiet Talks on Prayer* (1904; repr. Marshall Pickering, 1984).

Gorgan, G. W., 'Psalms', *NDBT*, pp. 203–208.

Gray, Tony, and Christopher Sinkinson (eds.), *Reconstructing Theology: A Critical Assessment of the Theology of Clark Pinnock* (Paternoster, 2000).

Green, Joel B., 'Persevering Together in Prayer: The Significance of

Prayer in the Acts of the Apostles', in Longenecker, *Into God's Presence*, pp. 183–202.

—— *The Gospel of Luke*, NICNT (Eerdmans, 1997).

—— *The Theology of the Gospel of Luke* (CUP, 1995).

Green, Michael, *2 Peter and Jude*, TNTC (IVP, 1968).

Grudem, Wayne, *Systematic Theology: An Introduction to Christian Doctrine* (IVP/Zondervan, 1994).

Gundry, Robert H., *Mark: A Commentary on his Apology for the Cross* (Eerdmans, 1993).

Guthrie, D., *The Pastoral Epistles*, TNTC (IVP, 1957).

Guthrie, D., and R. P. Martin, 'God', *DPL*, pp. 354–369.

Haenchen, Ernst, *John 2*, Hermeneia, tr. Robert W. Funk (Fortress, 1984).

Hagner, Donald A., *Matthew 1–13*, WBC 33a (Word, 1993).

Hallesby, O., *Prayer* (IVP, 1948).

Hamilton, Tim, *Your Kingdom Come: Praying for the Poor* (Tearfund, 1994).

Hamilton, Victor P., *The Book of Genesis Chapters 1 – 17*, NICOT (Eerdmans, 1990).

—— *The Book of Genesis Chapters 18 – 50*, NICOT (Eerdmans, 1995).

Hanes, David (ed.), *My Path of Prayer* (Walter, 1981).

Hawthorne, Gerald F., *Philippians*, vol. 43, WBC (Word, 1983).

Heiler, F., *Prayer: A Study in the History and Psychology of Religion* (OUP, 1966).

Helm, Paul, *The Providence of God* (IVP, 1993).

Hiebert, Paul, 'Spiritual Warfare: A Biblical Perspective', *Mission Focus* 20.3 (September 1992), pp. 41–46.

Hill, David, *The Gospel of Matthew*, NCB (Eerdmans/MMS, 1972).

Hodge, A. A., *Evangelical Theology: Lectures in Doctrine* (1890; repr. Banner of Truth, 1976).

Hodge, Charles, *Systematic Theology*, vol. 3 (James Clarke, 1960).

Hofius, O., 'Father', *NIDNTT*, vol. 1, pp. 615–621.

Holt, Bradley P., *A Brief History of Christian Spirituality* (Augsburg, 1993/Lion, 1997).

Hooker, Morna D., *The Gospel According to St Mark*, BNTC (A. & C. Black, 1991).

—— *The Message of Mark* (Epworth, 1983).

Horn, H. J. (ed.), *The Puritan Remembrancer* (Stanley Martin, 1928).

Houston, James, *The Transforming Friendship* (Lion, 1989).

Huggett, Joyce, *Listening to God* (Hodder & Stoughton, 1986).

Hurtado, L. W., 'God', *DJG*, pp. 270–276.

—— *Mark*, NIBC (Hendrickson, 1983).

Hybels, Bill, *Too Busy Not to Pray: Slowing Down to Be with God* (IVP, 1988).

Jensen, Phillip, *The Prayer Tapes*, audio tapes (St Matthias, 1986).

Jeremias, Joachim, *The Prayers of Jesus*, tr. J. Bowden et al. (SCM, 1967).

Jung, Kyu Nam, 'Prayer in the Psalms', in Carson, *Teach us to Pray*, pp. 35–57.

Kaiser, Otto, *Isaiah 13–39*, OTL, tr. R. A. Wilson, 2nd ed. (SCM, 1980).

Keddie, Gordon J., *Dawn of a Kingdom: The Message of 1 Samuel*, Welwyn Commentary Series (Evangelical Press, 1988).

Kelly, J. N. D., *A Commentary on the Epistles of Peter and Jude*, BNTC (A. & C. Black, 1969).

—— *The Pastoral Epistles*, BNTC (A. & C. Black, 1963).

Kidner, Derek, *Ezra and Nehemiah*, TOTC (IVP, 1979).

—— *Genesis*, TOTC (IVP, 1967).

—— *Psalms 1 – 72*, TOTC (IVP, 1973).

Knight, George W., *The Pastoral Epistles*, NIGTC (Eerdmans/Paternoster, 1992).

Köstenberger, Andreas J., *The Missions of Jesus and the Disciples According to the Fourth Gospel* (Eerdmans, 1998).

Kuzmič, Peter, 'Integral Mission in a World of Conflict', in Chester, *Justice, Mercy and Humility*, pp. 150–161.

Ladd, George Eldon, *A Theology of the New Testament* (Lutterworth, 1974).

Lane, William L., *Hebrews 1 – 8*, WBC (Word, 1991).

—— *The Gospel According to Mark*, NICNT (Eerdmans, 1974).

Laws, Sophie, *A Commentary on the Epistle of James*, BNTC (A. & C. Black, 1980).

Leopold, H. C., *Exposition of Genesis Volume 1 Chapters 1 – 19* (Evangelical Press, 1942).

—— *Exposition of Isaiah* (Baker/Evangelical Press, 1968).

Lewis, C. S., *A Grief Observed* (Faber, 1961).

—— *Letters to Malcolm Chiefly on Prayer* (Geoffrey Bles, 1964).

Lewis, Peter, *The Lord's Prayer: The Greatest Prayer in the World* (Hodder & Stoughton, 1995).

Lincoln, Andrew T., *Ephesians*, WBC (Word, 1990).

—— 'God's Name, Jesus' Name, and Prayer in the Fourth Gospel', in Longenecker, *Into God's Presence*, pp. 155–180.

—— *Truth on Trial: The Lawsuit Motif in the Fourth Gospel* (Hendrickson, 2000).

Lloyd-Jones, D. Martyn, *God's Ultimate Purpose: An Exposition of Ephesians 1:1–23* (Banner of Truth, 1978).

—— *Preaching and Preachers* (Hodder & Stoughton, 1971).

———— *Studies in the Sermon on the Mount*, vol. 2 (IVP, 1960).

Lohmeyer, Ernst, *The Lord's Prayer*, tr. John Bowden (Collins, 1965).

Longenecker, Richard (ed.), *Into God's Presence: Prayer in the New Testament* (Eerdmans, 2001).

———— 'Prayer in the Pauline Letters', in Longenecker, *Into God's Presence*, pp. 203–227.

Lucas, R. C., *The Message of Colossians and Philemon*, BST (IVP, 1980).

Lucas, R. C., and Christopher Green, *The Message of 2 Peter and Jude*, BST (IVP, 1995).

Luther, Martin, *Early Theological Works*, ed. James Atkinson, Library of Christian Classics (SCM, 1962).

Malina, Bruce J., and Richard L. Rohrbaugh, *Social-Science Commentary on the Synoptic Gospels* (Fortress, 1992).

Marshall, I. Howard, 'Jesus – Example and Teacher of Prayer in the Synoptic Gospels', in Longenecker, *Into God's Presence*, pp. 113–131.

———— *The Gospel of Luke*, NIGTC (Eerdmans, 1978).

Martin, Ralph P., *Colossians and Philemon*, NCB (Eerdmans/MMS, 1973).

———— *Ephesians, Colossians and Philemon*, IBC (John Know, 1991).

———— *James*, WBC (Word, 1988).

———— *Philippians*, NCB (Eerdmans/MMS, 1976).

———— *The Epistle of Paul to the Philippians*, TNTC (IVP, 1959).

McGrath, Alister E., *Christian Spirituality: An Introduction* (Blackwell, 1999).

———— *Luther's Theology of the Cross* (Blackwell, 1985).

Michaels, J. Ramsey, 'Finding Yourself an Intercessor: New Testament Prayer from Hebrews to Jude', in Longenecker, *Into God's Presence*, pp. 228–251.

Milne, Bruce, *The Message of John*, BST (IVP, 1993).

Moloney, Francis J., *Glory Not Dishonor: Reading John 13 – 21* (Fortress, 1998).

Moltmann, Jürgen, *The Crucified God* (ET SCM, 1974).

Moo, Douglas J., *James*, TNTC (IVP, 1985).

———— *The Epistle to the Romans*, NICNT (Eerdmans, 1996).

Morris, Leon, *The Epistle to the Romans* (Eerdmans/IVP, 1988).

———— *The Gospel According to John*, NICNT (Eerdmans, 1971).

Morrison, C. D., *The Powers that Be* (SCM, 1960).

Motyer, J. A., *The Message of Philippians*, BST (IVP, 1984).

———— *The Prophecy of Isaiah* (IVP, 1993).

Mounce, William D., *Pastoral Epistles*, WBC (Thomas Nelson, 2000).

Mowinckel, Sigmund, *The Psalms in Israel's Worship*, tr. D. R. Ap-Thomas (Blackwell, 1962).

Murray, Andrew, *The Ministry of Intercession* (James Nisbet, 1899).

—— *With Christ in the School of Prayer* (Spire, 1953).

Murray, John, 'Man in the Image of God', *Collected Writings*, vol. 2 (Banner of Truth, 1977), pp. 34–46.

—— *The Epistle to the Romans*, NICNT (Eerdmans, 1974).

—— 'The Heavenly, Priestly Activity of Christ', *Collected Writings*, vol. 1 (Banner of Truth, 1976), pp. 44–58.

Myers, Ched, *Binding the Strong Man: A Political Reading of Mark's Story of Jesus* (Orbis, 1988).

Newbigin, Lesslie, *The Gospel in a Pluralist Society* (SPCK, 1989).

Ng, Esther Yue L., 'Prayer in Revelation', in Carson, *Teach us to Pray*, pp. 119–135.

Nolland, John, *Luke 1 – 9:20*, WBC (Word, 1989).

—— *Luke 9:21 – 18:34*, WBC (Word, 1993).

Nygren, Anders, *Commentary on Romans*, tr. Carl C. Rasmussen (SCM, 1952).

O'Brien, Peter T., *Colossians, Philemon*, WBC (Word, 1987).

—— *Gospel and Mission in the Writings of Paul: An Exegetical and Theological Analysis* (Baker 1993/Paternoster, 1995). Also published as *Consumed by Passion* (Anzea, 1993).

—— 'Principalities and Powers: Opponents of the Church', in Carson, *Biblical Interpretation and the Church*, pp. 110–150.

—— *The Epistle to the Philippians*, NIGTC (Eerdmans, 1991).

Olyott, Stuart, *Dare to Stand Alone* (Evangelical Press, 1982).

Oswalt, John N., *The Book of Isaiah Chapters 1 – 39*, NICOT (Eerdmans, 1986).

Owen, Huw Parri, 'The Basis of Christian Prayer' (unpublished manuscript).

Owen, John, 'A Discourse on the Work of the Holy Spirit in Prayer', in Goold, *Works of John Owen*, vol. 4, pp. 235–350.

—— *Communion with God*, abridged by R. J. K. Law (Banner of Truth, 1991).

—— 'A Memorial of the Deliverance of Essex County and Committee', in Goold, *Works of John Owen*, vol. 8, pp. 77–126.

Packer, J. I., *Knowing God* (Hodder & Stoughton, 1973).

—— *Prayer*, audio tapes (Proclamation Trust, 1995).

Pannenberg, Wolfhart, *The Apostles' Creed: In the Light of Today's Questions*, tr. Margaret Kohl (SCM, 1972).

Payne, Tony, *Bold I Approach: The Why and How of Prayer* (Matthias Media, 1996).

Peskett, Howard, 'Prayer in the Old Testament Outside the Psalms', in Carson, *Teach us to Pray*, pp. 19–34.

Peterson, David, *Engaging with God: A Biblical Theology of Worship* (Apollos, 1992).

—— 'Prayer in Paul's Writings', in Carson, *Teach us to Pray*, pp. 84–101.

—— 'Prayer in the General Epistles', in Carson, *Teach us to Pray*, pp. 102–118.

Peterson, Eugene H., *Living the Message* (HarperCollins, 1996).

Pinnock, Clark H., *Most Moved Mover: A Theology of God's Openness* (Baker/Paternoster, 2001).

Pinnock, Clark H., and Robert C. Brow, *Unbounded Love: A Good News Theology for the Twenty-First Century* (IVP/Paternoster, 1994).

Piper, John, *Desiring God* (IVP, 1986).

Rahner, Karl, *Happiness Through Prayer* (ET Burns & Oates, 1958).

Reid, Andrew, *Salvation Begins: Reading Genesis Today* (Aquila, 2000).

Ridderbos, Herman, *Paul: An Outline of his Theology*, tr. John Richard de Witt (ET SPCK, 1975).

—— *The Gospel of John: A Theological Commentary*, tr. John Vriend (Eerdmans, 1997).

Sanders, J. N., and B. A. Mastin, *The Gospel According to St John*, BNTC (A. & C. Black, 1968).

Satterthwaite, Philip E., 'David in the Books of Samuel: A Messianic Expectation?' in Philip E. Satterthwaite, Richard S. Hess and Gordon J. Wenham (eds.), *The Lord's Anointed: Interpretation of Old Testament Messianic Texts* (Paternoster/Baker, 1995).

Schlier, Heinrich, '*parrēsia, parrēsiazomai*', *TDNT*, vol. 5, pp. 871–886.

Shrenk, G., '*patēr*', *TDNT*, vol. 5, pp. 974–1022.

Seitz, Christopher R., 'Prayer in the Old Testament or Hebrew Bible', in Longenecker, *Into God's Presence*, pp. 3–22.

Sergeant, John, *Lion Let Loose: The Structure and Meaning of St Mark's Gospel* (Paternoster, 1988).

Spurgeon, C. H., *The Early Years*, vols. 1, 2 (Banner of Truth, rev. ed. 1962).

Spykman, Gordon J., *Reformational Theology: A New Paradigm for Doing Dogmatics* (Eerdmans, 1992).

St Helen's Church, Bishopsgate, *Read Mark Learn: John's Gospel* (Marshall Pickering, 1999).

—— *Read Mark Learn: Romans* (Marshall Pickering, 2000).

Stott, John R. W., *The Essential John Stott* (IVP, 1999).
—— *The Message of 1 Timothy and Titus*, BST (IVP, 1996).
—— *The Message of Ephesians*, BST (IVP, 1979).
—— *The Message of Romans*, BST (IVP, 1994).
—— *The Message of the Sermon on the Mount*, BST (IVP, 1978).
Stroup, George (ed.), *Reformed Reader*, vol. 2: *Contemporary Trajectories 1799–Present* (Westminster/John Knox, 1993).
Surin, Kenneth, *Theology and the Problem of Evil* (Blackwell, 1986).
Teal Trust, *On our Knees?* (1998).
Tertullian, *De oratione* in *The Early Church Fathers: Ante-Nicene Fathers*, ed. A. Roberts and J. Donaldson, vol. 3 (Eerdmans, 1951).
Thielicke, Helmut, *I Believe: The Christian's Creed* (ET Paternoster, 1968).
—— *The Prayer that Spans the World: Sermons on the Lord's Prayer*, tr. John W. Doberstein (ET James Clarke, 1960).
Tidball, Derek, *The Message of the Cross*, BST (IVP, 2001).
Tiessen, Terrance, *Providence and Prayer: How Does God Work in the World?* (IVP, 2000).
Timmis, Stephen G., *Reading James Today* (Aquila, forthcoming).
Tomlin, Graham, *The Power of the Cross: Theology and the Death of Christ in Paul, Luther and Pascal* (Paternoster, 1999).
Turner, M. M. B., 'Prayer in the Gospels and Acts', in Carson, *Teach us to Pray*, pp. 58–83.
Urquhart, Colin, *Anything you Ask* (Hodder & Stoughton, 1978).
VanGemeren, Willem A., *The Progress of Redemption: From Creation to New Creation* (Baker, 1988/Paternoster, 1995).
von Hügel, Friedrich, *The Life of Prayer* (J. M. Debt, 1927).
von Rad, Gerhard, *Old Testament Theology*, tr. D. M. G. Stalker, vol. 1 (Oliver & Boyd, 1962).
Wagner, C. Peter, 'Territorial Spirits', in Wagner and Pennoyer, *Wrestling with Dark Angels*, pp. 83–102.
Wagner, C. Peter, and F. Douglas Pennoyer (eds.), *Wrestling with Dark Angels: Supernatural Forces in Spiritual Warfare* (Monarch, 1990).
Wakefield, Gordon S. (ed.), *A Dictionary of Christian Spirituality* (SCM, 1983).
Wallace, Ronald S., *The Message of Daniel*, BST (IVP, 1979).
Watts, John D. W., *Isaiah 34 – 66*, WBC (Word, 1987).
Webb, Barry, *The Message of Isaiah*, BST (IVP, 1996).
Weiser, Artur, *The Psalms*, tr. Herbert Hartwell, OTL (SCM, 1962).

Wenham, Gordon J., *Genesis 1 – 15*, WBC (Word, 1987).

———— *Genesis 16 – 50*, WBC (Word, 1994).

White, John, *People in Prayer* (IVP, 1977).

Wiesel, Elie, *Night* (Fontana, 1972).

Wilcock, Michael, *The Message of Psalms 1 – 72*, BST (IVP, 2001).

Williams, Roy, 'Lessons from the Prayer Habits of the Puritans', in Carson, *Teach us to Pray*, pp. 272–288.

Williams, Stephen N., *Revelation and Reconciliation: A Window on Modernity* (CUP, 1995).

Williamson, H. G. M., *Ezra, Nehemiah*, WBC (Word, 1985).

Wink, Walter, *Engaging the Powers: Discernment and Resistance in a World of Domination* (Fortress, 1992).

———— *Naming the Powers: The Language of Power in the New Testament* (Fortress, 1984).

———— *Unmasking the Powers: The Invisible Forces that Determine Human Existence* (Fortress, 1986).

Witherington III, Ben, *John's Wisdom: A Commentary on the Fourth Gospel* (Lutterworth, 1995).

Woodhouse, John, *Preaching Christ from the Psalms*, audio tapes (Proclamation Trust, 2000).

Wright, Chris, *Knowing Jesus through the Old Testament: Rediscovering the Roots of our Faith* (Marshall Pickering, 1992).

———— 'The Old Testament and Christian Mission', *Evangel* 14.2 (summer 1996), pp. 37–43.

Wright, N. T., *Colossians and Philemon*, TNTC (IVP, 1986).

———— *Luke for Everyone* (SPCK, 2001).

———— *Mark for Everyone* (SPCK, 2001).

———— *The Lord and his Prayer* (Triangle, 1996).

———— 'The Lord's Prayer as a Paradigm of Christian Prayer', in Longenecker, *Into God's Presence*, pp. 132–154.

Yoder, John Howard, *The Politics of Jesus* (Eerdmans, 1972).

Young, Edward J., *Genesis 3* (Banner of Truth, 1966).

Part 1
The foundations of prayer

Genesis 1 to Revelation 22
1. The conversation of friends

Prayer is the conversation of friends. It is not a mere convenience for letting God know what we are thinking or what we want. Prayer is that for which we were made. It is at the heart of God's plan of salvation. To understand the tremendous privilege and import of prayer we need to see it in the context of God's purpose to have a relationship with his people. 'It is not possible for us to say, I will pray, or I will not pray, as if it were a question of pleasing ourselves; to be a Christian and to pray mean the same thing, and not a thing which can be left to our own wayward impulses. It is, rather, a necessity, as breathing is necessary to life.'[1] In other words, prayer is part of the definition of what it means to be a Christian. A Christian is someone who knows God through Jesus Christ, and to know God is to converse with him. In this chapter we shall explore the theological context of prayer, namely God's gracious purpose to have a relationship with a people who are his people.

1. The riddle of creation

In the account of creation in Genesis 1 we read:

> Then God said, 'Let us make man in our image, in our likeness, and let them rule over the fish of the sea and the birds of the air, over the livestock, over all the earth, and over all the creatures that move along the ground.'
>
> So God created man
> in his own image,

---

[1] K. Barth, *Prayer and Preaching*, p. 19.

> *in the image of God*
> *he created him;*
> *male and female*
> *he created them.*
>
> (Gen. 1:26–27)

The plural pronoun in verse 26 is suggestive. Instead of saying, '*I will*', God says, 'Let *us*'. It suggests a conversation *within* God,[2] revealing a God who is plural and communal. God creates through his word and now that word is addressed to himself. God is personal and he exists in community. 'God addresses himself, but this he can do only because he has a Spirit who is both one with him and distinct from him at the same time. Here are the first glimmerings of a trinitarian revelation.'[3]

Whereas the plants and animals are made *according to their kinds* (Gen. 1:11, 12, 21, 24, 25), the man and woman are made according to God's *likeness*. What constitutes the image of God in man is a much debated issue, but one element is this communal nature. The God who is relational makes us relational beings. He did not make us solitary but as *male and female*. We are made to exist in community and we are made for community with God. The trinitarian community graciously extends its communal life. God did not make us because of a lack within himself. God exists, as he has for all eternity, in the fulfilled, complete relationships of the Trinity – Father, Son and Holy Spirit in perfect unity. God had no need of a relationship outside himself. Yet, in an act of sheer grace, he created us to share the trinitarian life. Karl Barth puts it powerfully in his exposition of the Apostles' Creed:

> If we make even a slight effort to look on God, to conceive Him as He reveals Himself to us, as God in mystery, God in the highest, God the Triune and Almighty, we must be astonished at the fact that there are ourselves and the world alongside and outside Him. God has no need of us, He has no need of the world and heaven and earth at all. He is rich in Himself. He has fullness of life; all glory, all beauty, all goodness and holiness reside in Him. He is sufficient unto Himself, He is God, blessed in Himself. To what end, then, the world? … How can there be something alongside God, of which He has no need? This is the riddle of creation. And the doctrine of creation answers that God, who does not need us, created heaven and earth and myself, of

---

[2] See Blocher, *In the Beginning*, pp. 79–97; and Clines, 'Image of God in Man', pp. 53–103, for discussions of both the image of God and the plural *Let us*.
[3] Blocher, *In the Beginning*, p. 84.

'sheer fatherly kindness and compassion, apart from any merit or worthiness of mine; for all of which I am bound to thank and praise Him, to serve Him and to be obedient, which is assuredly true'. Do you feel in these words Luther's amazement in the face of creation, of the goodness of God, in which God does not will to be alone, but to have a reality beside Himself? Creation is grace: a statement at which we should like best to pause in reverence, fear and gratitude.[4]

The riddle of creation is not: Is there a God who made this world? That is to get things round the wrong way. Our starting point should not be the reality of the world but the reality of God. In effect, then, the riddle is this: Why is there a world made by such a God? Why should God make us when he was 'rich in himself'? The answer to the riddle is *grace*. Creation is an act of grace in which God invites us to share the love of the trinitarian life. God graciously purposes to have a relationship with people. The riddle of creation is that God should desire to enter into a relationship with his creatures outside his trinitarian being. And this riddle is the foundation of prayer – and not only of prayer but of human existence.

> We have not a God, like the Absolute of the thinkers, alone in His absolute Being, uncommunicating and non-communicative, who 'broods' in that silence ... but a God who emerges from this silence and solitude by creating us as His counterparts and communicating Himself to us. And His will is that this creature should make use of this communication and call upon Him. To answer to the creative loving call of God with responsive love; this is the destiny for which man was created, and this call is the foundation of his being.[5]

We are created to be God's 'counterparts' and to answer his loving self-communication with 'responsive love'. God is not some abstract absolute force or sense of transcendence; he is personal: he hears, sees, smiles. He is the God who inclines his ear and opens his eyes (2 Kgs. 19:16; Dan. 9:18 ESV). Although this is anthropomorphic language by which God accommodates himself to our limited understanding, it nevertheless speaks truly of God's nature and enables us to experience prayer as personal and relational.

---

[4] K. Barth, *Dogmatics in Outline*, pp. 53–54.
[5] Brunner, *Dogmatics*, vol. 3, p. 328.

2. A broken relationship

The community with God for which mankind is made is pictured in the walking of God with Adam and Eve in the cool of the evening (Gen. 3:8). It is hard for us to imagine what this involved, but we can perhaps be guided by the later theophanies in which God accommodates himself to people by appearing in human or angelic form. However it happened, it beautifully expresses the relationship with God for which we were made. Yet, while the Hebrew of Genesis 3:8 suggests a habitual activity,[6] the walking together in the garden is mentioned in the narrative at the point at which the experience is lost. For this time, when God comes to walk with Adam and Eve, they are hiding. Their futile attempts to hide from God are a stark indication that their act of rebellion has immediately broken their relationship with him. Because of sin we can no longer appear before one another naked – as we are – without feeling shame (Gen. 3:7). Still less can we appear before God. H. C. Leopold says, 'Mistrust and fear have ... taken the place of the trust and the free communion with Yahweh, that had previously prevailed. Instead of running to Him they run from Him. Communion with the heavenly Father is no longer their highest delight. It is shunned as an evil and vexatious thing.'[7]

The root problem is not, however, that mankind now shuns the presence of God but that God excludes us from his presence. Humans rejected the rule of God and the fellowship of God. We determined to live in our own way outside a relationship with God. Thus we are cut off from Eden. The angel with the flaming sword becomes a symbol for our separation from God (Gen. 3:23–24). When Cain murders his brother we read, *So Cain went out from the LORD's presence and lived in the land of Nod, east of Eden* (Gen. 4:16). In Genesis 3:23 Adam and Eve found themselves east of Eden. Now Cain is further east. In Genesis 11:2 mankind is still moving eastward – away from Eden – this time to the plain of Shinar where they erect the tower of Babel in defiance of God. The geography of humanity's early movements highlights their distance from God. In every sense, we are a long way from walking with God in the garden.

3. The promise of a people

In Genesis 12 God begins the movement back to the presence of God. The story begins with a promise. This promise to Abraham is

---

[6] See V. P. Hamilton, *Genesis 1 – 17*, p. 192.
[7] Leopold, *Genesis*, p. 156.

that which shapes the story of the Bible and salvation, and ultimately the history of the world, and beyond history the consummation of all things. At the heart of that promise is the promise of a people. Abraham will have offspring who will become a nation (Gen. 12:2). In Genesis 17 God makes it clear that the promise is not just for a people but a people who will be God's people. *I will establish my covenant as an everlasting covenant between me and you and your descendants after you for the generations to come, to be your God and the God of your descendants after you* (Gen. 17:7). The sign of circumcision is given as a sign that Abraham's descendants are God's own people (Gen. 17:9–14). At the heart of God's saving purposes are a people who are God's people. God is creating a people who know him and are known by him. His purpose is to restore the broken relationship of Eden.

By the time we come to the opening chapter of Exodus the single man Abraham has become a great nation as God promised. But they are a people in slavery and exiled from the Promised Land. When God meets with Moses in the burning bush he says, *I have indeed seen the misery of* my people *in Egypt* ... *I am sending you to Pharaoh to bring* my people *the Israelites out of Egypt* (Exod. 3:7, 10; my emphasis). God promises to rescue his people and bring them to the land promised to Abraham. Again at the heart of the promise is the restoration of relationship: *I will take you as my own people, and I will be your God* (Exod. 6:7). Their redemption *from* slavery is also a redemption *to* something. They are rescued *to* know and worship God. The land is to be the place where God lives with his people. The promise that 'I will be their God and they will my people' runs throughout the biblical narrative and is the foundation for the Bible's understanding of prayer. 'Prayer in the Old Testament is not special content, particular technique, or the quality of a person's spirituality,' says Christopher Seitz. 'Rather, it is talk with the living God!'[8] It is this covenant relationship that gives biblical prayer its rich texture.

> Covenant partnership means that God cannot and does not use the divine prerogatives of power to reduce Israel's response to monotones of praise, submission, or silence. Such limitations on human response effectively eviscerate genuine covenant relationship, substituting instead enforced obedience and passive devotion. Covenant partnership also means that Israel cannot and does not withhold from God the full range of human experience.[9]

[8] Seitz, 'Prayer in the Old Testament', pp. 5–6.
[9] Balentine, *Prayer in the Hebrew Bible*, p. 263.

God redeems his people from slavery through the exodus and brings them to Sinai, where he makes a covenant with them and gives them his law. Together the exodus and Sinai define Israel's identity as a nation, constituting them as the people of God. God's purpose to restore his relationship with mankind is focused on one nation. But his intent is that by being *near* this people the nations will be drawn to life under his gracious rule (Deut. 4:5–8). At Sinai the people meet with God. Or rather they almost meet God. For rescue from Egypt is only a picture of the redemption God intends for his people, a redemption from the root problems of sin, judgment and death. When they encounter God at Sinai it is a long way from the experience of Adam and Eve walking in the garden. They must ritually purify themselves, reminding them that their sin cuts them off from God. Limits are placed around the mountain because those who step on to it or press forward to see the Lord will die – the Lord *will break out against them* (Exod. 19:12, 21, 24). As the firestorm of God's presence covers the mountain, we read, *Everyone in the camp trembled* (Exod. 19:16). God is present with his people, but it is hardly the intimate relationship for which we were made.

The instructions for the construction of the tabernacle, and later the temple, capture this sense of presence and distance. The tabernacle represents God's presence with his people, but at the same time its various courts and the curtain in front of the Holy of Holies keep people from the consuming presence of God. God's presence with his people at this point is mediated by symbols. The pillars of cloud and fire, the ark of the covenant and the tent of meeting express God's presence with his people to protect and guide them. When the people of God break camp, the tabernacle is taken down and goes with them so that God 'travels' with his people. But it is a mediated presence. He is with them through symbol and sign. The symbols point forward to something else. They partially fulfil the promise to Abraham that God will have a people who are his people. But the partial nature of the fulfilment points forward to a coming reality.

At Sinai, too, the people sin against God by constructing a golden calf. In response God says he will give them the land, *But I will not go with you, because you are a stiff-necked people and I might destroy you on the way* (Exod. 33:3). But, argues Moses as he intercedes for the people, there is no point in prosperity in the land without the presence of God (Exod. 33:15–16). The genius of Moses is to recognize that salvation *is* fellowship with God.

Because God is with his people they drive out the nations. The book of Joshua presents the conquest of the land as the battle of

God. Even when the people are repeatedly unfaithful to God, he does not disown them as his people. Instead he sends his judges to rescue them. Not until David has brought rest to the nation from its enemies and, more significantly, not until God has promised a 'house' (a dynasty) to David does David's son, Solomon, build a 'house' (a temple) for God. As the temple is consecrated God's glory descends, so that the priests have to evacuate the building (1 Kgs. 8:10–11). This is the place God has chosen for his Name to dwell (1 Kgs. 8:29). In his prayer of dedication, Solomon asks God to be attentive to prayer offered towards the temple (1 Kgs. 8:29–51). But we are not to mistake the temple for the reality to which it points, for the God whom the heavens cannot contain does not live in something made by human hands. The prayer made towards the temple is answered *from heaven* (1 Kgs. 8:27–30).

4. A tale of two psalms

Psalm 48 describes Mount Zion as *beautiful in its loftiness, / the joy of the whole earth* (48:2). The kings who advance against it are astounded at what they see, and flee in terror (48:4–5). The reader is invited to take a tour round the walls and marvel at its splendour (48:12–13). By the standards of geography and politics, however, these are ridiculous statements. Mount Zion was not the greatest mountain in the world and certainly not the loftiest. The city of Jerusalem was not of special significance in the economy or politics of the region. But the psalmist is reflecting a theological reality: what makes Jerusalem great is that God is with her; what makes her secure is God's presence. *God is in her citadels, / he has shown himself to be her fortress ... God makes her secure for ever ... Mount Zion rejoices ... because of your judgments* (48:3, 8, 11). What makes Jerusalem so special is that she is *the city of our God, his holy mountain* (48:1). Jerusalem, with the temple at its heart, is the symbol of God's presence with his people. Psalm 48 is a statement of Israelite faith. It is Israel's relationship with God that singles her out among the nations.

How poignant, then, to read Psalm 137. By the time Psalm 137 is written things have changed radically. Jerusalem has fallen. The temple has been destroyed. The people are once again in slavery. To remember Zion now is to weep (137:1). The books of 1 and 2 Kings, together with the great prophecies of Jeremiah and Ezekiel, are written to demonstrate that this has not happened because God was unfaithful to his promises but because the people were unfaithful. The destruction of the temple was the result of God's judgment – a fulfilment of the covenant warnings in Deuteronomy. At the point at which the temple is dedicated – the high point of the old covenant kingdom – the explanation of its collapse is given in a word from God to Solomon. If the people turn from God they and the temple will be destroyed: *all who pass by will be appalled and will scoff and say, 'Why has the LORD done such a thing to this land and to this temple?' People will answer, 'Because they have forsaken the LORD their God, who brought their fathers out of Egypt, and have embraced other gods, worshipping and serving them – that is why the LORD brought all this disaster on them'* (1 Kgs. 9:8–9).

In the end Israel presumed too much on God's presence. They mistook the sign for the reality. They put their trust in the bricks and mortar of the temple building – despite the warnings of Jeremiah (Jer. 7:1–15). But what Ezekiel sees in a poignant reversal of 1 Kings 8:10–11 is that the glory of God has departed from the temple building (Ezek. 10:18–19). Jerusalem has fallen. The temple has been destroyed. The people are exiled. All the symbols of God's presence with his people have gone. All that is left is the bare promise of God and it is on this promise that the prophets reconstruct hope for God's people. Jeremiah speaks of a new covenant in which not only will there be restoration after judgment but symbol will give way to reality. The law will be written on people's hearts and knowledge of God will be unmediated. At the heart of this new covenant is once again the promise of a relationship:

> *I will be their God,*
> *and they will be my people.*
>
> (Jer. 31:33)

Ezekiel sees a vision of a new temple in a new Jerusalem (Ezek. 40 – 48). His book closes in dramatic fashion with the name of the city: *THE LORD IS THERE* (Ezek. 48:35). Once again God will be with his people. Once again he will be their God and they will be his people.

When the returning exiles rebuilt the temple it was not Ezekiel's temple they built. It was not even a replica of Solomon's temple. Those who remembered the previous temple wept when they saw the meagre scale of the replacement (Ezra 3:11–13). This was not the fulfilment of God's promises. Even as they encouraged the people to complete the rebuilding (Ezra 6:14), the post-exilic prophets directed their attention beyond the replacement temple to a far greater work of God. Haggai promised that *the glory of this present house will be greater than the glory of the former house* (Hag. 2:9). The prophet Zechariah saw in a series of visions a greater building project that God himself is going to accomplish (Zech. 1 – 6). *Shout and be glad, O Daughter of Zion,* the Lord declares to Zechariah. *'For I am coming, and I will live among you,'* declares the LORD (Zech. 2:10).

5. The presence of God

Over five hundred years after the ministries of Ezekiel and Jeremiah a young woman from a backwater of an occupied territory gave birth to a child. The child was *Emmanuel,* which means *God with us* (Matt. 1:23). The child, of course, was Jesus and the angel who calls him Emmanuel was quoting from Isaiah (Is. 7:14). The promise to Abraham, reiterated by the prophets, was being fulfilled: God is with his people.

Describing the coming of Jesus, the apostle John says, *The Word became flesh and made his dwelling among us. We have seen his glory, the glory of the One and Only, who came from the Father, full of grace and truth* (John 1:14). *Made his dwelling* is literally 'tabernacled'. The signs of tabernacle and temple have given way to reality. The verse is also an allusion to Exodus 33 where Moses asks God to show him his glory. God allows Moses only a glimpse his glory: *you will see my back; but my face must not be seen* (Exod. 33:23). In contrast to this partial revelation, John says that in Christ *We have seen his glory ... full of grace and truth* (John 1:14). God's glory is revealed in the One who is *the exact representation of his being* (Heb. 1:3) and in whom *all the fulness of the Deity lives in bodily form* (Col. 2:9). *No-one has ever seen God, but God the One and Only Son, who is at the Father's side, has made him known* (John 1:18). The temple symbolized the presence of God, and in John's Gospel Jesus identifies himself as the true temple (John 2:19–22). Now the God who cannot be approached is among his people in human form in the person of his Son.

At the Last Supper Jesus makes a new covenant, constituting believers as the people of God. Through his death, which the bread and wine anticipate, Jesus is going to achieve God's saving plan to have a people who are his people. The Son is going to bring us into relationship with the Father. The apostle Peter can now say, *Once you were not a people, but now you are the people of God* (1 Pet. 2:10). To the Jews of the old covenant God had said – in a tragic reversal of the covenant promise – that they were no longer his people (Hos. 1:9). And the Gentiles were never a people – never the people of God. But now those who are in Christ – whether Jew or Gentile – have become members of God's family. All that the temple represented is now true of the community of believers, and the church is the place where God dwells on earth (Eph. 2:19–22).

Mark 11 records how Jesus enters Jerusalem in triumph and surveys the temple. Mark begins his Gospel with a quotation from Malachi that speaks of one who will prepare for the coming of the Lord (Mal. 3:1; Mark 1:2–4). The Malachi quotation continues, *Then suddenly the Lord you are seeking will come to his temple ... But who can endure the day of his coming?* (Mal. 3:1–2). In chapters 11 to 13 Mark portrays Jesus as the Lord who has come to his temple in judgment. Only animals bought in the temple courts could be sacrificed, and these animals could only be bought with temple currency. It was a scam to exploit those who came to sacrifice. Jesus clears the temple of the traders and moneychangers with a quotation from Isaiah:

Is it not written:

> '*My house will be called
> a house of prayer for all nations*'?

But you have made it 'a den of robbers'.

(Mark 11:17)

In the book of Isaiah God speaks of a time when he will bring *foreigners who bind themselves to the LORD* to his holy mountain and *give them joy in my house of prayer* (Is. 56:6–7). But the temple has become a place of exploitation rather than a place of welcome for the nations. Mark sandwiches this story between the cursing by Jesus of a fig tree and the discovery that it has withered (Mark 11:12–14, 20–25). The fig tree thus becomes a parable of God's judgment on the Jerusalem temple.

In Mark's Gospel a series of confrontations with the Jewish leaders then take place in the temple courts (Mark 11:27; 12:35, 41). They try to catch Jesus out, but it becomes clear that they are the ones being judged. They are like the tenants of the vineyard who reject the authority of the owner and kill his son, but will be judged by the owner (Mark 12:1–12). Then in Mark 13, in response to the disciples' praise of the temple, Jesus predicts its destruction (Mark 13:1–2). God will have a place of prayer for the nations, but it will not be the Jerusalem temple. Instead it will be the one to whom the temple pointed: Jesus Christ. In Christ all nations find fellowship with God, and in Christ's name all nations can pray to the Father.

As Jesus dies the curtain in the temple is torn from top to bottom (Mark 15:38). The symbol of God's inaccessibility becomes in that moment a symbol of his accessibility. Through the death of Christ God can be known. The writer to the Hebrews contrasts the terror of the encounter with God at the earthly Mount Sinai with the privilege that is now ours in Christ (Heb. 12:18–24). Unlike the Israelites of old we come gladly to the assembly of the heavenly Jerusalem. We come to God through the blood of his Son. The sin that once separated us from God has been cleansed through the sacrificial blood of Christ. The relationship is restored.

6. The conversation of friends

Jesus not only gives us access to God. He makes us family. He invites us to call God 'Father',[10] while he himself calls us his friends. But before Jesus came to earth, God had already entered into friendship with people. Abraham (2 Chr. 20:7; Is. 41:8; Jas. 2:23) and Moses (Exod. 33:11) were called the friends of God, and Job speaks of the friendship of God blessing his house (Job 29:4). Now God spectacularly widens his circle of friends. Jesus glories in the title *friend of sinners* (Matt. 11:19; Luke 7:34; see also Luke 5:20; 12:4; John 11:11). Shortly before his death he said to his disciples, *I no longer call you servants, because a servant does not know his master's business. Instead, I have called you friends, for everything that I learned from my Father I have made known to you* (John 15:15; see also 15:13–14).

It was for this we were made: to know God; to be with him; to enjoy friendship with him; to share the life of the trinitarian community. 'In obedience the Christian is the servant, in faith he is the child, but in prayer, as the servant and the child, he is the friend of God, called to the side of God and at the side of God, living and ruling and reigning with Him.'[11] 'God does not want us as objects, but as covenant partners, partners who can converse. He desires our conversation input, our spontaneous gratitude, our free concurrence, but also our patient or impatient questioning; and even our vehement protest is dearer to him than a silent, unconvinced acquiescence.'[12]

To say that we should seek friendship with the One who created the far reaches of the universe, who is the ruler of all history and who dwells in unapproachable light, sounds like outrageous hubris. Yet this is the gospel. Prayer is an expression of the very heart of God's eternal plan to have a people who are his people; to know us and to be known by us. We readily bask in the reflected glory of knowing someone even moderately important or famous – how much more can we glory in friendship with the trinitarian God!

[10] Bradshaw, *Praying as Believing*, p. 17.
[11] K. Barth, *CD* III/3, p. 286.
[12] Hendrikus Berkhof cited in Stroup, *Reformed Reader*, vol. 2, p. 231.

'Prayer means conversation with God, calling upon God ... The person who has grown up with the traditions of the Church takes this for granted. He is not conscious of the astonishing character, the boldness and "irrationality" of this act.'[13]

7. The fulfilment of prayer

But even prayer is not the reality – not ultimately. The Bible closes with John's vision of the new Jerusalem: *I saw the Holy City, the new Jerusalem, coming down out of heaven from God, prepared as a bride beautifully dressed for her husband. And I heard a loud voice from the throne saying, 'Now the dwelling of God is with men, and he will live with them. They will be his people, and God himself will be with them and be their God'* (Rev. 21:2–3).

All that Jerusalem represented to the old covenant people of God, and which was celebrated in Psalm 48, is fulfilled in the new creation. God has come to dwell with people, to protect and to be with them. The covenant promise of a people who are God's people is fulfilled and consummated. God enters into an eternal relationship of intimacy and security with his people. Revelation 21 echoes the language of Ezekiel's vision of a new Jerusalem and a new temple, for this is the fulfilment of God's purposes: *I did not see a temple in the city* says John, *because the Lord God Almighty and the Lamb are its temple* (Rev. 21:22). Prayer is not ultimate but penultimate, a pointer to the day when we shall see God face to face. It directs our attention forward to our participation in the trinitarian community. Prayer is an anticipation of the day when we shall truly know even as we are truly known (1 Cor. 13:12). *Come, Lord Jesus* (Rev. 22:20).

---

[13] Brunner, *Dogmatics*, vol. 3, p. 325.

Luke 11:1–13
2. Praying to the Father

Every time we read of Jesus praying he addresses God as Father
(Mark 14:36 par. Matt. 26:39, 42 and Luke 22:42; Matt. 11:25–26
par. Luke 10:21; 23:34, 46; John 11:41; 12:27–28; 17:1, 5, 11, 21, 24,
25), with only one exception (Mark 15:34 par. Matt. 27:46). In
Luke 11, as he teaches the disciples to pray, Jesus teaches them to
address God as Father. Indeed throughout the New Testament
prayer is addressed to the first person of the Trinity. The unity of
the Trinity means we can address prayer to the Son and the Spirit
– the Son and the Spirit are truly God and so can truly receive
prayer.[1] But the norm in the New Testament is to address prayer *to*
the Father *through* the Son *by*, or with the aid of, the Holy Spirit.
The following chapters explore this trinitarian pattern to our
prayers.

1. The Father of Israel: the liberating Father

What does it mean when Jesus invites us to call God 'Father'? The
language of divine fatherhood was not new to Jesus.[2] Its roots are in
the Old Testament where Israel was called God's *son*. It expressed
God's electing love towards the nation. The first description of
Israel as God's son comes when Moses is told to demand of Pharaoh
that he should let the Hebrew slaves go free: 'Then say to Pharaoh,
"This is what the LORD says: Israel is my firstborn son, and I told
you, 'Let my son go, so that he may worship me.' But you refused
to let him go; so I will kill your firstborn son"' (Exod. 4:22–23).

When the disciples are invited to call upon God as their Father
they are invited to see themselves as the new Israel. To call God

---

[1] On prayer to the Son see C. Hodge, *Systematic Theology*, vol. 3, p. 701.
[2] Heiler, *Prayer*, pp. 49, 59–61.

Father was to call upon the One who sets his people free to worship him. The disciples are invited to address the liberating Father.

The exodus became central for the people of Israel. It defined how they understood God – he was the God who rescued them from slavery. It defined their own identity – they were the people whom God had chosen and redeemed. It defined how they were to live – they were to care for the vulnerable because they themselves were once slaves in Egypt. But the exodus also defined their hope. Because of God's judgment on their faithlessness the people of Israel were once again enslaved and ruled by other nations. Jeremiah speaks of Israel's faithlessness towards God as a refusal to see him as a Father. God says:

> I thought you would call me 'Father'
> and not turn away from following me.
>
> (Jer. 3:19–20)

God yearns for 'Ephraim my dear son' (Jer. 31:20). Israel's only remaining hope is that God is her Father (Is. 63:15–16). So the prophets speak of God's salvation in terms of another, greater exodus. But this exodus will go beyond the first for it will deal with the underlying causes of exile and judgment. The exodus from Egypt pointed forward to a greater redemption – the redemption from sin and death, and the victory over Satan.

With the development of the monarchy in Israel, the term 'son' became focused on the king (Ps. 2:7). In his covenant with David God promises that David's sons will be God's sons (2 Sam. 7:14; Ps. 89:26). The act of liberation to which the exodus pointed and which the failure of God's people necessitated would be fulfilled by a royal Son. Freedom from bondage would come through the liberating work of the Messiah. Through the exile and beyond, down to Jesus' day, the Jews retained this hope that a messianic King would set them free. This messianic liberator would be the One of whom God said:

> You are my Son;
> today I have become your Father.
>
> (Ps. 2:7)

As Jesus invites his disciples to call upon the liberating Father, to use the language of Moses as he addressed Pharaoh, he is inviting them to pray for the promised liberation and see it being fulfilled in himself. When Jesus was transfigured he talked with Moses and Elijah of 'his departure' – literally 'his exodus' (Luke 9:30–31). Jesus celebrated the Passover with his disciples on the night before he died (Luke 22:7–20). But this celebration of the liberation from slavery became the first Lord's Supper in which Christians celebrate the liberation Christ achieved on the cross. Jesus was about to achieve the greater exodus promised by the prophets. Jesus never calls God the Father of Israel because he sees himself and his community as the new family of God. In John 8 Jesus says, 'I tell you the truth, everyone who sins is a slave to sin. Now a slave has no permanent place in the family, but a son belongs to it for ever. So if the Son sets you free, you will be free indeed' (John 8:34–36). In a similar way Paul says Christians are no longer slaves, but have become sons able to cry 'Abba, Father' through the Spirit (Gal. 4:4–7).

Seen against this background, it is no cosy thing to call upon God as Father: it is a subversive act. Tom Wright says, 'The very first word of the Lord's prayer, therefore, contains within it not just intimacy, but revolution. Not just familiarity; hope.'[3] To begin prayer by calling on the liberating Father was to recognize in Jesus the beginning of a new exodus – a new act of liberation. As it looks back to the exodus, so the prayer looks forward to a new exodus. Calling on God as Father in this way was a way of aligning oneself with this act of liberation. You were siding with God or, as Tom Wright puts it, 'signing on for the kingdom of God'.[4] It was a truly revolutionary start to prayer – not because it was a new way of talking about God but because it was a way of talking about God that evoked the promised liberation.

2. The Father of Jesus: the loving Father

Israel was an unfaithful son of God. God wanted to adopt the nation and treat it like a son, but it spurned his fatherhood. Jesus, as we have seen, is the true of son of God because he is the faithful person of God. He is the One of whom the Father says, 'You are my Son, whom I love; with you I am well pleased' (Mark 1:11 par. Matt. 3:17 and Luke 3:22; Matt. 17:5). Adam, too, was called the son of God and Luke portrays Jesus as the faithful Adamic son of God (Luke 3:38) who, in contrast to Adam, remains faithful to God when tempted by the devil (Luke 4:1–12): Jesus fulfils the filial identity of Adam and Israel.

But Jesus is also uniquely the pre-existent son of the Father. While Luke portrays Jesus as the faithful son in the way that Adam and Israel were intended to be, he is fully aware of a greater sonship

---

[3] N. T. Wright, *Lord and his Prayer*, p. 15.
[4] Ibid., pp. 19–20.

(Luke 3:23). Jesus is the second person of the eternal Trinity. In the language of John's Gospel he is the 'only begotten' (John 1:14, 18; 3:16, 18). While the Synoptic Gospels start with Jesus as the fulfilment of human Adamic and Israelite sonship (Mark 1:11; see also Ps. 2:7), John's Gospel starts with Jesus as the eternal Word through whom all things were created (John 1:1–3). Jesus is both the faithful son of God as Israel was called to be and the pre-existent son of God, eternally begotten of the Father.

So, as the faithful one of God, Jesus makes it possible for us to share in the divine family. It is our identity through faith with Jesus who is both the faithful human son and the fully divine son that enables us to share in the eternal trinitarian relationships. When we call on God as Father we call on him as the Father of Israel, but also as the Father of our Lord Jesus Christ.

> Seen with Christian hindsight – more specifically, with trinitarian perspective – the Lord's Prayer becomes an invitation to share in the *divine* life itself. It becomes one of the high roads into the central mystery of Christian salvation and Christian existence: that the baptized and believing Christian is (1) incorporated into the inner life of the triune God *and* (2) intended not just to believe that this is the case, but actually to experience it.[5]

This is the language of the New Testament. The apostolic writers speak of the first person of the Trinity as the 'Father of our Lord Jesus Christ' (Rom. 15:6; 1 Cor. 1:3; 2 Cor. 1:3; 11:31; Eph. 1:3; Col. 1:3; 1 Pet. 1:3). Before he is *our* Father (Matt. 6:9), he is the Father of Jesus Christ. Indeed he becomes our Father only through Jesus. 'God has revealed himself as Father in Jesus Christ and can hence be recognized as such only in him.'[6]

God is not universally Father.[7] God as Creator is Father, even of the heavenly lights (Jas. 1:17) and Luke traces his genealogy of Jesus back to 'Adam, the son of God' (Luke 3:38; see also perhaps Eph. 3:15). But for the most part in the Bible the language of fatherhood is associated with salvation rather than creation. Even in his genealogy Luke contrasts the flawed disobedient sonship of Adam with the new sonship of Jesus.[8] Mankind has forfeited its status as children of the Creator (Deut. 32:5–6). God is not the father of all people – he is the father of *his* people. God's fatherhood is based not on nature but on divine intervention. God is the father of the family

---

[5] N. T. Wright, 'Lord's Prayer', p. 132.
[6] Hofius, 'Father', vol. 1, p. 620.
[7] Carson, *Sermon on the Mount*, p. 63; and Packer, *Knowing God*, pp. 181–182.
[8] Nolland, *Luke 1 – 9:20*, p. 173.

he has called into being through his grace.[9] The descriptions of God as a 'Father to the fatherless' are set in this covenantal context (Ps. 68:5).

The teaching of Jesus follows the same pattern. He speaks of 'your Father' only when talking to his disciples. The fatherhood of God and the kingdom of God are intertwined so that Jesus gives God's fatherhood an eschatological focus.[10] Rather than looking back to creation, the fatherhood of God in the teaching of Jesus looks forward to the inclusion of many people into the family of God through the gospel. The fatherhood of God is linked to a person's relationship to Jesus himself. 'No-one knows who the Son is except the Father, and no-one knows who the Father is except the Son and those to whom the Son chooses to reveal him' (Luke 10:22), says Jesus in the previous chapter of Luke's Gospel (see also John 14:6–11; 17:20–26).

Throughout the New Testament we can call on God as Father only because he has become our Father in Christ. 'The NT witnesses, especially Paul and John, are unanimous in making the fatherhood of God rest upon a basis of christology and soteriology.'[11] Those 'in Christ' can call on God as Father, for as we are united to Christ by faith we become family. Paul takes up the image of adoption to express this. This means that to pray to the Father is to evoke the mediation of Christ. 'In calling God "Father", we put forward the name "Christ".'[12]

Although we can legitimately say, 'My Father' (just as David said, 'The Lord is my Shepherd'), in Matthew's account of the Lord's Prayer Jesus teaches the disciples to say, 'Our Father' (6:9). In Luke (11:1) Jesus introduces the prayer by saying, When you [plural] pray (i.e. when you pray together). It is striking that we cannot pray the Lord's Prayer on our own – it must be prayed with others. Or, at least, when we do pray it on our own, it forces us to recognize that we pray as part of a wider family. Luther said that the Lord's Prayer 'binds people together within one another, so that each prays for the other and with the other'.[13] Given a choice between praying on my own and praying with someone else, I would normally choose to pray with others, as my public prayer is stronger and more sustained than my private prayer. And while I wish my private prayer were better, I do not regard this as hypocritical, but as a recognition that I need other people to help me pray: we pray as members of a family.

[9] Hofius, 'Father', vol. 1, p. 617.
[10] Ladd, *Theology of the New Testament*, pp. 84–87.
[11] Hofius, 'Father', vol. 1, p. 620; see also Shrenk, *'patēr'*, vol. 5, pp. 990–991.
[12] Calvin, *Institutes*, 3.20.36.
[13] Cited in Heiler, *Prayer*, p. 246.

We know God as Father through our participation in Christ. United with Christ, the Father of our Lord Jesus Christ becomes our Father. When we call upon God as Father we are expressing our inclusion in the trinitarian relationships. This, I suspect, is how we should view Isaiah's description of Jesus as 'the everlasting Father' (Is. 9:6). Evangelicals too readily conceive of Father, Son and Spirit as separate entities, but biblical trinitarianism holds the 'threeness' of God in tension with his 'oneness'. We must not forget the 'oneness' of the Father and Son – a unity not only of purpose but also, according to the ancient creeds, of substance. Father and Son are not the same, nor are they different modes of expression of the one God. Yet they are one. In the Son we see the Father. Indeed we do not experience God as Father apart from the Son. It is through the Son, and only through the Son, that we know the Father. The sonship of Jesus defines for us the fatherhood of God.

In Mark 14:36 Jesus uses the Aramaic term *Abba* to address God as does Paul in Romans 8:15 and Galatians 4:6. The words of Jesus in the Gospels are a Greek translation of the Aramaic that he would have spoken during his ministry. Only rarely are Aramaic words retained, and *Abba* is an example of this. The significance of this has been the subject of debate. Joachim Jeremias said that *Abba* was drawn from the nursery and that its use by Jesus suggested a new perspective on God.[14] Jeremias's ideas have entered popular theology with the claim that we can call God 'Daddy' – a conclusion from which Jeremias distanced himself. Moreover James Barr has challenged the work of Jeremias, showing, for example, that *Abba* was also used by adults in the Judaism of the time.[15] Perhaps the key point is this: while the use of *Abba* clearly does suggest intimacy, we should not confuse intimacy with indulgence. A father in Palestine was a figure of respect. The one time the Gospels record Jesus using *Abba* is in Gethsemane, which is the antithesis of indulgence (Mark 14:36).

We lose the wonder of this new relationship if we isolate the truth of God's fatherhood from the wider reality of God. God is the majestic Creator of all things, the One who dwells in unapproachable glory, who consumes those who come near him. It is this One who through Christ has now become Father. But he is not any less Lord or Judge.[16] We have not moved from an old conception of God to a new conception. Rather we have come into relationship with the awesome God. Now we come with *both* the fear and reverence

[14] See e.g. Jeremias, *Prayers of Jesus*.
[15] Barr, 'Abba, Father'.
[16] Shrenk, '*patēr*', vol. 5, pp. 995–996, 1010–1011.

of a subject and the ease and confidence of a child. Jesus is not informing us of another way of addressing God: he is giving us a new relationship with God. Jesus does indicate a radically new perspective on our relationship with God – not so much through the language he used but through his own attitude to 'sinners'. The new perspective is not that God is Father – the Jews spoke of God as Father (John 8:41). What is new is that Jesus invited individual sinners to share this fatherly relationship with God. God is still our Creator, but now he is also our Father. We view God not only from outside, as it were, as creatures looking upon their Creator. We now view God from the inside as children within his family. The invitation of the Father, which he extends to us through his Son, is the beginning of prayer. 'Christian prayer', says P. T. Forsyth, 'is our word answering God's'.[17] Prayer is thus a response to the word of the Father.

a. The motherhood of God

Before we move on, we must consider why God is addressed as 'Father' and not as 'Mother' or 'Parent'. The God of the Bible is without gender. 'He' is not female, but neither is 'he' male. When God made mankind in his image he made them 'male and female' (Gen. 1:27). The Bible shows no reluctance to use motherly images of God (Deut. 32:18; Is. 42:14). Jesus speaks of himself as a mother hen gathering her chicks (Matt. 23:37; Luke 13:34). Yet the Bible never speaks of God as 'Mother'. God is described as like a Mother, but known always as Father. Can we address 'God our Mother' in prayer? The example of the Scriptures suggests we should not. The names of God in the Bible are not the result of human speculation or redundant cultural norms: they are a revelation by God of himself. The cultures surrounding Israel had female deities, but the writers of the Old Testament chose not to adopt such language to describe Yahweh. The language of motherhood may have been avoided to prevent any confusion with notions in Babylonian myths of god giving birth to the world – notions that are still with us in the ideas associated with Mother Earth. Instead God relates to his people as a husband relates to his wife.[18]

In exploring the fatherhood of God we have ranged beyond Luke 11 to examine its historical background in the history of redemption and its theological background in the trinitarian relationships. Let

[17] Forsyth, *Soul of Prayer*, p. 68.
[18] See Frame, *Doctrine of God*, pp. 378–386.

us return now to examine Jesus' own expansion of God's father-hood in Luke 11.

3. A willing and generous Father (11:5–13)

Jesus continues his teaching on prayer by telling a parable. We are to imagine a Palestinian family sleeping together in their small home. Suddenly there is frantic knocking on the door. A friend has come asking for bread because he has received an unexpected visitor. In the culture of the time there was a strong expectation that generous hospitality should be shown to visitors. Failure to do so would be a cause of shame – something to be avoided at all costs. But most food was prepared daily and there were no preservatives. The only resort of the guest without food is to beg it from someone else. Hence the late-night call. But the man is reluctant. His children are sleeping with him – to get up will disturb them.

Jesus was speaking of a situation his hearers would understand. They could appreciate both the desperation of the man outside and the reluctance of the man inside. They could imagine hoping the caller would go away, but they could also imagine conceding to his request. The word translated 'persistence' (NIV) is *anaideia*, which actually means 'boldness' or 'shamelessness'. It could refer to the man outside who knocks shamelessly, but it is more likely to refer to the man inside. He answers because he does not want to bring shame on himself by refusing the request and tarnishing the village's reputation for hospitality. He is the centre of the parable and is the one whose attitude casts light on the attitude of God.[19]

Jesus is arguing from the lesser to the greater. He is not saying that God is like a reluctant neighbour who has to be nagged before he will do anything for us. Rather, he is saying, if a reluctant human being will give you what you want out of concern for his reputation, *how much more* will your loving heavenly Father? If a man will answer your cry even though he is asleep with his family, *how much more* will he who never sleeps? God is ready to hear us. Our Father is willing to hear our prayers.

So Jesus applies the parable with a threefold promise: *Ask and it will be given to you; seek and you will find; knock and the door will be opened to you. For everyone who asks receives; he who seeks finds; and to him who knocks, the door will be opened* (9–10).

The leader of any nation is surrounded by various levels of security. Downing Street, the home of the British Prime Minister, is protected by iron gates. A policeman stands outside. Security

---

[19] Marshall, *Luke*, p. 465; and Turner, 'Prayer in the Gospels and Acts', pp. 66–67.

officers are positioned inside and travel everywhere with him. If you want to see him you need an appointment, but only a few people get an appointment with the Prime Minster. His time is too precious and his security too important. But imagine you are one of the Prime Minister's children. The policeman at the door opens it for you. The secretary lets you see him without an appointment.

That is what it means for us to pray to our Father. Although our God is far more powerful than presidents and far more important than prime ministers, we can go to him at any time because he is our Father. We pray to someone who is always willing to listen. 'God is not a timeless truth or ideal floating in the heavens, to which we try to make our lives correspond here below. The flesh and blood realities of what actually happens in history concern the heavenly Father deeply.'[20]

In verses 11–13 Jesus is again arguing from the lesser to the greater. If our earthly fathers give good things to their children, *how much more* will our heavenly Father. Queen Elizabeth I, when Sir Walter Raleigh was asking for yet another favour, is said to have asked, 'When will you leave off begging?', to which Raleigh replied, 'When your Majesty leaves off giving.' We have a greater Majesty who delights to give us good things. 'We must not hesitate', says Jim Packer, 'to imitate the sublime "cheek" of the child who is not afraid to ask his parents for anything, because he knows he can count completely on their love.'[21] We pray to one who loves us and cares for us. He delights to answer our prayers and give us good things even if those good things are not always the good things we want or think we need.

We should note, too, that Jesus says all human fathers are to some extent *evil* (13). Although many people's experience of fatherhood has been deficient, our *Father in heaven* is not like an abusive, distant or manipulative human father. 'Father' is not simply an image drawn from human life, but rather divine fatherhood provides the pattern for human fatherhood (Eph. 3:17). Our pain at poor parenting is an expression of the realization that this is not how it should be: God is the loving, generous Father whom human fathers should be like.

That God gives good things to his children is plain, but this story contains surprises that require further reflection. The parallel story in Matthew's Gospel speaks of a stone instead of bread and a snake instead of a fish (Matt. 7:9–11). Bread and fish are obvious choices for they were staple foods (Luke 9:13) and a stone and serpent are

---

[20] Bradshaw, *Praying as Believing*, p. 16.
[21] Packer, *Knowing God*, p. 192.

chosen because of the similarity in appearance with a loaf and fish. Why, then, does Luke's account replace the bread and stone couplet with an egg and scorpion? Furthermore why does Luke replace Matthew's general promise of *good things* with the specific promise of *the Holy Spirit*? The answer lies in the previous chapter. When the seventy-two return from their mission, Jesus says, 'I saw Satan fall like lightning from heaven. I have given you authority to trample on snakes and scorpions and to overcome all the power of the enemy' (10:18–19). Luke continues:

> At that time Jesus, full of joy through the Holy Spirit, said, 'I praise you, Father, Lord of heaven and earth, because you have hidden these things from the wise and learned, and revealed them to little children. Yes, Father, for this was your good pleasure. All things have been committed to me by my Father. No-one knows who the Son is except the Father, and no-one knows who the Father is except the Son and those to whom the Son chooses to reveal him.'
>
> (10:21–22)

Serpents and scorpions represent Satans's power, which the disciples have overcome through Jesus' authority. In contrast, Jesus 'rejoiced in the Holy Spirit' (esv) who works in the disciples, revealing the Father to them through the Son. In the passage immediately after the simile of 11:11–13 Jesus is accused of casting out demons by the prince of demons (11:14–15). 'The simile itself is intended to assure the disciples that when they ask God for his power in their mission alongside Jesus, the power they receive will not be an *evil* spirit. God is sure rather to give them "a good spirit", i.e. a share in the Holy Spirit by which Jesus is anointed.'[22]

In other words, the prayer these verses presuppose is a prayer for power in mission and God promises to answer this through the Holy Spirit. But the ultimate gift is not 'that the spirits submit to you, but ... that your names are written in heaven' (10:20). The Father gives the Spirit so that through the Spirit 'those to whom the Son chooses to reveal him' may know God as Father (10:22) and call upon him in prayer (11:2).

4. Conclusion

The Father–child relationship into which the gospel brings us is the fundamental fact of prayer. To understand prayer, argues Karl

---

[22] Turner, 'Prayer in the Gospels and Acts', p. 68.

Barth, we must not see it as primarily worship, nor as confession. Rather 'in the first instance, it is an asking'.[23] 'It is the fact that [a man] comes before God with his petition which makes him a praying man. Other theories of prayer may be richly and profoundly thought out and may sound very well, but they all suffer from a certain artificiality because they miss this simple and concrete fact, losing themselves in heights and depths where there is no place for the man who really prays, who is simply making a request.'[24]

The heart of prayer is not the greatness of God, nor the unworthiness of mankind. It is, rather, that the great God has come near to unworthy people 'with the nearness of Father and child'.[25] So, it is in coming as a petitioner before God that the praying person 'makes the most genuine act of praise and thanksgiving, and therefore worship; and again, that in so doing he makes the most genuine act of penitence. By coming before God as one who asks he magnifies God and abases himself.'[26]

I have been frustrated by members of my congregation who could not be exhorted to focus on the praise of God or on confession without moving on to petition. It is an attitude of which I now repent. We too easily think of those who move into contemplative modes of praying or those who make worship or confession the focus of their praying as those who are advanced prayers. It is not so. We must recognize that it is the 'unsophisticated', simple prayers who truly express trust in divine Majesty, who truly acknowledge their own need before God, and who have truly grasped the freedom of the Father–child relationship. Many books on prayer exhort us to search for deeper experiences in prayer or more sophisticated modes of prayer that breed a sense of inadequacy in some and of superiority in others. The Bible invites us to find the model of prayer in the simple petitioning of a child before a father. This leads to freedom and peace.

[23] K. Barth, *CD* III/3, p. 268.
[24] Ibid., p. 268.
[25] Ibid.
[26] Ibid., p. 270; see also p. 274.

Hebrews 4 – 5
3. Praying through the Son

My experience of celebrities is decidedly limited, but I think it would be rather fun to work for one. I would introduce myself to people as plain Tim Chester and then enjoy seeing their attitude change when I eventually let slip that I was acting in the name of my boss. I suspect that a restaurant reservation or special request refused a moment ago would suddenly become possible. Such is the power of a name. Imagine you hear someone knocking on your door in the middle of the night. You stick your head out of the window to find out who it is. If they say, 'It's John Smith,' you will probably tell them to get lost. But if you see a policeman and he says, 'Open up in the name of the law!' your attitude will be very different. When Christians pray we do so in the powerful name of Jesus, and his name, as the writer of Hebrews explains, gives us access to the throne of heaven.

The letter of Hebrews was written to Christians who were tempted to turn back to Judaism. The book is punctuated by calls to keep trusting in Jesus and his sufficiency (see e.g. Heb. 4:11, 14). Imagine those Jewish believers. Christianity is alarmingly simple: no paraphernalia, none of the trappings of religion (no rituals, no sacred places, no holy people, no special times), just the simple truth of the gospel. To match all the glories of Judaism – temple, priesthood, sacrifice – there is just the person of Jesus. To match all the splendour of what one can *see* in religion there is simply the memory of the cross. The writer addresses these issues through a series of expositions showing how the Old Testament is fulfilled in Jesus: Jesus is superior to all that has gone before.

The radical simplicity of the gospel continues to trouble people. Christians have always been tempted to turn back to religion, ritual or mysticism. This is so even today, perhaps especially today, and particularly in the area of prayer. Among evangelicals we have seen in recent years a growing interest in contemplative prayer, mystical prayer, warfare prayer and so on. People hunger for something more, something deeper, something higher than the stark simplicity of the gospel. So they look into Celtic spirituality, Ignatian spirituality, the wisdom of the desert Fathers, creation spirituality. While we have much to learn from the saints who have gone before, the pursuit of such things sometimes reveals a desire for something in addition to the gospel. The message of the writer to the Hebrews is *Jesus is better*. In Hebrews 4 and 5 the writer expands on this central theme by exploring how Jesus is our High Priest, introducing ideas that he develops in the central section of chapters 5 – 10. All to which the priesthood in the Old Testament pointed has been fulfilled in Jesus, and this fulfilment more than exceeds all that preceded it.

1. Jesus is our High Priest

Having introduced the theme in 4:14–16, the writer characteristically explains the Old Testament background (5:1–4) and then shows how it is fulfilled in Jesus (5:5–10). The structure of the passage is as follows:[1]

A. The old high priest (5:1)
   B. Requirement: from among men (5:2–3)
      C. Requirement: appointed by God (5:4)
      C^1. Fulfilment: Jesus is appointed by God (5:5–6)
   B^1. Fulfilment: Jesus is from among men (5:7–8)
A^1. The new high priest (5:9–10)

a. Jesus is from among men

In 5:2–3 the writer says the high priest had to be *from among men* for two reasons. First, he was a man so that he could act as the representative of the people before God. He had to be one of us. Second, his humanness meant he could deal gently with those who were going astray. He shared their weakness and so he would correct them with sympathy.

In 5:7–8 the writer explains how these features are fulfilled in Jesus. Prima facie *the Son of God* (4:14) is ill-equipped to fulfil these requirements. That is the implication of the phrase *Although he was a son* (5:8). The lack of a definite article does not mean it refers to sonship in some general sense. It is a reference to divine sonship in

---

[1] Adapted from Lane, *Hebrews 1 – 8*, p. 111.

the sense captured by F. F. Bruce's suggested translation 'Son though he was'.[2] How can the all-powerful One understand our weaknesses? How can the sinless One understand our struggles with temptation? In 4:15 it would have been simpler to say, 'We have a high priest who is able to sympathize', but the writer uses a double negative (not ... unable), which suggests there were those who thought Jesus was unable to sympathize with our weaknesses.

But, says the writer to the Hebrews, Jesus learned obedience from what he suffered (5:8). There is a play on the words learned (emathen) and suffering (epathen). This does not mean Jesus was disobedient and then became obedient, for in 4:15 the writer says that Jesus was without sin. Rather Jesus learned obedience in the sense that he learned what obedience felt like for a human being. 'The transition is not from rebellion to obedience but rather one of maturing in the task imposed on him.'[3]

There is a sense in which Jesus endured more temptation than any of us. At one time or another each has put an end to temptation by giving in to it. But Jesus never succumbed to temptation. So Jesus has been tempted in every way, just as we are – yet was without sin (4:15). Indeed he experienced obedience to the full by remaining obedient through suffering even to the point of death. The anguish of Gethsemane ultimately reveals the extent and reality of Jesus' temptations. The word translated 'suffering' (epathen) is used in Hebrews of suffering to death (Heb. 2:9; 9:26; 13:12).[4] Reverent submission in 5:7 (apo tēs eulabeias) could refer to fear (of death) or reverence (to God).[5] The latter best fits the context, suggesting submission to the will of God in the face of suffering and death. The joyful obedience of heaven was replaced by the painful obedience of Gethsemane. However one resolves the vexed question of whether sin was a genuine possibility for Jesus or not,[6] it is clear that temptation involved a real struggle for him. When in our struggles and pain we cry out to God, we do so in the name of the One who offered up prayers and petitions with loud cries and tears (5:7). Calvin adds that his tears and cries also 'commend to us a zeal and a closer application in prayer'.[7]

The writer says that Jesus was made perfect (5:8; see also 2:10). Again, this does not mean Jesus was imperfect in the sense of sinful. It means he became complete – 'fully qualified to be the Saviour and

[2] Bruce, Hebrews, pp. 102–103.
[3] Berkouwer, Person of Christ, p. 248.
[4] See also Phil. 2:8 and Lane, Hebrews 1–8, p. 121.
[5] Ellingworth, Hebrews, pp. 289–291.
[6] See Berkouwer, Person of Christ, pp. 239–264.
[7] Calvin, Hebrews and First and Second Peter, p. 64.

High Priest of His people'.[8] He became man and experienced what it was like to be a man. The wonder of the incarnation is that God himself now perfectly meets the qualification of being *from among men* (5:1; see also 2:17). The High Priest had to be a man to represent men to God. Jesus became perfectly suited for the task – truly human, subject to human frailty and having experienced *loud cries and tears*.

b. Jesus is appointed by God

In 5:4 the writer gives a second condition for being a priest. A priest must not only be human. He must be appointed by God. He must be human to represent humans, but he must also be approved or appointed by God to make representation before God.

In 5:5–6 the writer shows how this is fulfilled in Jesus. But there is a problem. Although Jesus is descended from the tribe of Judah, which legitimizes his claim to the throne of David, the priesthood belonged exclusively to Aaron's descendants in the tribe of Levi (7:11–14). After the Maccabean wars in the second century BC the Jewish nation had been divided when, for political reasons, certain men had assumed the priesthood without this hereditary claim.[9] Christ, however, did not exalt himself (5:5). Instead he was appointed by God. Thus his claim to the priesthood came from the throne of God.

The writer of Hebrews makes good this claim by going back, via Psalm 110, beyond Aaron to a more ancient priest of God: Melchizedek. Melchizedek is first mentioned in Genesis 14. Abraham returns from winning a battle to be met by Melchizedek, the king of Salem and a priest of God, to whom Abraham makes an offering. But this brief, elusive encounter has an important wider significance in the Bible. Melchizedek, which means 'king of Righteousness', is also described as the 'king of Peace' or 'King of [Jeru]Salem'. In Psalm 110 this mysterious figure reappears:

> The LORD has sworn
>   and will not change his mind:
> 'You are a priest for ever,
>   in the order of Melchizedek.'
>
> (Ps. 110:4)

It is this that Hebrews 5:6 quotes. The psalm speaks of David's royal

---

[8] Bruce, *Hebrews*, p. 105.
[9] Ibid., pp. 92, 95–97.

line; the king on David's throne is the king of Salem (= Jerusalem) and so, it seems, he inherits the role of priest after the order of Melchizedek. In Joshua 10 a previous (evil) king of Jerusalem is titled Adonai-Zedek, which means Lord of Righteousness – similar to the name Melchizedek.

In Psalm 110 David is looking forward. As Jesus reminded the Pharisees, in Psalm 110 David calls this future priest-king 'My Lord' (Mark 12:35–37). For all the glory of his reign, David knew he was not the real thing – he was looking for a greater king. In Zechariah 6:9–15 the coming together of kingship and priesthood in one person is anticipated. This vision is, of course, fulfilled in Jesus who is both our king and priest. Psalm 110 is the passage of the Old Testament most frequently quoted by the writers of the New Testament who do so to demonstrate that Jesus is both the promised greater king and the promised priest of the order of Melchizedek. 'The appeal to Melchizedek, who as the first priest mentioned in Scripture is the archetype of all priesthood, validates Jesus' priesthood as different from and superior to the Levitical priesthood.'[10] In other words, the appeal to Melchizedek is not just a cunning way of sidestepping the problem of Levitical descent. It is an appeal to a more ancient and more foundational priesthood.

In Hebrews 7 the writer returns to Melchizedek to demonstrate that Jesus is a greater priest by virtue of what he has accomplished. Jesus is the greater priest whose sacrifice saves completely. The old Levitical priesthood was insufficient – it could save neither completely nor eternally, for they had to keep repeating the sacrifices. So God promised a new priest-king. It is the fulfilment of that promise in Jesus that we see explained in 7:11–28. Jesus is a priest because of the oath or the promise of God (7:20–22). It is not that Jesus is descended from Melchizedek (7:15–16) but rather that God appoints him priest after the order of Melchizedek, so that he is a priest by the word of God (5:5–6).

The result is that Jesus offers a 'better' guarantee (7:22) – one based on the oath of God. Jesus is a better priest offering a salvation that all our efforts could never achieve. We cannot be right with God by trying to live a good life. We cannot be right with God through religious observance. Even the very best of religion – the old priesthood appointed by God – could not achieve salvation. It was only ever a pointer to the reality to come. The writer to the Hebrews draws out the contrast in chapter 10: 'Day after day every priest stands and performs his religious duties; again and again he offers the same sacrifices, which can never take away sins. But when

[10] Lane, *Hebrews 1 – 8*, p. 123.

this priest had offered for all time one sacrifice for sins, he sat down at the right hand of God. Since that time he waits for his enemies to be made his footstool, because by one sacrifice he has made perfect for ever those who are being made holy.'

The conclusion of 7:23–28 is that Jesus is a better priest because he is:

1. *Eternal* (7:23–25). As an 'eternal priest', Jesus *became the source of eternal salvation for all who obey him* (5:9). His salvation never expires, for he saves to the end. His once-for-all sacrifice is sufficient now and will be sufficient for ever. He ever lives to intercede for us. He will never die, leaving us without a priest.

2. *Faultless* (7:26–27). The Aaronic priests had first to offer for their own sin (5:3). But, as a 'faultless priest', Jesus the perfect One offers us perfect righteousness and complete cleansing. Nothing is left out and there are no loose ends to be sorted out, no purgatorial cleansing to be undergone.

3. *Appointed by God* (7:28). As a 'priest appointed by God', Jesus operates with the authority of God. God is satisfied. The demands of his justice and holiness are met and met completely by the death of Jesus in our place.

So Jesus *saves completely* (25). There is nothing we can do to jeopardize what he has done, no sin we can commit that will put us outside his salvation. His perfect sacrifice means every sin is covered.

2. Jesus our High Priest gives us confidence in prayer

The key word in 4:16 is *confidence*. William Lane translates it as 'bold frankness'.[11] In secular Greek it was used to denote free speech, while in the private sphere it meant 'candour'.[12] Because Jesus is our High Priest we can have confidence. He has secured us the right of free speech before God. We do not need to choose our words with the care of a subject for whom a slip of the tongue might mean the disfavour of the king. We do not need to hold back our thoughts for fear of censure. We can speak freely and candidly before our God.

It is significant that this call to come before God with confidence is preceded by these words: *For the word of God is living and active.*

---

[11] Ibid., p. 115.
[12] Schlier, *'parrēsia, parrēsiazomai'*, vol. 5, pp. 871–886.

Sharper than any double-edged sword, it penetrates even to dividing soul and spirit, joints and marrow; it judges the thoughts and attitudes of the heart. Nothing in all creation is hidden from God's sight. Everything is uncovered and laid bare before the eyes of him to whom we must give account (4:12–13).

The word of God exposes us before God in all our guilt and shame (4:12–13). There can be no worse position than to be *naked and exposed to the eyes of him to whom we must give account* (4:13 ESV). But it is in this very position, exposed before the throne, that we have confidence without guilt and without shame. One of the blessings of prayer is that as we talk to God we must be honest with the one from whom *nothing in all creation is hidden* about things that in other moments we hide even from ourselves. Prayer can be a process of self-illumination, revealing our true motives and thoughts. But no matter what we find within ourselves, we can still come before God with confidence. Jesus our High Priest fulfils the criteria of being truly human and appointed by God, and so we can speak freely before the throne of grace. The writer to the Hebrews offers three reasons for this confidence.

a. Jesus understands us

Because Jesus is truly human he understands our struggles. He has learnt what it means for human beings to be obedient: *For we do not have a high priest who is unable to sympathize with our weaknesses, but we have one who has been tempted in every way, just as we are – yet was without sin* (4:15). In the next verse the writer applies this great truth. What are the implications of a priest who is truly human and a God who understands what it is for us to struggle? *Let us then approach the throne of grace with confidence, so that we may receive mercy and find grace to help us in our time of need* (4:16).

The writer urges us to come before God *in our time of need*. We can do so with confidence because God himself knows what it is to be in need. Indeed not only that, he knows what it is like to struggle in prayer in those times: *During the days of Jesus' life on earth, he offered up prayers and petitions with loud cries and tears* (5:7). God himself has cried out in prayer during difficult times. It is part of the perfection of Christ that he has learnt what it means to wrestle before God with human suffering and human frailty (5:7–9). So God will not respond, 'Just pull yourself together. What interest have I in your puny problems?' Instead he will *deal gently* with us (5:2).

Why can we come before the throne of grace with confidence? Because God knows what it is to find life tough – he understands our weakness. The one who has entered heaven on our behalf has carried real humanity there, so that he knows how we feel.

b. Jesus represents us before God

It was the role of the priest to represent people before God (5:1) and that is what Jesus now does for us. 'Therefore he is able to save completely those who come to God through him, because he always lives to intercede for them' (7:25).

Jesus' intercession does not consist of petitions to God.[13] This might imply a deficit in the cross that Jesus makes up by his constant prayers on our behalf. No, Jesus intercedes by being in heaven on our behalf. 'The presence of the crucified and yet glorified Christ with God is the reality behind the concept of his heavenly intercession.'[14] By his presence he reminds the Father – as if the Father needed reminding – of the finished work of the cross. Jesus, as it were, says by his presence, 'I am here in heaven and my people are united with me – they have access to God.' Later in the letter of Hebrews the writer says, 'For Christ did not enter a man-made sanctuary that was only a copy of the true one; he entered heaven itself, now to appear *for us* in God's presence' (9:24; my emphasis). Jesus appears in heaven 'for us'. He is before God with his wounded side and his pierced hands as if to say, 'These are the reasons why you should hear my people and show them mercy.'

Why can we come before the throne of grace with confidence? Because Jesus is already there at the right hand of the throne with his pierced hands and his wounded side – he is there as our representative.

c. Jesus gives us access to God

In 4:14 the writer says that we have a great High Priest *who has gone through the heavens, Jesus the Son of God*. The temple was a big picture of the inaccessibility of God. God is so great and incomprehensible that he cannot be known. God is so holy and glorious that we cannot come into his presence without being destroyed. So the temple consisted of a series of courts beyond which different people could not go. Finally you came to the Holy of Holies, the symbol of God's presence, into which only the high priest could go, only once a year and only through the shedding of sacrificial blood. In front of the Holy of Holies was a thick curtain separating the people from

[13] For a contrary view see Grudem, *Systematic Theology*, pp. 627–628.
[14] D. Peterson, 'Prayer in the General Epistles', p. 104.

the presence of God. But when Jesus died that curtain was torn from top to bottom (Mark 15:38). The way to God was opened.

Yet the curtain and the temple were a shadow of the real thing. In Hebrews 9 the writer says that the real action was going on heaven. The earthly temple was a picture of the heavenly presence of God. That is why the writer says Jesus has *gone through the heavens*. When Jesus entered heaven he presented himself as the true sacrifice to God. Jesus bears the judgment we deserve. He absorbs the holy glory of God. His blood cleanses us. Now through Jesus the way to God is open, the curtain torn in two. We can know God and be near him.

Why can we come before the throne of grace with confidence? Because Christ has opened the way for us through his sacrifice and his sacrifice is final and complete (10:11–14).

Donja proudly showed me round her new house in the slums of Mexico City. She had built it herself with the help of a local church to replace the shack made from cardboard milk cartons that she had shared with her nine children. She told me how she had discovered the power of prayer, how God had heard her prayers for a house and a job. It was humbling to pray with her, holding hands on the street outside her home. Before she became a Christian her home had been full of images of Mary and the saints. Now they were all gone. She did not need them. With Jesus as her High Priest no-one has better access to the eternal God than Donja, a poor single mother from the slums of Mexico City.

3. Prayer and the gospel

Have we been thinking about prayer or have we been thinking about how we can be right with God? The answer is, both. The basis of prayer is the gospel. John Owen said that in prayer the Holy Spirit is 'copying' the pattern of his general work in a believer.[15] There is no 'advanced' teaching on prayer. There is no 'higher' spirituality. Prayer is continually rooted in the gospel. The basis of Christian prayer is the basis of Christian salvation. The access to God through the Son that we experience in prayer is a snapshot of the gospel. And so the solution to prayerlessness is the gospel. The reason we do not pray more is that sinners do not want to come before a holy God – we shrink from the light. But in Christ we have been declared righteous. We need not shrink back but can approach God boldly.

[15] Cited in Ferguson, *John Owen*, p. 225.

To pray in the name of Jesus is not to end each prayer with those words – though that can be a helpful reminder of the basis on which we pray. The name of Jesus is not a talisman or invocation. Rather it is a reminder that we have access to God through the once-for-all sacrifice of Jesus. And this defines the spirit in which we should pray. To pray in the name of Jesus is to pray recognizing our dependence on Christ's meditorial work. It means not praying in such a way as to suppose God will hear our prayers because of our goodness, the style of our praying or the length of our prayers.

Here is the test of whether you have grasped the radical simplicity of the gospel. Do you think your prayers are more likely to be answered if you are living a more godly life or if you are also fasting or if you bind demons in your prayer or if you pray for two hours rather than one hour? If we are inclined to answer yes to any of these questions then we have not grasped the grace of God in the gospel. We have not grasped the sufficiency of Christ's mediatorial role.

Fasting and times set aside for prayer may all help us as we pray. We should not discourage such things. But, while they help *us*, they do not persuade God. Hallesby says, 'We do not need definite seasons of prayer for God's sake. He does not need them. On the contrary, it is we who need them.'[16] In a similar vein Calvin commends regular times of prayer not because we thereby repay our debt to God but as 'a tutelage for our weakness'.[17] The same can be said of fasting. We should not suppose that fasting makes our prayers more winsome to God. If fasting is of benefit it is not of benefit to God. It may be of benefit to us as praying people, perhaps providing a way of concentrating the mind, but it can add nothing to the finished work of Christ.

Much of the devotional literature on prayer is focused on those things that help us to pray – posture, exercises, liturgies, habits. But, while they may be helpful, none of them is necessary. The focus of the Bible is instead on Christ and his sufficiency. There is nothing we can do to make our prayers more effective before God. Any such notions are a return to paganism – it is to suppose that we can manipulate or placate God. As Ronald Dunn puts it, the floor of the throne room is sprinkled, 'not with the sweat of my good works, but with the blood of his sacrifice'.[18] The 'posture' that the Bible commends is a humble and contrite heart (Pss. 34:18; 51:17; Is. 57:15; 66:2).

We can also have confidence in prayer despite our mixed motives. If we pray with entirely wrong motives God may not hear us – he

[16] Hallesby, *Prayer*, p. 74.
[17] Calvin, *Institutes*, 3.20.50.
[18] R. Dunn, *Don't Just Stand There*, p. 43.

will not share his glory with another (Jas. 4:2–6). But often our motives are mixed and confused. We long for people to be saved, but we also want our church to be 'successful'. We should acknowledge those mixed motives before God and ask him to purify our motives. But we can still have confidence in prayer. God does not hear our prayers because our motives are pure but because of the blood of Jesus Christ. It is as if the rather murky prayers that leave us are transformed by the work of Christ into fragrant incense as they reach God.

Christ does not stand before the Father. He sits beside him, for his work is completed. There is nothing we can do to make his sacrifice more effective or to improve his work as our mediator. Our only claim before the throne of God is the blood of Jesus. But what a claim that is! The writer of Hebrews begins his great section on the high priestly work of Jesus with these words: *Let us then approach the throne of grace with confidence, so that we may receive mercy and find grace to help us in our time of need* (4:16). And the section ends in a similar way: 'Therefore, brothers, since we have confidence to enter the Most Holy Place by the blood of Jesus, by a new and living way opened for us through the curtain, that is, his body, and since we have a great priest over the house of God, let us draw near to God with a sincere heart in full assurance of faith, having our hearts sprinkled to cleanse us from a guilty conscience and having our bodies washed with pure water' (10:19–22).

The central section of Hebrews on Christ's priesthood and sacrifice is thus embraced by these two exhortatory passages, and both have as their focus a call to confidence in prayer. If our prayers were made more effective through fasting, or godliness, or length we could never be sure they had been heard or would be answered. We could never be sure we had done enough to satisfy the Father. But the Father is entirely satisfied by the work of the Son and the Son's work is entirely finished. That is the confidence we have before God, and it is a confidence that can never be shaken.

> Before the throne of God above
> I have a strong, a perfect plea;
> a great High Priest, whose name is Love,
> who ever lives and pleads for me.
> My name is graven on His hands,
> my name is hidden in His heart;
> I know that while in heav'n He stands
> no tongue can bid me thence depart.[19]

[19] Charitie Lees de Chenez (1841–1923), 'Before the throne of God above'.

In a similar vein Calvin says:

Since no man is worthy to present himself to God and come into his sight, the Heavenly Father himself, to free us at once from shame and fear, which might well have thrown our hearts into despair, has given us his Son, Jesus Christ our Lord, to be our advocate and mediator with him, by whose guidance we may confidently come to him, and with such an intercessor, trusting nothing we ask in his name will be denied us, as nothing can be denied to him by the Father.[20]

God himself has given us Christ to 'free us ... from shame and fear' so that we can 'confidently come to him'. This is surely all the encouragement to prayer we need. The climax of this wonderful explanation of Jesus as our High Priest in Hebrews 4 – 10 is the exhortation to pray. The writer describes the section as *solid food* (5:14). But its application is simple: use the privileges for which Christ died; come before God in prayer; call out to him in time of need. Let us approach the throne of grace. Let us draw near to God.

[20] Calvin, *Institutes*, 3.20.17.

Romans 8 and Jude
4. Praying by the Spirit

The role of the Spirit in prayer has been an issue of controversy in recent years. This is a pity, for what the New Testament says about the subject offers great encouragement to us in our struggle to pray. The sad irony is that many Christians are made to feel inadequate by talk of praying in the Spirit, whereas in reality the Spirit wonderfully ensures the adequacy of our prayers.

1. The Spirit and the object of prayer (Rom. 8:14–17)

The object of prayer is the God who invites us to call him 'Father'. But, says Paul, we can only call upon God in this way through the Spirit of adoption, who witnesses to our spirits that we are children of God. It is the Spirit who enables us to perceive the God who is the object of prayer as our Father. Through the Spirit we enjoy the freedom, experience and confidence of God's children.

a. The freedom of children

In the first half of Romans 8 Paul draws a contrast between two ways of life or two spheres of government: life according to the flesh and life according to the Spirit. The way of the flesh leads to death and is hostile to God (5–8). The way of the Spirit leads to life and peace with God (6, 9–11). Christians are like a workplace under the new, benevolent management of the Spirit. But the habits of the old regime die hard and must be consciously eradicated. This is what Paul means when he says *by the Spirit you put to death the misdeeds of the body* (13). To be led by the Spirit (14), then, is not some ecstatic experience but to battle against our sinful habits – what previous generations called 'mortifying the sinful nature'.

Those who are thus led by the Spirit, says Paul, are sons of God

(14). On a visit to India I saw children who were bonded labourers working to repay the debts of their parents. Shackled in chains, they spent their days hammering rocks into pieces. Christians are like children who after years in bonded labour have been adopted into a family. The rules of the old master together with the fear of punishment have been replaced by the freedom of a loving family. While our years in slavery continue to affect us and sometimes cause friction in the new family, they cannot undermine the security we now enjoy. 'In the Roman world of the first century AD an adopted son was a son deliberately chosen by his adoptive father to perpetuate his name and inherit his estate; he was no whit inferior in status to a son born in the ordinary course of nature, and might well enjoy the father's affection more fully and reproduce the father's character more worthily.'[1]

That 'sons' is inclusive of men and women is evident from the use of 'children' (*tekna*) in verses 16–17. But it is significant that both men and women are adopted as 'sons' (*hyioi*) in verses 14–15, for sons were the ones with a claim on the inheritance (17). Far from being exclusive, Paul is saying that before God, women have a status as co-heirs with men, which Roman society denied them.

In this passage Paul uses the language of exodus.[2] James Dunn says that in this section 'continuity with and fulfilment of the promises to Abraham and Israel is the hidden current which carries Paul's thought forward'.[3] Once we were slaves just as the Israelites were slaves in Egypt. But Christ has effected a new exodus. He has broken the power of sin and the fear of death.[4] His death and resurrection – re-enacted in baptism – are like the escape through the Red Sea (1 Cor. 10:2). Now we are led by the Spirit just as the Israelites were led by the pillars of cloud and fire (14). The God who called on Pharaoh to liberate Israel his 'son' now enables us through the Spirit to call him Father (15). Just as they received an inheritance in the Promised Land, so we are heirs (17). The Spirit is the liberating Spirit. He gives us the experience of freedom that is ours through the liberating work of Christ. One sign of this is that we can call upon God as Father without fear.

b. The experience of children

The objective work of the Son, reconciling us to God and giving us access into his presence, is matched by the subjective work of the

[1] Bruce, *Romans*, p. 157.
[2] See N. T. Wright, 'Lord's Prayer', p. 153.
[3] J. D. G. Dunn, *Romans 1 – 8*, p. 449.
[4] On 'a spirit of slavery' see Moo, *Romans*, pp. 499–500.

Spirit. *The Spirit himself testifies with our spirit that we are God's children* (16). The Spirit makes the mediatorial work of the Son a living experience in the life of the believer. God sends the Spirit of the Son to the believer so that what is true in fact becomes real in experience. Verse 16 could mean the Spirit witnesses *together with* our spirit, but it is more likely to mean the Spirit witnesses *to* our spirit.[5] Paul is not simply talking about a truth that comforts us but a phenomenon we experience in *our spirit*. The Spirit makes prayer a real experience of communication rather than an empty charade. The conviction that prayer is more than talking to oneself is the work of the Spirit within us. We should not underestimate the importance of the reality of prayer in providing assurance. 'Paul stresses that our awareness of God as Father comes not from rational consideration nor from external testimony alone but from a truth deeply felt and intensely experienced. If some Christians err in basing their assurance of salvation on feelings alone, many others err in basing it on facts and arguments alone.'[6]

True prayer is thoroughly trinitarian and can only be trinitarian. The Father invites us to call upon him through the Son by the Spirit. The relationship between God and mankind only works because God is at work on both sides of the relationship: both to accept prayer and to inspire prayer. The Father is the one to whom we pray and who graciously hears our prayers. The Son is the one who mediates, giving us access to the Father. The Spirit is the one who enables us to pray, disposing us to pray to God where once we were hostile towards him (6–7). 'For through [Christ]', says Paul to the Ephesians, 'we both have access to the Father by one Spirit' (Eph. 2:18). Through the obedience of the Son we can call upon God as Father. The Son makes us family. The Spirit is the Spirit of the Son (9) and so he is the Spirit of sonship or adoption (15). The Spirit is sent by the ascended Christ to mediate his presence so that those united to the Son can participate in the trinitarian relationship. Through the Spirit we join with the Son in calling upon God as Father.

In practice this means that the Spirit is the only 'mechanism' or 'means' we need in prayer. We do not need special words, tone, place or times. At any time and in any place we can direct our attention to God and call upon him as Father. It is the Spirit who makes this possible. We learn to pray by living in friendship with God through the Spirit, not by reading a manual. Billy Bray, the

---

[5] See Cranfield, *Romans*, vol. 1, p. 403; and Morris, *Romans*, pp. 316–317.
[6] Moo, *Romans*, p. 502.

nineteenth-century Cornish evangelist, when faced with a problem would simply say, 'I must go and talk to Father about it.'

Most of us spend over twenty hours each day on the ordinary, routine things of life: work, chores, eating, sleeping, commuting. But most of what we think of as discipleship – Bible study, quiet time, church meetings, ministry activities – belongs in the remaining four hours. And for most people it is much less than four hours. Exhortations to discipleship simply result in us trying to squeeze more into an already full pot. What is more, in common with our culture, we Christians value the extraordinary over the ordinary. Whether it is conferences, spiritual experiences, revivals – we are looking for the extraordinary. But the message of the incarnation is that God meets us not in the earthquake, wind or fire, but in the ordinary. Meals, journeys, homes – these are the places where Jesus conducted his ministry. The Spirit of God has been given so that the routine is filled with God's presence. The fruit of the Spirit is not the characteristic of high achievers but of those who serve faithfully in the commonplace things of life (Gal. 5:22–23). We can pray without ceasing – not by being always on our knees but by living each moment for God in the presence of God. To be spiritual is not to have attained esoteric experiences but to walk with the Spirit in the everyday (Gal. 5:25). Jesus suggests that on the day of judgment we may well be surprised to discover who the truly spiritual are (Matt. 7:21–24; 25:31–46).

c. The confidence of children

Paul urges us not to slip back into the old mindset of a slave but to live according to our new status as adopted children. *For you did not receive a spirit that makes you a slave again to fear, but you received the Spirit of sonship* (15). It is the mindset of a slave to cringe in fear before one's master. It is the mindset of a child to cry out Abba, *Father.* We do not have a spirit of fear. We do not have to look over our shoulders, wondering whether God is going to give up on us. Instead we have a Spirit of sonship who testifies that we are part of God's family. Dick Lucas tells of an occasion in a shop when he overheard a young Jewish boy call out to his father, 'Abba, Abba.' Lucas says that in that moment 'I bowed and worshipped' – he realized with new force the intimacy with God that is ours through the Spirit. Paul has already said that 'God has poured out his love into our hearts by the Holy Spirit, whom he has given us' (Rom. 5:5) for it is by the Spirit that we see in the cross the demonstration of God's love (Rom. 5:6–8). If God loved us at our worst – when we were powerless, ungodly, sinners and his enemies – then he will continue to love us to the end (Rom. 5:6–11). In this way the Spirit 'pours ... confidence into our hearts' and this confidence 'opens our mouths' in prayer.[7]

Some have interpreted the testimony of the Spirit as a distinct, dramatic experience subsequent to conversion. But, as John Stott, says, 'I have an uneasy feeling that it is the experiences which have determined the exposition.'[8] Verses 14–17 read most naturally as a description of the ordinary experience of *all* believers. Stott concludes, 'There is no indication in these four verses that a special, distinctive or overwhelming experience is in mind, which needs to be sought by all although it is given only to some. On the contrary, the whole paragraph appears to be descriptive of what is, or should be, common to all believers.'[9]

In his book exploring the growth of evangelical Christianity, *The Hallelujah Revolution*, the journalist Ian Cotton describes how Lloyd Kuehl, an American Christian, travelled from the United States to join a group of British Christians praying for the healing of John, who was suffering from liver cancer. Lloyd arrived to find that John was already dead. But Lloyd felt God say to him, 'I will raise him from the dead,' so the group continued to pray that John would be brought to life. Four days later they gave up and John was cremated. Whatever else one might say about those involved, they had understood the outrage of Christians dying. Paul says that Christians are *free from the law of sin and death* (2). How can God promise us life (Rom. 5:17–21; 6:23; 8:1–2) and then leave us to die? The same is true of sin. Paul says we are free from sin (Rom. 6:6–7, 14, 18, 22; 8:1–2) and yet we know all too well that sin is part of our lives every day. When I sin I am left asking whether I have truly been saved or alternatively whether the gospel can deliver what it promises.

Romans 8 is written to give Christians confidence in the gospel in the face of sin and death. Our response should not be to pray that Christians might be spared death as Lloyd Kuehl and his friends did. Instead through the chapter Paul weaves three responses: (1) the presence of the Holy Spirit, (2) the promise of glory, and (3) the ultimate purposes of God. The Spirit's role in prayer is part of the assurance we have in the face of sin and death. Our sin and mortality throw the gospel into question, but our experience of the Spirit reassures us that we are God's adopted children. 'Anyone who is seriously struggling to put to death the sin in his life is clearly being led by the Spirit, and those who are led by

[7] Calvin, *Romans and Thessalonians*, p. 170.
[8] Stott, *Romans*, p. 236.
[9] Ibid.

the Spirit are sons of God.'[10] To struggle with sin should not make us doubt, for the very fact that we experience sin in terms of struggle is a sure sign of the Spirit's work. Prayer itself reminds us that as God's children we need not fear sin and death, for one day we shall enjoy the inheritance of sons. Prayer is founded on, and is a sure sign of, 'something prior to it and independent of it, namely the fact that no less an authority than God Himself in His Spirit has assured us – and continues to assure us – that we are His children'.[11]

2. The Spirit and the content of prayer (Rom. 8:26–27)

The hope of an inheritance with which Romans 8:14–17 ends is qualified: *if indeed we share in his sufferings in order that we may also share in his glory* (17). The pattern of suffering followed by glory that we see in the cross and resurrection is the pattern of Christian discipleship (see e.g. Mark 8:31–38; 10:35–45; Phil. 3:9–10; 1 Pet. 1:10–11; 4:13; 5:10). We live in the overlap of two ages: the old age of death and the new age of grace (Rom 5:12–21). In the second half of Romans 8 Paul talks about the tension of living between these two ages; between the now and the not-yet of Christian hope. In verse 15 Paul says we *received the Spirit of sonship*, but in verse 23 he says *we wait eagerly for our adoption as sons*. Christian hope makes no sense unless the freedom from sin and death promised in the gospel are future realities (24). The correlate of New Testament hope is often patience (25).

Paul says the creation groans as it experiences the frustration of bondage and awaits its liberation (22). In the same way we groan inwardly as we await full redemption (23). Tasting the first fruits of salvation through the Spirit only heightens the expectation of what is to come. And Paul says that even the Spirit of God groans (26). We would not talk this way if the Word of God did not give us precedent. God experiences the tension of life between the two ages, and through the Spirit joins us in longing for the liberation of the new age.

When our groans express the tension of life between the ages, the Spirit, as it were, offers them as a prayer to God. In our weakness the Spirit prays for us. This is a wonderful and surprising truth, for we often feel inadequate compared to those we consider Spirit-filled. We pray in the Spirit, however, not in moments of high emotion but when we are weak: the Spirit comes to our aid not when our spiritual senses are heightened but when they are dull.

[10] St Helens, *Romans*, p. 123.
[11] Cranfield, *Romans*, vol. 1, p. 402.

The Spirit is not the sole possession of the spiritually strong but is God's gift to the spiritually feeble! Such a truth, however, finds no place in a spirituality of human design, for we focus on attainment. This is the spirituality of grace.

A deeper hold on this truth would deliver many evangelicals from the grip of a secret legalistic bondage, according to which failure to pray brings ostracism or excommunication from the family of God, necessitating a kind of re-conversion. But on the contrary, the New Testament stresses the care of the Spirit for the tired and struggling disciple. This guidance removes the temptation to import an alien 'justification by quiet times' into evangelical spirituality ... Here lies the message of true freedom, that God the Spirit even upholds us in our fear, failure, and unfaith.[12]

This does not mean we can dispense with duty and discipline. *We have an obligation* (12) and that obligation is to be led by the Spirit into conformity with the Son who said no to some things so that he could spend time with his Father (Luke 5:16). Those who would share the Son's glory must also share his suffering (17).

Neither are these verses just about moments of crisis. The weakness to which they refer is the weakness of all those living in the tension between the two ages. It is the weakness of fallen human beings not yet fully redeemed (23). The phrase *in the same way* (26) suggests that just as the Spirit causes us to feel the overlap of the ages as a tension, so he helps us pray in that tension. Just as the Spirit causes us to wait both eagerly and patiently (23, 25), so he helps us when we do not know whether to pray for deliverance or endurance. This is a description of prayer between the ages and so it is a description of all Christian prayer.

The problem is *we do not know what we ought to pray for* (26). The issue is the content of prayer.[13] 'All praying of Christian men, in so far as it is *their* praying, remains under the sign of this not-knowing, of real ignorance, weakness and poverty, and that even in their prayers they live only by God's justification of sinners.'[14] We can always pray to some extent in accordance with God's will because his great purpose to conform us to Christ and bring us to glory is revealed in his Word, as Paul reminds us in verses 28–30. But we do not know the route to this end in any given situation. We do not know what is best for us, still less how it might be achieved.

But such ignorance need not inhibit prayer. The logic of verses

[12] Bradshaw, *Praying as Believing*, pp. 82–83.
[13] Moo, *Romans*, p. 523.
[14] Cranfield, *Romans*, vol. 1, p. 422.

26–27 is compelling. Our words may be wrong. Words may even fail us. But the Spirit prays for us without words. God does not need our words to be right for he *searches our hearts*. At the same time, God does not need words from the Spirit for *he ... knows the mind of the Spirit*. God knows that the Spirit desires what God desires. C. S. Lewis says, 'Prayer in its most perfect state is a soliloquy ... If the Holy Spirit speaks in the man, then in prayer God speaks to God.'[15] Every prayer we offer is a prayer offered in weakness and ignorance. But every prayer we offer is partnered by the Spirit who prays in full knowledge of God's will. These verses, then, are a wonderful incentive to pray.

> Our failure to know God's will and consequent inability to petition God specifically and assuredly is met by God's Spirit, who himself expresses to God those intercessory petitions that perfectly match the will of God. When we do not know what to pray for – yes, even when we pray for things that are not best for us – we need not despair, for we can depend on the Spirit's ministry of perfect intercession 'on our behalf'.[16]

When we are so perplexed that our prayers become confused, God makes sense of them. When pain obscures coherent thought, God interprets the heart. When we try to pray publicly and our words come out wrong, God hears our true intent. Moreover when we fail in prayer – as we do to a greater or lesser extent every time we pray – the Spirit prays for us and his prayers always hit the mark. Every prayer we pray is a flawed prayer, but through the Spirit every prayer becomes a prayer *in accordance with God's will*.

I occasionally help international students with the English of their assignments. One student had only recently learnt English and her work was full of mistakes, sometimes making no sense at all. Nevertheless I was able to take her intentions and turn them into a piece of (reasonably) polished English prose. I wondered what her tutor would make of such an uncharacteristic piece of work! In a similar way, our prayers are riddled with mistakes and lack good sense, but the Spirit takes and presents them as they should be before God.

3. The Spirit and the practice of prayer (Jude 20)

Jude tells his readers to *pray in the Holy Spirit* (20). We often

[15] Lewis, *Letters to Malcolm*, p. 93.
[16] Moo, *Romans*, p. 526.

interpret this in the light of our experience – or our assumptions of what that experience should involve. But to understand what Jude meant by it we need to read it in the context of the epistle as a whole. Jude's desire was to have written a positive letter of encouragement but the circumstances demanded a letter of warning (3). False teachers have infiltrated the church but their false teaching is in fact a cover for false living. *For certain men whose condemnation was written about long ago have secretly slipped in among you. They are godless men, who change the grace of our God into a licence for immorality and deny Jesus Christ our only Sovereign and Lord* (4).

The false teachers advocated a form of antinomianism. They argued that since we are saved by grace rather than by good works it does not matter how we live. They abused the freedom we have in Christ and made it an excuse for immorality. In so doing they denied the lordship of Christ. They wanted Christ as Saviour but they would not accept his authority as *Sovereign and Lord* in their lives. In verses 5–16 Jude presents a series of examples from the Old Testament and extra-biblical literature to show how dangerous this is. He identifies the false teachers as those about whom the apostles warned (see e.g. Acts 20).

a. Self-controlled prayer

It is in this context that Jude talks about the role of the Spirit. The false teachers *follow mere natural instincts and do not have the Spirit* (19). Without the Spirit they follow ungodly desires. The implication is that the Christians to whom Jude writes should be controlled by the Spirit, and if they are controlled by the Spirit they will exercise self-control. Those with the Spirit do not follow *mere natural instincts* but build one another up and pray in the Spirit.

This is not how we often think of the role of the Spirit, especially in prayer. To pray in the Spirit, it is supposed, is to pray led by your instincts or using ecstatic gifts.[17] But the immediate context makes it clear that for Jude to pray in the Spirit is to pray with self-control. It is to subdue our natural instincts. If we follow our natural instincts we shall watch the television rather than join the prayer meeting. We shall stay in bed rather than rise to pray. We shall measure prayer by how it makes us feel or how spectacular the signs that accompany it. But when we pray in the Spirit we shall exercise self-control. We shall seek to build others up as we pray with them. We

[17] Bauckham, *Jude, 2 Peter*, p. 113; see also J. D. G. Dunn, *Jesus and the Spirit*, pp. 239–240.

shall submit to others just as the spirits of the prophets are to be controlled by them (1 Cor. 14:32). We shall pray for lives brought under the authority of Christ our Sovereign (4).

Prayer is difficult. John Stott speaks of the battle of the threshold of prayer.[18] Often, he suggests, the struggle in prayer comes as we approach prayer when distractions, weariness and weakness divert us. Sometimes, of course, prayer is pure delight, but we must not allow our feelings to determine when we pray. The fruit of the Spirit within us includes the self-control needed to pray when we are disinclined to do so (Gal. 5:22–23).

> To cultivate the ceaseless spirit of prayer, use more frequent acts of prayer. To learn to pray with freedom, force yourself to pray. The great liberty begins in necessity. Do not say, 'I cannot pray. I am not in the spirit.' Pray till you are in the spirit ... So if you are averse to pray, pray the more. Do not call it lip-service. That is not the lip-service God disowns. It is His Spirit acting in your self-coercive will, only not yet your heart.[19]

b. Corporate prayer

The Spirit is not our only companion in the battle. Contending for the faith (3) is a corporate activity. Jude's readers are to *build yourselves* and *keep yourselves* (20–21): literally build 'one another' and keep 'one another'. 'Building up' is an allusion to the image of church as a temple, which the New Testament uses to reinforce the corporate nature of our relationship with God (see e.g. Eph. 2:19–22). It is through mutual exhortation and correction that we guard the church. While the false teachers divide the church (19), we are to be united in the truth. So when Jude talks about praying in the Spirit he is not talking about an individual alone with God (see also Eph. 2:17–18). Instead this is the prayer of the prayer meeting – we pray *together* in the Spirit.

c. Selfless prayer

Most commentators understand the call to *wait for the mercy of our Lord Jesus Christ to bring you to eternal life* (21) as a reference to the return of Christ who will mercifully grant eternal life to those who are his. But it could refer instead to waiting for God mercifully to answer our prayers. While the NIV adds 'to bring you', the ESV reads,

---

[18] Cited e.g. in Bewes, *Talking about Prayer*, p. 55.
[19] Forsyth, *Soul of Prayer*, pp. 62–63.

waiting for the mercy of our Lord Jesus Christ that leads to eternal life. If building one another and keeping one another in verses 20 and 21 are parallel statements, then praying in the Spirit and *waiting for the mercy of our Lord Jesus Christ* may also be parallel. To wait on God is used in the Scriptures as a synonym for prayer:

> I waited patiently for the LORD;
> he turned to me and heard my cry.
>
> (Ps. 40:1)[20]

To pray in the Spirit is matched by seeking God's mercy towards those affected by the false teachers, so that they are rescued for eternal life (21). The theme of mercy continues in verses 22–23. These verses contain difficult textual problems about which 'it is probably impossible to reach an assured conclusion'.[21] Some manuscripts describe three groups – *those who doubt*; those whom we are to *snatch from the fire*; and those to whom we should show mercy *mixed with fear* – while other manuscripts omit the first group (*those who doubt*). It is also not clear whether Jude's readers are to 'convince' or 'show mercy' to this first group. If three groups are mentioned, Jude's readers are to show mercy to those wavering in their faith (22) and to rescue those who have already succumbed to the false teachers (23). But they are also to show mercy to *others*. This final group is probably the false teachers themselves or those thoroughly influenced by them. Therefore their mercy is *mixed with fear*, for this group represents a threat to faithful Christians. They are to hate *even the clothing stained by corrupted flesh* (23). The picture is of showing mercy to people with whom they are not to have contact. How else can this be done except through prayer? Jude's readers show mercy to the false teachers by praying for them to be rescued from their error. They pray for God's mercy, which leads to eternal life (23) rather than the judgment to which these teachers' error tends (15).

The *snatching* of others *from the fire* and *the clothing stained by corrupted flesh* are both references to Zechariah 3 to which Jude has already alluded (9). These allusions suggest that the prayers of Jude's readers may not be in vain. In Zechariah 3 Joshua the high priest stands before God with Satan at his side accusing him. The Lord rebukes Satan because Joshua is 'a burning stick snatched from the fire' (Zech. 3:2). The Lord then instructs an angel to 'take off his filthy clothes' because, he explains to Joshua, 'I have taken away

---

[20] See also Pss. 62:1, 5; 63:3; 130:5–6; Prov. 20:22; Is. 33:2; 40:31.
[21] Bauckham, *Jude, 2 Peter*, p. 108.

your sin'. God shows mercy to Joshua, overruling the accusations of Satan, sparing him from judgment and removing his sin. By using the description of Joshua to describe those influenced by the false teachers, Jude implies that God may be merciful to them as he was to Joshua.

To pray in the Spirit, then, is to pray for others – even those who threaten us. This is certainly not our natural inclination. When other people cause us problems our tendency, if we pray at all, is to seek our vindication. But those controlled by the Spirit will pray for their opponents to receive mercy from God and escape his judgment. In this we echo the prayer of him who said, 'Father, forgive them, for they do not know what they are doing' (Luke 23:34).

4. Conclusion

The letter of Jude is written with a sense of urgency – this is not the letter Jude wanted to write. He warns his readers of danger, urging them to contend for the faith. Yet, while this is the language of struggle and threat, these warnings are enclosed by two lovely statements of eternal certainty:

To those who have been called, who are loved by God the Father and kept by Jesus Christ.

(1)

To him who is able to keep you from falling and to present you before his glorious presence without fault and with great joy – to the only God our Saviour be glory, majesty, power and authority, through Jesus Christ our Lord, before all ages, now and for evermore! Amen.

(24–25)

In Romans 8:23 Paul describes the Spirit as the *firstfruits* of the new age, and in Ephesians 1:14 as 'a deposit guaranteeing our inheritance'. When the realities of sin and death in our lives undermine our confidence in the gospel, or when our faith is threatened, the Spirit assures us that God will keep us and complete his eternal purposes. The Spirit is the foretaste and guarantee of the life to come.[22] We taste heaven on earth through our life together as the community of the Holy Spirit. Through the Spirit prayer itself is an assurance and anticipation of the day when we participate fully in the trinitarian relationships.

[22] See John Stott, *The Contemporary Christian* in *The Essential John Stott* (IVP, 1999), p. 648.

James 1 and 5
5. Praying with faith

> Once, the word providence efficiently communicated the idea that God loved us, ruled time to its minute details, and was himself a historical agent. That time is gone, however, and the word has rusted up through misuse beyond utility.[1]

Belief in the providence of God – the belief that God lovingly rules time and history – has endured a twin assault in recent centuries. Advances in science in the eighteenth and nineteenth centuries led to a growing perception that natural cause and effect could provide a sufficient explanation of the universe. People no longer looked to God as the hand behind events. The natural sciences explained the patterns of the physical world, while the rise of social sciences offered a way of explaining history. Darwinism took this to a further level, providing not only an alternative explanation of human origins but also of purpose in history. If confidence in human reason undermined providence in the eighteenth and nineteenth centuries, it was human brutality in the twentieth century that led the second assault on providence. Two world wars, nuclear destruction, the Jewish holocaust, Stalinism, a myriad of national, regional and genocidal wars, and a global awareness of famine and poverty have made it still harder to affirm the hand of a benevolent Deity in the affairs of mankind.

Yet faith in the providence of God is a prerequisite of prayer. Prayer has no meaning without a God who intervenes in human affairs. A. A. Hodge acknowledges that prayer 'does produce valuable subjective effects upon the state of mind and character of the person praying'. But, he argues, the Bible encourages us to pray for 'temporal and material benefits', and it only makes sense to pray

---

[1] Jonathan Tucker Boyd, cited in Tiessen, *Providence and Prayer*, p. 16.

for a material good if 'we may really and truly influence the mind of God to give it to us'.[2] *Prayer presupposes that God acts in history for our good in response to our requests.* In James 1:5–6 James tells his readers to make their requests to God without doubting. If they doubt they will not receive (1:7). Effective prayer must be prayed in faith.

1. The situation: economic hardship

James writes *to the twelve tribes in the Dispersion* (1:1 ESV; *among the nations* in the NIV is not in the original). Although the twelve tribes no longer existed, it had become a way of referring to a renewed Israel (Ezek. 47:13; Matt. 19:28), and as far as the early church was concerned the new Israel had been reconstituted in Christ (see 1 Pet. 2:4–10). James is probably referring to Jewish believers who had been scattered from Jerusalem as a result of persecution (see Acts 8:1; 11:19). He refers to them as *my brothers* and *my dear brothers* (Jas. 1:16, 19; 2:1, 5, 14; 3:1, 10, 12; 5:12, 19). Douglas Moo says, 'These could well have been former "parishioners" of James whom he now addresses in a "pastoral letter".'[3]

The recipients of James's letter were facing *trials of many kinds* (see also 1:2, 12). These trials seem to have found expression in different forms, so that James can talk about *many kinds* of trials (literally 'multicoloured'), but at root they appear to have been economic.[4] Acts 11:27–30 describes a famine that hit Palestine and which prompted the first gift from Gentiles to Jewish believers. Many in the congregations would have been subsistence farmers or agricultural labourers facing hardship and exploitation as the value of their labour fell.

Evidence for this is found within the letter itself. James says the rich in society are exploiting the poor within the congregation (2:6). He talks about *the brother in humble circumstances*; that is, someone who is poor and marginalized in society (1:9). He says, 'Has not God chosen those who are poor in the eyes of the world to be rich in faith and to inherit the kingdom he promised those who love him?' (2:5). His warning against favouritism makes sense given how easy it would have been to treat a rich visitor with special honour as a potential benefactor (2:1–5). When James famously links faith and deeds the example he gives matches the situation in the congregation: a wealthy Christian who mouths empty words of comfort to a needy brother or sister without doing anything to help them

[2] A. A. Hodge, *Evangelical Theology*, p. 91.
[3] Moo, *James*, p. 58.
[4] See Timmis, *Reading James Today*.

(2:15–17). Those with greater economic mobility are to trust God rather than their own capabilities (4:13–16). They are to identify with the beleaguered congregation and do the good they know they ought to do (4:17). The community is not to aspire to be like the rich landowners who face God's judgment (5:1–6), but to *be patient … until the Lord's coming* (5:7).

It is easy to feel we are missing out when we see the wealth of others. If God is at work in history, then his actions do not seem fair. For some people the problems become serious, leaving them exploited by employers, robbed of dignity by welfare or impoverished by their marginalization. James is writing to just such people.

2. The response: faith in God (1:2–4)

The response of James to the economic hardship of his readers is to call on them to trust God and to keep on trusting God. On the one hand he calls them to live what they claim to believe – their faith is dead if it is not accompanied by works commensurate with that faith. But he also encourages them to believe that they can live the radical lifestyle to which he calls them because God is trustworthy. James says that they *can* have works that match their faith because their faith is in a reliable and generous God. They need not show favouritism to potential rich benefactors (2:1–5) because they already have a rich benefactor – the God who has chosen them to be rich and inherit the promised kingdom (2:5). They need not aspire to be like the rich exploiters (5:1–6) because the Lord is coming (5:7–8). The God they trust is the One who gives *every good and perfect gift* (1:17).

In verses 2–3 James says, *Consider it pure joy, my brothers, whenever you face trials of many kinds, because you know that the testing of your faith develops perseverance.* The problem is not their trials per se but how they respond to them. Trials are to be viewed as an occasion for joy because they have a purpose and that purpose is *perseverance.* Perseverance is faith that keeps on going. It is faith that keeps on trusting. In the parable of the Sower the seed sown on rocky ground springs up but then withers away. 'Those on the rock are the ones who receive the word with joy when they hear it, but they have no root. They believe for a while, but in the time of testing they fall away' (Luke 8:13). James's readers are facing just such a time of testing and he urges them not to fall away. The seed sown on good soil represents those 'who hear the word, retain it, and by persevering produce a crop' (Luke 8:15). Perseverance *in the time of testing* is the sign of true faith. But perseverance itself is not the end product. *Perseverance must finish its work so that you may be mature and complete, not lacking anything* (4). The NIV obscures the fact that this is a command: James's readers are to let perseverance complete itself in maturity. Persevering means to keep *going* as a Christian, but it also means to keep *growing* as a Christian. The goal is Christian maturity. 'The joiner, when he glues together two boards, keeps them tightly clamped till the cement sets, and the outward pressure is no more needed; then he unscrews. So with the calamities, depressions, and disappointments that crush us into close contact with God. The pressure on us is kept up till the soul's union with God is set.'[5]

So James starts his letter with this amazing statement: *Consider it pure joy, my brothers, whenever you face trials of many kinds* (2). Trials should make us rejoice with *pure* joy because they produce perseverance and perseverance leads to maturity. James is not being glib here. The word *count* implies reason and persuasion – reaching a conscious decision. James knows that circumstances throw God's providence into question. But James says they can look beyond appearances. That is the nature of faith. Faith looks beyond what can be seen to the promises and character of God. They are to *persuade* themselves that their trials are producing maturity in them.

3. The means: prayer for wisdom (1:5–8)

To trust in the providence of God when times are difficult is not easy. To count trials pure joy can seem impossible. So James exhorts his readers to ask God to help them understand. *If any of you lacks wisdom, he should ask God* (5). Wisdom in the Bible is about making connections. The book of Proverbs, for example, is about seeing the connections between cause and effect in an ordered universe. Here James wants his readers to pray for the ability to make connections between the trials they are enduring, and the purposes and character of God. Suffering leads to Christian maturity, but we need divine wisdom to realize this.

This request for wisdom requires faith. *Let him ask in faith*, says James, *without doubting* (6 ESV). We do not have to get everything sorted out in our mind before we pray, but we have to get at least this sorted out: we have to trust in God and his goodness. If we do not trust God, then every new circumstance will change our view of God. We shall be like someone who, when life is good, thinks well of God, but when life is hard, thinks ill of him. Such a person is like *a wave of the sea, blown and tossed by the wind* (6). Such people are *doubled-minded* (8). They are people who hedge their bets. They

[5] Forsyth, *Soul of Prayer*, p. 17.

trust God when things are good but look elsewhere when things are difficult. It prepares the way for what James will say in 4:4–8 where he calls worldly Christians *double-minded* because they want both God *and* the world. These are people for whom God is one option among others for getting what they want. If we treat God in this way we should not be surprised if prayer is unsatisfactory (7). The double-minded man is *unstable*. He is like an investor who keeps moving his stock around as share prices fluctuate. In contrast we are to keep our stock firmly placed in God through thick and thin, confident in a good return.

The 'multicoloured' trials of life often raise big questions in our mind. James invites us to pose those questions to God himself. We are invited to pray for understanding, perhaps even to interrogate God as the psalmists often did. But underlying this questioning must be faith in God. Faith in God does not mean we have all the answers in a neat package. But if there is not an underlying faith the questions will take us further from wisdom rather than closer to it.

James gives us this promise: when we pray for wisdom, God will enable us to see our troubles as opportunities to mature and to see beyond them to glory. When we ask for this, says James, God will give generously without finding fault, neither begrudging nor criticizing us (5).

Faith is confidence in the goodness of God. Wisdom is the application of that confidence to everyday life. In the Jewish mind 'wisdom meant practical righteousness in everyday living'.[6] Wisdom sees in the trials of life opportunities for Christian growth. Wisdom makes the connection between affliction and perseverance and maturity. Wisdom translates faith in the goodness of God into confidence in his providential rule over current circumstances.

4. Wisdom to discern the good purposes of God (1:9–12)

James expands on this wisdom in the next two sections. He says, *The brother in humble circumstances ought to take pride in his high position* (9). This is an act of the mind that employs the wisdom received in verse 5.

We rejoice in trials not only because they lead to maturity but because they direct our attention beyond the trials to what lies ahead. In verses 9–11 James speaks of a great eschatological reversal. The poor will be exalted – not all the poor, but those who recognize that in God they find *a high position* (9). They recognize they have nowhere to go but to God. They have turned from trusting in

[6] Martin, *James*, p. 17.

wealth to serving God – even if that means hardship. No doubt the poor felt like they were fading away under the pressure of their adversity, but in fact it is the rich who will *pass away* (10). The poor will be exalted and the rich will be brought low. Verse 10 is ironic: all the rich can really take pride in is that they will be brought low. Their position looks so secure, but in reality they are as transient as blossom. These verses are an allusion to Isaiah 40:6–8 where the grass and flowers fade while the Word of the Lord endures forever. Those who trust in riches or who exploit the poor will pass away, but those enriched by the gospel (2:5) will stand the test (12). History has often testified to the transient nature of wealth and power, but these historical reversals are merely pointers to the eschatological reversal of the final judgment.

These verses recall the many announcements of reversal in the ministry of Jesus: 'The last will be first, and the first will be last' (Matt. 20:16). They recall, too, Mary's song:

> He has performed mighty deeds with his arm;
>   he has scattered those who are proud in their inmost
>   thoughts.
> He has brought down rulers from their thrones
>   but has lifted up the humble.
> He has filled the hungry with good things
>   but has sent the rich away empty.
>
> (Luke 1:51–53)

Mary's experience is paradigmatic. God has chosen this lowly peasant girl to be the one through whom the Saviour came. Everything is being turned upside down in God's kingdom. We can *consider it pure joy* because we have this end in sight – fortunes are going to be reversed. You may be missing out now, James is saying, but if you keep trusting God you will not miss out on heaven. *Blessed is the man who perseveres under trial* (1:12). Those who keep going until the end will be rewarded with *a crown of life* – the victor's garland, the gold medal. The wisdom for which we should pray is the ability to look beyond circumstances to see the ultimate purposes of God. It is to be able to say with Paul, 'I consider that our present sufferings are not worth comparing with the glory that will be revealed in us' (Rom. 8:18).

James orients faith to the eschatological future. Faith is not convincing ourselves that God will necessarily relieve our problems in the present. How could such faith consider trials to be pure joy? Faith oriented to the present cannot coexist with trials. Trials become a sign that faith is weak. But James says trials are an opportunity to persevere and mature. Faith is challenged by trials, but it is challenged to look beyond them to the promise of a crown of life.

Some of us readily moan about our problems, while others are full of joy as they endure acute affliction. The difference is rarely the extent of the suffering they endure but their focus on the goodness of God. I remember a friend called Ruth who had been disabled for many years and was now suffering from cancer. She was in constant pain so that you often saw her wince. Yet I remember her smile to this day. She always had a positive word and a testimony to God's goodness. To talk to her was to be encouraged – and challenged. She told me once how God had pursued her for over ten years before she finally put her faith in Christ. She was stubborn, she told me, by way of explanation. Now in her pain she was once again stubborn – stubbornly trusting in the goodness of God and the future he had for her.

5. Wisdom to discern the good character of God (1:13–18)

When trouble comes there are two options, two ways of connecting what is going on.

a. Option one: things are bad because God is at fault (13–15)

This is the option James addresses in verse 13: *When tempted, no-one should say, 'God is tempting me.' For God cannot be tempted by evil, nor does he tempt anyone.* God is not trying to wreck our faith by tempting us. God does allow bad things to happen, but never does so to tempt us away from faith. 'While God may test or prove his servants in order to strengthen their faith, he never seeks to induce sin and destroy their faith.'[7] God cannot be tempted, because he cannot be induced to sin, and, so the logic of James goes, he cannot be thought of as inducing someone else to sin either.

If we are tempted it is because of our own evil desires (14–15). In other words, if trials become an occasion for temptation that is because trials ignite our evil desires. We cannot blame God. The Greek word translated 'trials' in verse 2 and 'temptations' in verse 13 is the same. Trials become temptations when we blame God rather than rejoicing in his good purposes for us. 'At the beginning of his letter, James writes about a demanding though positive process: *trial* leading to *perseverance* leading to *maturity* and ultimately leading to *life* (12). In these verses, he writes about

[7] Moo, *James*, pp. 71–72.

another process, only this time one far more disturbing: *desire* leading to *temptation* leading to *sin* and ultimately leading to *death*.[8]

What makes the difference between following one route and not the other is praying for the wisdom to discern God's purposes in our trials.

b. Option two: things are bad, but God is good (16–18)

Even when we are surrounded by trials we can trust in the goodness of God. We see his goodness in the good things he gives us. Indeed ultimately *every* good thing comes from God (17). James reminds his readers that God is a *Father*. He treats us as his children. Normally human fathers seek the best for their children. They will not always give their children what they want, but at their best they act for the good of their children. God's goodness is a fatherly goodness.

The providence of God, however, involves not only his goodness but also his power. So James asserts that God is a proven giver of good gifts. It is not the heavenly bodies that determine our fate for good or ill, but the One who is the 'Sovereign Ruler of the skies, / ever gracious, ever wise'.[9] Through the sun and moon God's goodness to mankind quite literally shines forth (Gen. 1:14–18). Furthermore, God *does not change like shifting shadows* (17). We should not assume when good things happen God is being good to us and when bad things happen God is being ill-disposed towards us. God *does not change like shifting shadows*, but his goodness shines as constant – more constant – than the *heavenly lights* of which he is the Creator.

Ultimately our confidence in the goodness of God is rooted in the gospel. Through the gospel – *the word of truth* – he has given us new *birth* (18). While sin *gives birth to death* (1:15), through the gospel God chose to *give us birth* to new life. We can trust in the goodness of God in the midst of hardship because we have already received the greatest possible gift – the gift of new life through the gospel. Our experience of new life through the word of truth is a foretaste of God's cosmic purposes. We live in a world of pain and suffering, but one day God will recreate that world – he is going to put right all that is bad. We can be confident in this because we have received the *firstfruits* in our new birth.

---

[8] Timmis, *Reading James Today*.
[9] John Ryland (1753–1825), 'Sovereign Ruler of the skies'.

6. The prayer of faith (5:13–20)

James 1:5 is not the only time James links prayer and faith in his letter. In 5:15 he says, *And the prayer offered in faith will make the sick person well; the Lord will raise him up. If he has sinned, he will be forgiven.* The section has occasioned a lot of discussion. Some argue that if we have the faith, God will heal sickness – the implication being that if someone is not healed it is because they or the praying person have insufficient faith. Others speak of an occasional God-given inner certainty, which comes in prayer, that in this instance God wills the person being prayed for to be healed. Some see in this justification for 'a ministry of healing'.

It is important to note two preliminary things before we look at what the section is saying.[10] The first is to remember the socio-economic context of the letter. This is a Christian community in which many are suffering deprivation, but some have greater economic freedom and mobility. They need to be reminded of their obligation to the wider Christian community (Jas. 2:15–17; 4:13–17). Second, the NIV translates 5:15 as *And the prayer offered in faith will make the sick person well; the Lord will raise him up. If he has sinned, he will be forgiven.* But the word translated 'if', the Greek word *kan*, can also be translated 'even though'.[11] This would give the sense of the translation in the GNB: *This prayer made in faith will heal the sick; the Lord will restore them to health, and the sins they have committed will be forgiven.* It is the context that determines the meaning of *kan* and the context of James 5 suggests we should see a link between the sickness and a particular sin.

Throughout the book James has been calling his readers back to true faith in God expressed in concrete ways. That is how he begins this section. If you are in trouble, then faith in God is expressed in prayer. If you are happy, then faith in God is expressed in praise. The reality of God and his goodness is to impinge constantly on everyday life. It is a lovely picture of a church in which people naturally turn bad news into prayer and good news into praise.

But there is a third category that merits more attention because it is an immediate and pressing concern in the community – those who are sick. The troubled and the happy are to turn to God, but the sick person is to turn to the congregation. It suggests that their problem lies in their relationship to the Christian community. When we read 'even though' instead of 'if' in 5:15 the situation becomes clearer.

[10] This interpretation owes much to discussions with Stephen Timmis. See Timmis, *Reading James Today.*
[11] BAGD, p. 402. E.g. in John 10:38 *kan* is translated 'even though' in the NIV, RSV, NRSV and GNB, and 'though' in the NASB and AV.

Someone has sinned against the Christian community – perhaps by blatantly disregarding the needs of its poorer members. As a result they are being judged by God. This is not to suggest that all sickness is the result of particular sins (see John 9:1–3), but in the Bible sickness is sometimes a judgment against sin (see 1 Cor. 11:27–30). The remedy is to express repentance towards the community represented by its leaders (5:14). The *oil* recalls the oil of unity in Psalm 133, for unity is now being restored. *The prayer offered in faith* restores the person *because* they have sinned and have now been forgiven.

It is a prayer *of faith* because, as in James 1, it is offered with confidence in the character of God. James probably highlights it as prayer offered in faith to recall the promise of chapter 4. James 4:4–10 is a rebuke and promise to those members of the congregation – some of whom may be among those sick – who have neglected their obligation to its poorer members. They have chosen friendship with the world over God (4:4). They have been motivated by envy, but have found that God opposes the proud (4:5–6). Now they are invited to come back to God, to be purified and grieve for their sin (4:7–9). They are promised, *Humble yourselves before the Lord, and he will lift you up* (4:10). There is an echo of the lifting up of the penitent of 4:10 in the raising up of the sick Christian in 5:15. Faith in the promise of 4:10 is fulfilled in the restoration of 5:15.

James 5:16 further links confession and healing: *Therefore confess your sins to each other and pray for each other so that you may be healed.* When James says that *the prayer of a righteous man is powerful and effective* (5:16) he is not referring to some spiritual elite but to those who pray with single-minded trust in God (1:6–7). The example of Elijah is the example of a man *just like us.* The elders are to pray for the restoration of health after the repentance of the sinner just as Elijah prayed for the restoration of rain after the repentance of Israel (1 Kgs. 18). And the elders do so through faith in the promises that James has spoken of in James 4, just as Elijah prayed for restoration on the basis of the promises of the covenant (cf. Deut. 28:12, 23–24). The end of the letter continues the theme with an encouragement to restore sinners to the way of truth (5:19–20).

7. Conclusion

James exhorts us to pray for wisdom – wisdom to make connections aright. We are to pray for wisdom to see in trials God's purposes to make us mature in Christ. We are to pray for wisdom to look beyond trials to the eschatological purposes of God. We are to pray for that wisdom which persuades us of the goodness and generosity of God. So James invites us to pray something like this: 'Loving Father, help us to keep trusting in your goodness and generosity even though we are surrounded by problems. Help us to see our problems as an opportunity for growth and maturity. Good God, help us to keep the end in sight so that we keep rejoicing in our heavenly reward. Amen.'

This is how we should pray for one another. Sometimes we do not know how to pray when people are facing troubles. Should we pray that their problems will go away? That is a proper thing for which to pray, but we cannot be sure it is God's will in any particular situation. In such situations we should be humble enough to say, 'if it be your will'.[12] But we *do* know that it is God's will that Christians should keep on trusting him and keep the end in sight; that we should persevere and mature. God does not promise to give us health and plenty, but he does promise to give us the wisdom to remain faithful in all circumstances.

James's readers faced economic hardship and exploitation, but the response that James urges on them is *the gospel*. He calls on them to keep trusting God and looking to the future glory that he promises. Faith is a precondition for prayer. Luther says prayer is 'the hardest work of all – a labour above all labours since he who prays must wage a mighty warfare against the doubt and murmuring excited by the faintheartedness and unworthiness we feel within us'.[13] Calvin talks about 'the presumption of faith', which consists of 'the firm assurance of mind that God is favourable and benevolent'.[14]

Praying in faith does not mean convincing ourselves that God will give us whatever we ask. It does not mean working up our expectation of specified outcomes until we reach the quantity of faith to which God responds. We do not have faith in faith itself but in the character of God. It is rather to pray, trusting in the character of the One to whom we pray. 'Petitionary prayer depends on the character of the one petitioned rather than on the effort of the petitioner to have the right attitude of faith. Prayer is the expression of a relationship with a God whom we are learning to trust because he is faithful and good.'[15]

The story of Peter's release from prison in Acts 12 contradicts the notion that God only answers when we have confidence that he will respond in the manner we specify. James has been beheaded and now Peter is about to be tried – his fate appears clear. The church, we are told, 'was earnestly praying to God for him' (Acts 12:5).

---

[12] See Stott, *Romans*, pp. 389–390.
[13] Cited in Heiler, *Prayer*, p. 263.
[14] Calvin, *Institutes*, 3.20.12.
[15] Marshall, 'Jesus', pp. 122–123.

During the night an angel sets Peter free. When Peter goes to the house in which the church are praying the servant girl who answers the door is so overjoyed that she leaves him standing outside while she goes to tell the praying Christians. ' "You're out of your mind," they told her. When she kept insisting that it was so, they said, "It must be his angel." But Peter kept on knocking, and when they opened the door and saw him, they were astonished' (Acts 12:15–16). They are praying for Peter and when God answers their prayer they do not believe it. Yet God has answered their prayer.

To pray in faith is not to anticipate God's answer to our prayers. To pray in faith is to pray trusting in the goodness and generosity of God. Once we grasp this we can pray with confidence and freedom. We can pray confident that – whether God gives us that for which we ask or not – his response will be for our ultimate good. The following verse is attributed to an unknown soldier of the American civil war:

> I asked for strength that I might achieve;
> he made me weak that I might obey.
> I asked for health that I might do great things;
> he gave me grace that I might do better things.
> I asked for riches that I might be happy;
> he gave me poverty that I might be wise.
> I asked for power that I might have the praise of others;
> he gave me weakness that I might feel a need of God.
> I asked for all things that I might enjoy life;
> he gave me life that I might enjoy all things.
> I received nothing I had asked for;
> he gave me all that I had hoped for.

Part 2
The practice
of prayer

Genesis 18 and 32
6. Praying with the Patriarchs

Abraham, Isaac and Jacob experienced prayer, if indeed that is the right word for it, in a way very different from our experience as new covenant believers. They appeared to engage in direct dialogues with God. We could look back on such experiences with envy or claim an echo of them in our own experience. But we would be mistaken to do so. Consider the opening words of Hebrews: 'In the past God spoke to our forefathers through the prophets at many times and in various ways, but in these last days he has spoken to us by his Son ... The Son is the radiance of God's glory and the exact representation of his being' (Heb. 1:1–3).

'In the past', says the writer, God spoke 'in various ways'; that is, in dreams, visions and direct encounters. But now something radically new has happened that renders these *various ways* redundant – God has spoken through his Son. It literally says that 'he has spoken to us in Son', in, as it were, the pure language of the Son. And the Son is the perfect revelation of God, his 'exact representation'. Poets always express something of themselves in their work. God so perfectly expresses himself in his Word that he and his Word are one (John 1:1–3). So Jesus is a better Word even than the dialogues experienced by the Patriarchs. To look for dreams, visions and voices is to imply that the revelation of God in Jesus is inadequate. There are wonderful stories of converts from Islam and animism for whom dreams and visions have been significant, but those of us with ready access to God's Word should not trade the greater revelation for the lesser. It is to say that Jesus in whom 'all the fulness of the Deity lives in bodily form', and in whom we 'have been given fulness' (Col. 2:9–10), is not enough for us. Peter makes the same point (1 Pet. 1:10–12): we might wish we could hear God's voice as the prophets did or entertain angels as Abraham did, but we know more of God's saving grace through the sufferings and glories of Christ than they did. The prophets searched and angels long to look, but we have been told.

However, the 'better covenant' (Heb. 7:22; 8:6) that Jesus inaugurates does not render the Old Testament irrelevant – quite the opposite. The Old Testament testifies to what Jesus was to do so that his work is illuminated by it. And this is true of the dialogues of the Patriarchs. We should not expect imitations of their experience. But, seen in the light of Christ, their experience informs our own experience of prayer.

1. Genesis 18

In Genesis 18 Abraham entertains three strangers, though it is clear this is an appearance of the LORD (1). The LORD reiterates his promise of a child to Abraham and Sarah (9–15). As Abraham walks with the strangers (16) God discloses his intention to destroy the nearby cities of Sodom and Gomorrah (20–21). Abraham's nephew, Lot, is living in Sodom, although no reference is made to this in Genesis 18. On hearing God's intentions, Abraham embarks on an audacious dialogue with God (22–33). He asks if God will spare the city if he finds fifty righteous people within it. And if not fifty, then what about forty-five? And if not forty-five, then what about forty? And so on down to ten. God confirms that he will not destroy the city for the sake of ten righteous people. And then the conversation breaks off.

This *dialogue* between a man and God should be read in the light of the *monologue* of God in verses 17–19. In these verses God talks to himself, giving us what we might call pure, unmediated theology. In this divine soliloquy we are allowed to overhear something of God's eternal purposes in salvation. The dialogue of Genesis 18 is set in the context of God's saving purposes that come to us in the gospel. So, while we should be wary of making Abraham's 'prayer' a model for our own, this monologue and dialogue do teach about what it means to pray in the context of our covenantal relationship with God.

a. God's grace makes prayer bold

I have chosen him (19) says God of Abraham. This is what we call 'election' and it is made up of three interwoven themes. The first is *the initiative of God*. God chose Abraham before Abraham chose God. In the same way Jesus said to the disciples, 'You did not choose me, but I chose you' (John 15:16). 'We love because he first loved us' (1 John 4:19). God initiates salvation. The second strand of election is *the promise of the gospel*, which is the sign of God's choice. The conversation comes after God has confirmed his promise of a people. God recalls this promise in verse 18: *Abraham will surely become a great and powerful nation, and all nations on earth will be blessed through him.* Paul describes the promise to Abraham as the gospel 'announced ... in advance' (Gal. 3:8). Just as the sign of election to Abraham was the promise of God, so the sign of election for us is the gospel of Christ. The sign that God has chosen us is that we receive the gospel through faith (Eph. 1:3–14). Third, at the heart of election is *grace*. Salvation is not based on our merit but upon God's loving choice. We see these interweaving themes of God's initiative, promise and grace in the way Paul describes what God did for Abraham: 'God in his grace gave [the inheritance] to Abraham through a promise' (Gal. 3:18). Paul says that salvation starts with the gift of God. God gave it 'through a promise' – the promise is the sign of God's choice and the means by which he fulfils his purposes for us. Finally God gave it 'in his grace'.

God chooses Abraham for a relationship. *Shall I hide from Abraham what I am about to do?* is an amazing statement (17). Friends share their thoughts with one another. Now the God of the universe reveals his intentions with Abraham. Election is not about the moves of a cosmic chess master, pushing pieces round the board at his whim: it is the gracious intent of God to have a people who are his people.

Abraham reciprocates with boldness in prayer. If our relationship with God is based on God's prior choice, sealed in the gospel and rooted in grace, then there is nothing we can do that will undo God's determination to have a relationship with us. If he chose us when we were his enemies (Rom. 5:6–11), there is nothing we can now do that will undo that choice. So the certainty of election gives a proper boldness in prayer. Abraham acknowledges the audacity of his questions (27, 31), yet he does question God. Some manuscripts read, 'the LORD stood before Abraham' (22), like an accused before an accuser.[1] God chose us for a relationship, so we can be bold before him. The King of the universe sits on the throne of heaven and none can come before him to plead the case of Sodom – except those he has chosen to be his children.

b. God's justice makes prayer trusting

The assurance that election and grace give us is not an excuse for sin. God says, *For I have chosen him, so that he will direct his children*

---

[1] See Brueggemann, *Genesis*, p. 168; and V. P. Hamilton, *Genesis 18–50*, pp. 23–24.

and his household after him to keep the way of the LORD *by doing what is right and just* (19). Ethics are not contrary to election – they are its purpose. When Jesus said to his disciples, 'You did not choose me, but I chose you', he added, 'and appointed you to go and bear fruit – fruit that will last' (John 15:16; see also Eph. 1:4; 2:8–10). Ethics are also defined by grace. Abraham is to direct his children and his household *to keep the way of the* LORD. We are to be like our gracious God. The Hebrew word translated by the NIV as *chosen* (19) is the same as that translated 'have sex' in 19:5. God graciously chooses to know Abraham while the men of Sodom aggressively demand to know the two divine messengers. The contrast could not be more stark: the promise of Genesis 18 offers an alternative way of life to the wickedness of Genesis 19. 'In the context of a world going the way of Sodom, God wanted a community characterized by the "way of the Lord".'[2]

God chose Abraham to direct the children of promise throughout the generations in the ways of the Lord. This means *doing what is right and just*. But are the ways of the Lord just? If the promise of verses 17–19 is to be formative for God's people, then the dialogue of verses 22–33 is crucial. God's people must walk in his ways, but those ways include the wholesale destruction of two cities (20–21). Abraham must determine that God does what is right. The issue at the heart of this conversation is whether God is just.

The phrase *far be it from you* (25) is stronger than the English translation suggests. In Ezekiel 20:9, where it is translated *profane*, God rescues Israel so that his name will not be profaned. In Genesis 18 Abraham wants to be sure that God is not being profane – that he is not compromising his reputation by being ungodlike. Will he treat the wicked and the righteous alike? Will the righteous die because of the wicked or is there the possibility that the wicked might be saved because of the righteous? 'It is not the fate of Sodom that is the issue in Abraham's prayer, but the character of God.'[3] At first sight Abraham and God seem to be playing a numbers game as if Abraham is haggling with God. In reality Abraham is exploring the depths of God's mercy and righteousness.[4] He is not trying to strike a bargain with God – 'I will do this if you hear my prayer.' Abraham is ensuring that *the Judge of all the earth does right*.

The people of God must be able to trust God's purposes and trust those purposes when circumstances suggest that God is not doing what is right. The righteous suffer with the wicked and often at the

[2] C. Wright, 'Old Testament and Christian Mission', p. 40.
[3] White, *People in Prayer*, p. 18.
[4] Kidner, *Genesis*, p. 133.

hands of the wicked. Much heartfelt prayer takes up this tension and presents it in all our pain and perplexity before God. But here on behalf of God's people Abraham tests the justice of God. He discovers that God will not destroy the righteous with the wicked and may even spare the wicked for the sake of the righteous. Forever afterwards we can say – even when we do not comprehend God's purposes – the Judge of all the earth will do right. Samuel Balentine invites us to consider how the text of Scripture would feel if Abraham and others following his lead had not engaged in such 'loyal opposition' to God or if such accounts had been omitted as inappropriate. He suggests, 'Without these prayers and the model they encourage for engaging God authentically in the struggle for meaning in the midst of chaos, one would confront an intolerable inexorability that imposes monologue without dialogue, revelation without response, destiny and fate without hope.'[5] We should not fear prayer that takes the form of questioning God. This is where our doubts belong – not hidden away in our hearts but presented before the God who makes us his covenant partners.

Abraham not only examines God's justice. He discovers the depths of God's mercy. For the sake of how many will God save the city? For the sake of fifty down to ten he will show mercy. Then the conversation abruptly stops. We want to keep going. What about five? What about for the sake of Lot and his family? The question is left hanging until finally the answer comes: 'Christ died for sins once for all, the righteous for the unrighteous, to bring you to God' (1 Pet. 3:18). The questions of Genesis 18 are left open until they are answered by the cross. God spares the wicked – you and me – for the sake of one righteous person: Jesus Christ, the Righteous One. In Hosea God says:

> How can I give you up, Ephraim?
>> How can I hand you over, Israel?
> How can I treat you like Admah?
>> How can I make you like Zeboiim?
> My heart is changed within me;
>> all my compassion is aroused.
> I will not carry out my fierce anger,
>> nor will I turn and devastate Ephraim.
> For I am God, and not man –
>> the Holy One among you.
> I will not come in wrath.
>
> (Hos. 11:8–9)

[5] Balentine, *Prayer in the Hebrew Bible*, p. 145.

Admah and Zeboiim are references to Sodom and Gomorrah (14:2). God's people deserve the same fate, but God turns aside from anger. The word translated in the NIV 'changed' is the same word used of the 'overthrow' of Sodom and Gomorrah (19:25, 29). 'God has taken the earthquake into his own person rather than against the city.'[6] In this God proves himself godlike and holy: *For I am God, and not man.*

We discover how just God's justice is at the cross. His justice is met in full measure. He is not indifferent to sin and injustice. It is judged – and judged to the full. And we discover how merciful God's mercy is at the cross. He spares the wicked for the sake of one righteous man. He sends his Son to die in our place.

These are the ways of the Lord that we are to keep. Grace makes us bold in prayer. It allows us to ask questions of God. But with those questions we trust God's ways and have faith in his justice. 'It is not fair,' we often want to say to God in prayer, and grace allows our questions. But at the same time we can be confident that God's ways are just and merciful. 'You cannot have a relationship with God without standing, at one time or another, precisely where Abraham stood,' grappling with the purposes of God and discovering in prayer as Abraham did 'it was no monster that faced him but the familiar God of the covenant'.[7]

Abraham is to direct his family in the ways of God (19; see also Deut. 6:4–9). While the habit of family prayers is not easy in an age when many families congregate only in front of the television, we should not give up teaching our children the gracious ways of the Lord. However, descendants of Abraham are not his biological offspring but those who share his faith. Telling people the ways of the Lord means calling people to become Abraham's descendants by faith. It means mission.

c. God's purposes make prayer missionary

As the divine soliloquy reminds us, God chose Abraham so that *all nations on earth will be blessed through him* (18). One man is chosen for the sake of all nations. Election is not exclusive but inclusive, and mission is founded on God's electing purposes. The promise of blessing to the nations (18) will be fulfilled as Abraham's family keep the ways of the Lord (19) (see also Deut. 4:5–8).

But Abraham is also a blessing to the nations as he intercedes for them. He has previously intervened in the affairs of Sodom to rescue

---

[6] Brueggemann, *Genesis*, p. 173.
[7] White, *People in Prayer*, pp. 18–19.

her from defeat (14:8–16). Now Abraham blesses Sodom by interceding for her. 'The faithfulness of Abraham consists in boldly pressing God to be more compassionate.'[8] The possibility that judgment may be revoked (21), Gordon Wenham suggests, is an invitation to intercede for Sodom.[9] And, while Sodom is destroyed, God does accede to Abraham's requests. He agrees that he would not destroy the city for the sake of ten righteous people. The problem is that ten righteous people cannot be found in Sodom. Yet still God spares Lot because 'he remembered Abraham' (19:29) and the nearby town of Zoar is spared in response to Lot's intercession (19:20–21).

In Exodus 19 God says he has chosen Abraham's descendants to be *a kingdom of priests*. Peter picks up this language when he says, 'you are a chosen people, a royal priesthood, a holy nation, a people belonging to God, that you may declare the praises of him who called you out of darkness into his wonderful light' (1 Pet. 2:9). We bless the nations when we intercede on their behalf, representing them as priests before God. And we bless the nations as we declare the praises of God, directing the peoples of the world in the ways of the Lord. The nations should be part of our daily prayer routine.

2. Genesis 32

In Genesis 18 God again promises to give Abraham a son through whom all nations would be blessed, Isaac who in turn has twins. The firstborn – and therefore the expected inheritor of the promise – is Esau. The second born comes out clutching Esau's heel and so he is called Jacob, meaning 'he grasps the heel' or 'he deceives'. True to his name, Jacob tricks the dying Isaac into giving him the inheritance. Jacob is forced to flee from Esau. He has received the Abrahamic promise, but has had to leave the Promised Land.

He goes to his uncle, Laban, where he prospers until Laban's own sons become jealous. Laban and Jacob agree to live apart, setting up a stone that neither can cross. Jacob cannot go back. But ahead is Esau. So in Genesis 32 Jacob prepares to meet Esau, dividing his possessions so he will lose only half in an attack, and sending messengers ahead with gifts. Then he sends his family across the Jabbok river while he stays alone (33).

During the night, in one of the most intriguing stories in Scripture, an anonymous man comes and wrestles with him. There is a delightful play on words: the word for 'wrestle' is 'je-abeqed', so

---

[8] Brueggemann, *Genesis*, p. 176.
[9] Wenham, *Genesis 16–50*, p. 52.

Ja-acob je-abeqed by the Jabboq! This is not a scripted wrestling bout but a struggle lasting throughout the night. Yet Jacob is able to hold his own. The man cannot overcome him. What makes this so remarkable is that it becomes apparent that this mysterious wrestler is none other than God himself. With just a touch he cripples Jacob at the hip. But Jacob has spent his life struggling for blessing and is not going to stop now. Whereas Esau despises the blessing of God (Gen. 25:34; Heb 12:16–17), Jacob battles for it. The Jabbok marked the edge of the land of blessing (Num. 21:24; Deut. 2:37; 3:16; Josh. 12:2; Judg. 11:13, 22), but Jacob must wrestle that blessing from God. Jacob names the place 'Peniel', which means 'face of God', because he recognizes that he has met with God. As a permanent reminder of this meeting he lives the rest of his life with a limp. Every step he takes from then on reminds him of his struggle with God. It is an evocative encounter in which Jacob is wounded by God.

This night is clearly significant for Jacob. He acquires a limp and a new name. He meets with God and receives his blessing. Yet this event is also formative for all God's people. The wrestler says, *Your name will no longer be Jacob, but Israel, because you have struggled with God and with men and have overcome* (28). Jacob rarely used his new name, but *Israel* became the name by which God's people are usually known in the Old Testament. This encounter is formative for all God's people. In some sense it defines who we are. It defines something of our common experience of God. The origins of the term *Israel* are debated, but it probably means 'God fights' or 'God rules'.[10] Just as Jacob is the one who *struggled with God*, so all God's people are known as those who struggle with God. In Hosea 12 the prophet calls upon God's people in his day to strive with God as Jacob did (Hos. 12:2–6). God brings a charge against Jacob the nation (2) in response to which the people should emulate (6) the example of Jacob the person (3–5). Hosea interprets Jacob's experience as an experience that the people of God should follow in prayer. 'Israel', says Walter Brueggemann, 'is not formed by success or shrewdness or land, but by an assault from God.'[11] What are we to make of this?

a. God struggles with his people to strengthen our relationship with him

Jacob has spent his life searching for blessing, but avoiding God. By the Jabbok he is forced to deal with God in an encounter that

[10] Ibid., pp. 296–297.
[11] Brueggemann, *Genesis*, p. 269.

changes him forever. We find something similar in Judges 3. God judges the people by leaving the Canaanites in the land 'to teach warfare to the descendants of the Israelites' (Judg. 3:2). Just like Israel their father, each generation must struggle. Through conflict they are forced to commit themselves afresh to God and to look to him for victory. In the New Testament we are told that trials develop perseverance and maturity (Jas. 1:2–4), and refine our faith (1 Pet. 1:6–7).

The story reveals an important dimension to our relationship with God that our sentimental age often fails to see: God is dangerous. He is the aggressor in the narrative. He is not comfortable to have around. Yet in the struggle with God our relationship with him grows and our faith is immeasurably deepened. Calvin says we should think of 'all the servants of God in this world as wrestlers'. He continues:

> God himself ... as an antagonist descends into the arena to try our strength. This, though at first sight it seems absurd, experience and reason teaches us to be true. For as all prosperity flows from his goodness, so adversity is either the rod with which he corrects our sins, or the test of our faith and patience ... What was once exhibited under a visible form to our father Jacob, is daily fulfilled in the individual members of the Church.[12]

Hallesby says, 'Our striving is a struggle, not with God, but with ourselves.'[13] It is true that prayer is a struggle against our sinful nature, which retains its disinclination towards prayer, so that to wrestle in prayer is to struggle against ourselves. But prayer can also be a struggle against God. This was Jacob's experience and, as we have seen, his experience was defining for the people of God. It is not, of course, that a reluctant God can be won over by our persistence. It is rather that God also purposes for us to deepen our relationship with him – he wants us to engage with him at a profound level. He made us to share the intimacy of the trinitarian relationship, and rattling through a list of prayer requests falls far short of this purpose! 'We shall come one day to a heaven where we shall gratefully know that God's great refusals were sometimes the true answers to our truest prayer. Our soul is fulfilled even if our petition is not.'[14]

When my eldest daughter was young I used to play a game with her where I would grasp her in my arms and she had to wriggle free.

---

[12] Calvin, *Genesis*, vol. 2, pp. 195–196.
[13] Hallesby, *Prayer*, p. 87.
[14] Forsyth, *Soul of Prayer*, p. 14.

I always let her win eventually, but in the meantime I enjoyed a good cuddle. It was our way of expressing intimacy. While God does not need our intimacy, the Bible says he delights in his people (e.g. Zeph. 3:17). God lovingly gives us a relationship and graciously deepens that relationship – even if it means he must wrestle with us.

Jim Packer says that 'within evangelicalism a quietist stream of thought about communion with God flows steadily'.[15] He cites Hallesby's book *Prayer* as an example of this, as well as the lines

> Drop thy still dews of quietness
> till all our striving cease;
> take from our souls the strain and stress
> and let our ordered lives confess
> the beauty of thy peace.[16]

Hallesby says that 'to pray is to let Jesus come into our hearts'[17] and he returns often to this definition of prayer. In contrast Packer says:

> Biblical Christian experience, whatever else it is, is active battling throughout, inwardly against the flesh, outwardly against the world, and in both against the devil. Awareness and acceptance of the fight ... is itself a gauge of spiritual authenticity and vitality ... God may actually resist us when we pray in order that we in turn may resist and overcome his resistance, and so be led into deeper dependence on him and greater enrichment from him at the end of the day.[18]

It is not just Jacob who wrestles with God. We see the psalmists struggling with God. We see Jeremiah questioning God. Epaphras wrestles in prayer for the Colossians (Col. 4:12). Even Jesus himself did not submit to the will of the Father in Gethsemane until he had sweated blood. The writer of Hebrews says that Jesus 'offered up prayers and petitions with loud cries and tears' (Heb 5:7). Our relationship with God often involves struggle. Sometimes it is a struggle with temptation. Sometimes it is a struggle with the circumstances of life. Often it is a struggle with ourselves. But sometimes it is a struggle with God himself. God gives us this struggle to refine our faith and to deepen our relationship with him.

---

[15] In Hanes, *My Path of Prayer*, p. 58.

[16] From the hymn 'Dear Lord and Father of mankind', by John Greenleaf Whittier (1807–92).

[17] Hallesby, *Prayer*, p. 9.

[18] In Hanes, *My Path of Prayer*, p. 59.

He wants us to cling to him like Jacob did – holding out for blessing. As Forsyth says, 'too ready acceptance of a situation as His will often means feebleness or sloth'.

b. God comes to his people in weakness to fulfil his promise of blessing

Before God blesses Jacob, he asks him his name (names in the Old Testament often reveal a person's character). God, of course, knows Jacob's name, but he forces him into an act of confession. 'Jacob' means 'he grasps the heel' or 'he deceives'. Jacob has been a deceiver all his life, deceiving his father, defrauding Esau, cheating Laban. Earlier Esau said, 'Isn't he rightly named Jacob? He has deceived me these two times: He took my birthright, and now he's taken my blessing!' (27:36). But now *Jacob*, the deceiver, becomes *Israel*. Instead of a name that expresses his guilt, Jacob receives a name that expresses the promise and the grace of God towards him. As he stands on the edge of the Promised Land he must discover for himself the grace of God.

Jacob has inherited the promise of God. He has become a large group in fulfilment of the promise, including the sons who will form the twelve tribes of Israel. He himself acknowledges before God, *I am unworthy of all the kindness and faithfulness you have shown your servant. I had only my staff when I crossed this Jordan, but now I have become two groups* (10). But now Jacob stands on the edge of the land of promise. Will he survive the encounter with his brother? Will he enter the land safely? Will he live in it peacefully? In answer to these questions God gives him a new name, Israel, *because you have struggled with God and with men and have overcome* (28). Esau not only allows Jacob to enter, but runs to embrace him. Indeed Jacob says to his brother, 'to see your face is like seeing the face of God, now that you have received me favourably' (33:10). Jacob, as mentioned earlier, had called the place where he wrestled with God 'Peniel', because there he saw God face to face. The encounter with God seems to parallel the encounter with his brother. Walter Brueggemann suggests that 'in the night the divine antagonist tends to take on features of others with whom we struggle in the day'.[19] It is as if Jacob's encounter with God is a vicarious one. Perhaps Jacob realizes that his struggle with Esau will end in blessing just as his struggle with God did. Perhaps he realizes that by struggling with God in prayer he has avoided the struggle with Esau. 'The conflict brought to a head the battling and groping of a

---

[19] Brueggemann, *Genesis*, p. 267.

lifetime, and Jacob's desperate embrace vividly expressed his ambivalent attitude to God, of love and enmity, defiance and dependence. It was against Him, not Esau or Laban, that he had been pitting his strength, as he now discovered; yet the initiative had been God's, as it was this night, to chasten his pride and challenge his tenacity.'[20]

Who knows what problems we avoid because of our prayers – or what problems are left when we do not pray! Or perhaps more to the point, without prayer our problems bring us down rather than strengthening our relationship with God.

> O what peace we often forfeit!
> O what needless pain we bear!
> All because we do not carry
> Everything to God in prayer.
>
> Are we weak and heavy-laden,
> Cumbered with a load of care?
> Precious Saviour, still our refuge,
> Take it to the Lord in prayer.[21]

Every time the people of God heard the name 'Israel' it would remind them of this story. It would remind them that their forefather had overcome God and men. And if Jacob the deceiver had overcome, then so might they. It was a promise of God's help and deliverance.

But this is no comfortable God. What makes the story so enigmatic is the tension between God blessing Jacob while he attacks him. Jacob has to learn that God is more dangerous than men. Jacob is running from Laban. Jacob fears what Esau might do to him. But the One who is really to be feared is God (Matt. 10:28). Jacob uses all his wisdom and financial resources to get out of trouble, but this cannot prepare him to do battle with God.

God is against us. He is opposed to our sinful ways. According to Revelation 19, Christ is coming as a mighty warrior to conquer and defeat us. But the wonderful thing is that Jesus himself has also entered the struggle on our side. He came to us in weakness to bless us. He died on our behalf. If we take refuge in him, then we shall escape his coming wrath. God has come to his people in weakness to fulfil his promise of blessing. He came in the frailty of a baby. He let us beat and crucify him. But this weakness was his victory and it was our victory. In Christ we *have struggled with God and with*

---

[20] Kidner, *Genesis*, p. 169.
[21] Joseph M. Scriven (1819–86), 'What a friend we have in Jesus'.

men and have overcome. As Gordon Wenham says of the Israelites, 'Among all their trials and perplexities in which God seemed to be fighting against them, he was ultimately on their side; indeed, he would triumph, and in his victory, Israel would triumph too.'[22] We need not fear men, for God is on our side. And we need not fear God, for in Christ we have overcome.

3. Conclusion

In the National Gallery of Scotland hangs a painting by Paul Gauguin called *The Vision of the Sermon.* Gauguin believed art should represent not only what was there but the way it made you feel. In *The Vision of the Sermon* a group of devout Breton women have heard a sermon on Jacob wrestling with God. It is so real to them that they see it before their eyes. Gauguin distinguishes between the literal reality of the women and the reality of their vision. The grass is red and they are separated from the struggle by the line of a tree. Yet it is real. Indeed one of their cows has strayed into the fray. The reality of wrestling with God is as real as their cow. Wrestling with God is not some mythical reality or a reality for the spiritual elite. It is part of everyday life. It is, as it were, a domestic reality.

Writing to the Colossians, Paul tells them that Epaphras 'is always wrestling in prayer for you, that you may stand firm in all the will of God, mature and fully assured' (Col. 4:12). It has been my privilege to visit churches in Asia, Africa and Latin America. What they had in common was passion and energy in their praying. I shall not easily forget my experiences praying with Brazilians. For the most part in the West while someone leads in prayer others listen quietly. But when my Brazilian friends pray they all engage in prayer – it is a truly corporate exercise. As one person leads, others join in with constant and vigorous affirmations. It is a noisy affair! They truly pray together and together they wrestle with God. Charles Spurgeon, the Victorian preacher who saw great blessing in his ministry, wrote:

When I came to New Park Street Chapel, it was but a mere handful of people to whom I first preached, yet I can never forget how earnestly they prayed. Sometimes they seemed to plead as though they could really see the Angel of the covenant present with them, and as if they must have a blessing from Him. More than once, we were all so awe-struck with the solemnity of the

[22] Wenham, *Genesis 16 – 50*, p. 303.

meeting, that we sat silent for some moments while the Lord's power appeared to overshadow us ... Then down came the blessing; the house was filled with hearers, and many souls were saved. I always give all the glory to God, but I do not forget that He gave me the privilege of ministering from the first to a praying people ... Every one appeared determined to storm the Celestial City by the might of intercession, and soon the blessing came upon us in such abundance that we had not room to receive it.[23]

We, too, need to learn what it is to wrestle with God in prayer. People often look for something that will make prayer easy. But prayer is often difficult. 'The harder we find concentration to be,' says Calvin, 'the more strenuously we ought to labour after it.'[24] Like Abraham we should wrestle with boldness, confident in God's grace. We should wrestle for ourselves and for the nations. We should wrestle trusting that the Judge of all the world will do right even when we find his will perplexing. And, like Jacob, we should hold out for God's blessing, remembering that God came to us in weakness that we might overcome. Calvin says, 'We do not fight against him, except by his own power, and with his own weapons; for he, having challenged us to this contest, at the same time furnishes us with the means of resistance, so that he both fights *against* us and *for* us.'[25]

[23] Spurgeon, *Early Years*, p. 263.
[24] Calvin, *Institutes*, 3.20.5.
[25] Calvin, *Genesis*, vol. 2, p. 196.

Isaiah 37, Nehemiah 9 and Daniel 9
7. Praying with the Old Testament saints

From time to time competitions are held in which the prize is to get whatever you can put in a supermarket trolley in a limited period of time. People dash round the supermarket grabbing at this, scooping up some of that, dumping it all in the trolley before their time is up. Sometimes our prayers can be like that. We dash into the presence of God, grab a load of requests and then dash out again – time is up. However, it is not always that we have no time; more often it is that we do not have the inclination. Or maybe we do not know what to say beyond listing those requests.

But in prayer we can engage with God. The prayers recorded in the Bible invite us not only to make our requests to God but to present to him reasons why he should answer those requests. The Bible invites us, as it were, to argue with God. Prayer may well be hard work, but it can be real work. Prayer can be much more than reeling off requests. When we read of people in the Bible praying we find them expressing a genuine relationship. This chapter explores three examples of this from the Old Testament.

1. Isaiah 37

Sennacherib, the king of Assyria, has captured the fortified cities of Judah and then sent his army to Jerusalem. The commander of the Assyrian army meets a delegation from Hezekiah, the king of Judah (36:1–22). Resistance is futile, claims Sennacherib's commander. It is no good looking to Egypt (36:4–7). Nor can they look to the Lord because he has been alienated by the destruction of his shrines (36:7). Sennacherib's campaign has divine sanction (36:10). This is not good theology – the centralization of worship was commanded by God – but it is enough to make nervous Israelites jittery. Hezekiah has neither the weapons nor manpower to withstand the Assyrians. Even if the Assyrians give them horses the Israelites cannot find riders for them (36:8–9). The delegation from Hezekiah asks the commander to speak in Aramaic so that the Hebrew-speaking people of Jerusalem will not understand (Aramaic was the language of international diplomacy). Instead the Assyrian commander shouts defiantly to the city walls, questioning the power and honour of the Lord: 'Do not let Hezekiah mislead you when he says, "The LORD will deliver us." Has the god of any nation ever delivered his land from the hand of the king of Assyria?' (36:18).

Hezekiah sees clearly that the issue is the Lord's reputation (37:1–4). *It may be that the LORD your God will hear the words of the field commander, whom his master, the king of Assyria, has sent to ridicule the living God, and that he will rebuke him for the words the LORD your God has heard. Therefore pray for the remnant that still survives* (37:4).

Isaiah reassures Hezekiah (37:5–8). A report will come from Assyria leading to the withdrawal of the army. Sennacherib's commander has said, *This is what the king says …* (36:14). Now Isaiah says, *This is what the LORD says …* (37:6). The commander calls Sennacherib 'the great king' (36:13), as throughout the known world what Sennacherib said was done. But now a greater King has spoken. The word of Sennacherib comes into conflict with the word of God. Again Isaiah recognizes that the issue is God's reputation: *Isaiah said to them, 'Tell your master, "This is what the LORD says: Do not be afraid of what you have heard – those words with which the underlings of the king of Assyria have blasphemed me"'* (37:6).

The report in 37:8 that Sennacherib has left Lachish to fight against Libnah causes his commander to withdraw – just as Isaiah announced in 37:7.

Another report comes, suggesting a threat from Egypt. It prompts Sennacherib to increase the pressure on Hezekiah with the hope of getting a speedy resolution to his Judean problem. So Sennacherib threatens Jerusalem for a second time (37:9–13), precipitating a second cycle of threat, prayer and prophetic reassurance. Sennacherib sends Hezekiah a letter saying that he should not depend on God to rescue him from the might of Assyria. The focus on the honour of God that emerged in the first cycle of threat and response emerges again. Sennacherib says, *Do not let the god you depend on deceive you when he says, 'Jerusalem will not be handed over to the king of Assyria'* (37:10). Hezekiah again responds by turning to God (37:14–20). He spreads Sennacherib's letter out in the temple and prays. Before we look at Hezekiah's prayer, let us complete the story.

All the way through the story the reputation of God and the validity of his reign have been the central issues. They remain so as the story is resolved. The concern for God's glory is reinforced in God's response to Hezekiah's prayer, which Isaiah brings in 37:21–38:

> *Who is it you have insulted and blasphemed?*
> *Against whom have you raised your voice*
> *and lifted your eyes in pride?*
> *Against the Holy One of Israel!*
> *By your messengers*
> *you have heaped insults on the Lord.*
>
> (37:23–24)

The prophecy that Isaiah brings comes in two portions. The first is 37:22–32, which ends, *The zeal of the LORD Almighty will accomplish this*. God is zealous. He has a passion for his glory. The second portion of Isaiah's word is 37:33–35, which ends, *I will defend this city and save it, for my sake and for the sake of David my servant!* (37:35). Isaiah gives two reasons why God will defend the city. The first is *for my sake* – to vindicate his reputation. The second is *for the sake of David my servant* – God will be faithful to his promise that one of David's sons will always reign over God's people (see 2 Sam. 7).

Why should God deliver Israel? Not because the Israelites deserve to be saved – they do not. Not because the Israelites need to be saved – although they do. Deliverance will come for *God's* sake – for the sake of his reputation and to fulfil his promise to David. And indeed this happens: an angel of the Lord comes and kills 185,000 of the Assyrian army (37:36–37); Sennacherib withdraws and we read how his own sons later murder him (37:38).

a. Confidence in the reign of God

Hezekiah begins his prayer, *O LORD Almighty, God of Israel, enthroned between the cherubim, you alone are God over all the kingdoms of the earth. You have made heaven and earth* (37:16).

It is language familiar to us, perhaps too familiar. We need to remember the context to appreciate what a great statement of faith this is. Having Sennacherib turn up on your doorstep was like having the United States army turn up outside your house with hundreds of armoured personnel carriers, several battle tanks, a

105

couple of nuclear warheads all backed up by a squadron of fighter bombers. Assyria was the superpower of the day and Israel was powerless. Hezekiah faces a tough choice. He must choose between a king who is the greatest power in the world and whose army he can see surrounding his capital, and a God whom he cannot see. The fortified towns of Judah have already fallen. 'It is no use thinking that your God will save you,' says Sennacherib (37:11–13). 'The other nations thought that, but I defeated them. Why should you think you will be any different?' It is a powerful argument and Hezekiah acknowledges as much before God (37:17–19). Calvin says, 'The earnestness that pervades the prayer breathes an amazing power of anguish, so that it is easily seen that he had a struggle attended by uncommon difficulty to escape from the temptation.'[1] But still Hezekiah has confidence in God – a confidence that drives his praying.

This confidence is reflected in the opening to his prayer. The God of Israel is not some national deity but *the LORD Almighty*. He is *God over all the kingdoms of the earth* (37:16). This is not a case of Assyria's gods against another nation's gods. When Sennacherib came against Israel he was coming against the God who is *alone* (37:16). *Enthroned between the cherubim* (37:16) is a reference to the ark, which symbolizes God's presence with his people (Exod. 37:6–9). God is not an absentee Lord. He is with his people to rule and protect them. But the ark, and the temple in which it is placed, are a mirror of heaven where God is enthroned among the heavenly court. Unlike the gods of the nations, God does not dwell in temples made by human hands (1 Kgs. 8:27). Instead he is the One who *made heaven and earth* (37:16). Hezekiah's prayer is premised on a confidence in the present reign of God.

It is worth reflecting on the part this narrative plays in the predominantly prophetic book of Isaiah, especially since these chapters largely repeat the account in 2 Kings 18 – 19. Isaiah's concerns are clearly theological as well as historical. He omits the fact that Hezekiah initially tried to buy off Sennacherib with the temple treasures (2 Kgs. 18:13–16): Isaiah recounts only the triumph of Hezekiah.

In the earlier chapters of his book (especially chs. 6 – 12), Isaiah has announced that God will triumph through the Davidic king. God's anointed, his Messiah, will reign not only over Judah but over the world. But these great promises sound like empty words in the face of the realities of history. The present king had enough trouble reigning over Judah without outside interference, let

---

[1] Calvin, *Isaiah*, p. 486.

alone over the world. What is more, a time will come when Jerusalem will fall to a foreign king. Isaiah's words opened up a huge credibility gap. In this context the story of Hezekiah demonstrates that God can intervene to establish the rule of the Davidic king – the defeat of Sennacherib demonstrates the credibility of Isaiah's prophecies.

But in case we were tempted to think Hezekiah himself was the promised Messiah of chapters 9 and 11 we read in chapters 38 and 39 of Hezekiah's frailty and folly. In chapter 38 Hezekiah is granted fifteen more years of life. It is an amazing gift but some way short of the King who will reign forever! In chapter 39 Hezekiah shows off 'everything' to Babylonian envoys (39:4), sowing the seeds of an exile in which 'everything' will be carried off (39:6). The scene is set for Isaiah's prophecy of a servant of God who will end the exile and bring comfort to God's people (40:1–5). It is with Isaiah's words that Mark introduces John the Baptist (Mark 1:2–4). John announces the coming of the Messiah – the One who will truly deliver God's people from exile and deal with the underlying problems of sin and judgment.

These chapters reassure us that God can fulfil his promises. We can be confident that King Jesus will reign over the nations even when the events of history cast doubt on this. Indeed we trust in the one who not only defeated Sennacherib but has triumphed over sin and death. In the midst of the turmoil of history we can pray confidently to the God who keeps his promises. Without this confidence, prayer is reduced to wishful thinking. This trust in the promises of God and the reign of his Messiah is the foundation of prayer.

b. Concern for the reputation of God

All the way through this story the key issue has been God's reputation and glory. And this is the argument Hezekiah uses with God as he prays for deliverance: *Now, O LORD our God, deliver us from his hand, so that all kingdoms on earth may know that you alone, O LORD, are God* (37:20). Hezekiah did not spread Sennacherib's letter out in the temple to inform God. God already knew what was happening. Hezekiah spread the letter out to provoke God. He says, in effect, 'Look at this, Lord. You cannot ignore this. Your name is being dishonoured. Your power is being mocked. Your reputation is at stake.' Hezekiah's audacity is a challenge to us. We are to pray boldly that God will honour his name.

Hezekiah is not just concerned for God's glory: he is concerned for God's glory among the nations. He prays that *all kingdoms on earth* may recognize God's glory. Hezekiah's logic is simple: God saves his people. The nations hear and God is glorified. The same logic applies today. God has saved his people through Jesus Christ. The nations hear and God is glorified. God is glorified when the nations hear the gospel and turn to him.

There is no better way to pray for the glory of God than to pray for mission. And conversely there is no greater argument when praying for mission than the glory of God. When we pray for mission we pray for God's reputation. We pray that people will turn from neglecting and insulting God to worshipping and serving him. When we realize that the glory of God is central to prayer, then a concern for mission in our praying must follow. Hezekiah begins his prayer by affirming that *you alone are God over all the kingdoms of the earth*. This affirmation naturally translates into the request *that all kingdoms on earth may know that you alone, O LORD, are God*. Our prayers should be *God-centred* and *mission-centred*.

2. Nehemiah 9

Nehemiah was a cup-bearer in the court of the Persian king Artaxerxes. A century or so previously Judah had fallen to the Babylonians as the prophets Jeremiah and Ezekiel had warned. The cream of the Jewish establishment had been taken off to Babylon. Seventy years later the Persians had conquered Babylon and allowed some Jews to resettle Judah. Nehemiah is one of those who remain – until news comes from his brother, Hanani, that things are not going well in Judah: the people are in trouble and the walls of Jerusalem remain unrepaired (1:3). Nehemiah turns to God in prayer. He reminds a covenant-keeping God of his promises to Moses while confessing that the Jews have not been a covenant-keeping people. Nehemiah receives the blessing of Artaxerxes to go to Judah to see what can be done, and under his leadership the wall is rebuilt. But Nehemiah is concerned for more than bricks and mortar. The real threat is not the surrounding nations but God's holiness, and the real need is for spiritual renewal. With Ezra he gathers the people and for seven days the law is read and the people join together to renew the covenant. It is in this context that the prayer recorded in Nehemiah 9 is made.

This prayer is a response to God's Word. For most of the people this is the first time they have heard the law. They realize how the nation has fallen short of what is required and they weep with repentance. Only at the exhortation of Nehemiah, Ezra and the Levites does this sorrow turn to joy. Perhaps one of the Levites listed in verses 4–5 led the prayer, but no-one is specified.

Nehemiah wants to convey the sense that all the people were united in this prayer. It was not prayer *for* them, but *by* them. This is their response to God's Word as it had been read to them.

a. The story of God's promise

The first thing that strikes us as we read this prayer is that it is a story. In some ways it does not feel like a prayer at all – at least not the sort of praying in which most of us engage. Yet prayers that are stories are common in the Bible (see Pss. 104 – 107; Dan. 9; Acts 4). Most of us have been taught the truths of the Bible as timeless truths transcending history, and we can have a rather static view of its accounts. But it is first and foremost a story – the story of God's plan of salvation. The Bible is not an encyclopaedia nor a manual. We cannot look under *p* for 'prayer' or *s* for 'salvation' to find out what is what. Instead we read a story. It is the story of how God's promise is made first to Abraham; how it is partially fulfilled in the history of Israel; how it is reaffirmed in successive covenants; how its scope enlarges as the story progresses until we discover that only a new humanity in a new creation will fulfil God's purposes.

This prayer starts with that promise as the Creator God makes a covenant with Abraham (5b–8a). Verses 6 and 7 both begin in the same way: *You alone are the* LORD ... (despite absence of 'alone' in v. 7 of the NIV). The God who alone made all things is the God who alone makes a covenant with mankind. The One who receives the worship of heaven is the One who includes us in his plan of salvation. The key statement is verse 8: *You have kept your promise because you are righteous.* The word 'righteous' here means 'faithful' – 'One who keeps his promise'. The rest of the prayer recalls how God has indeed been faithful to his promise throughout Israel's history. The people are saying, in effect, 'This is the story so far. And here we are waiting for the next stage. Do not forget your promise. Remember your faithfulness.' 'They appealed to the contradiction between their present circumstances and what they perceived as God's immutable purposes toward them.'[2] There is a relentlessness about the prayer. The story ploughs on and the praying people stand in the way, waiting to be swept up into God's purposes, caught along by the flow of his promise. The argument is plain: *Hear us and keep your promise – as you have done before.*

As mentioned earlier, the promise made to Abraham, which forms the basis of this prayer, was the gospel 'announced ... in advance' (Gal. 3:6–9). The gospel is God's promise to us that we

---

[2] Williamson, *Ezra, Nehemiah*, p. 319.

shall share the inheritance of God's people in the new creation through the work of Christ: 'Through the gospel the Gentiles are heirs together with Israel, members together of one body, and sharers together in the promise in Christ Jesus' (Eph. 3:6). The promise comes to us with the same momentum that we see in this chapter. It is still driving forward to the climax of history. We, too, can cry, *Hear us and keep your promise – as you have done before.*

b. The story of God's mercy

There is a tension between the opening of the prayer – *You alone are the LORD* (6) – and its conclusion – *We are in great distress* (37). How can the people of the Sovereign Lord languish in distress? The answer is the sin of the people. Within the story of the progress of God's purposes there is a repeated cycle of redemption, sin and mercy.

Verses 9–21 describe events surrounding the exodus. Verses 9–15 recall the redemption from Egypt, while verses 16–17a recall the sin of the people, and verses 17b–21 describe how God had mercy on their sin. In verses 22–27 the same pattern is repeated in the conquest of Canaan. Verses 22–25 emphasize the land as God's gift and the conquest as God's victory. Verses 26–27a recall the sin of the people, while verse 27b describes God's mercy and redemption through the judges. In both cases – the exodus and the conquest – there is a pattern of redemption, sin and mercy. Verse 28 goes on to describe how this cycle becomes a repeated cycle of sin and mercy. Verses 29–31 once again describe the cycle, with the added element of God warning the people through his prophets.

The message is clear. Israel's history has been a history of sin and mercy. God has rescued his people time after time. And time after time they have turned from him. Yet he continues to have mercy upon them. The argument of the prayer is, in effect, *Hear us and be merciful – as you were to our sinful forefathers.* The prayer ends, *we are slaves today* (36–37). History has tragically come full circle: the people are back in slavery as they were in Egypt. They need a new exodus.

The people vindicate God in verses 33–35. They acknowledge that God has acted justly, faithfully and mercifully throughout their history. The only plea of the people is the undeserved mercy of God. This history reveals the character of God. God is the Saviour of his people. He is the *forgiving God, gracious and compassionate, slow to anger and abounding in love* (17) (see also Exod. 34:6–7; Ps. 103:8–18). The prayer began with a focus on the God who is the Creator of all things (6) and the keeper of promises (8). When in verse 32 the prayer turns to petition, these themes are picked up again: *Now therefore, O our God, the great, mighty and awesome God, who keeps his covenant of love, do not let all this hardship seem trifling in your eyes* ... (9:32)

We, too, can remind God of his mercy, for his character does not change. But we can also add a chapter to this story-prayer. God has again acted in unmerited mercy towards his people. This time in a climactic way. The God who created all things, the God who keeps his promises, the God who saves his people, the God of compassion and love has brought all these things to a climax in the gift of his Son and in the love of the cross. Christ effects the new exodus for which the people pray (36). So we can pray, 'You have shown mercy to us in sending your Son to die for us. Do not forsake us now. Remember his shed blood. Hear us and be merciful – as you did while we were still sinners, still powerless and still enemies' (Rom. 5:6–11).

3. Daniel 9

Hezekiah 'argues' with God in prayer on the basis of the reputation or glory of God. The people in Nehemiah 9 present before God his promise and his mercy. Daniel 9 brings together these three great arguments – the promise, mercy and glory of God.

a. The promise of God

Daniel is living in Babylon (1–3). Nehemiah is his younger contemporary. Nearly seventy years previously the Jews had been defeated by the Babylonians and many had been taken away into exile – including the young Daniel. Now Daniel reads in Jeremiah that the Jews will return to Jerusalem after seventy years (Jer. 25:8–14; 29:10–14; see also Zech. 1:12) – and so he prays. Daniel prays that the promise made through Jeremiah will be fulfilled. He prays in response to God's word for what he knows to be God's will. 'The fact that God has spoken through the prophets does not mean that all the believer does is sit, newspaper in hand, awaiting the outcome. The appropriate response is prayer.'[3] That God has promised a return from exile does not cause Daniel to think there is no need to pray. Rather the promise of God becomes the starting point of his prayer: 'When Daniel knew the time was come he prayed the more earnestly. You will say, "What need he pray for it when he knew the time was accomplished?" I answer, The more need. Prayer helps

---

[3] Goldingay, *Daniel*, p. 263.

the promise to bring forth. Because a woman's time is come, therefore shall she have no midwife? Nay, therefore give her one. He that appointed their return appointed that it should be a fruit of prayer.'[4]

The answer to Daniel's prayer is a vision of the future (20–27). The return from exile to Jerusalem that took place under Ezra and Nehemiah was a disappointment in many ways. The walls were rebuilt but Jerusalem was still threatened (Neh. 6:15 – 7:3). The people were reformed but it proved superficial (compare the promises of Neh. 10 with the sins of Neh. 13). As Gabriel puts it in verse 25, Jerusalem will be rebuilt *in times of trouble.* So Daniel is shown a vision of the two comings of Christ. In his first coming Christ deals with our alienation from God: he puts an end to sin, atones for wickedness, brings everlasting righteousness (24). In Matthew 24 Jesus interprets this chapter as a reference first of all to the fall of Jerusalem in AD 70: 'So when you see standing in the holy place "the abomination that causes desolation", spoken of through the prophet Daniel – let the reader understand – then let those who are in Judea flee to the mountains' (Matt. 24:15–16).

But Jesus sees the fall of Jerusalem as a pointer to the final judgment and the in-gathering of the elect (Matt. 24:30–31). Jesus will return to gather the exiled people of God from the four corners of the world and bring them home. Daniel prays according to the promise of God for the future return of God's people and the restoration of Jerusalem. What he does not realize is that the promise is ultimately fulfilled in people from every nation in the heavenly Jerusalem. In a sense he gets far more than he bargained for – he prays for the end of the exile but gets the end of the world!

b. The mercy of God

Verses 4–14 are a comprehensive confession of sin. The people of Israel have not obeyed God's law (5) and have not listened to his prophets (6). All – wherever they are (7) and whoever they are (8) – are implicated. The prayer moves back and forth between the righteousness of God and the sin of the people.

> *God ... keeps covenant and steadfast love*
>
> (4 ESV)

> *we have ... turn[ed] aside from your commandments and rules*
>
> (5 ESV)

[4] J. Owen, 'Memorial', pp. 85–86.

To you, O Lord, belongs righteousness

(7 ESV)

to us open shame ... To us ... belongs open shame

(7–8 ESV)

To the Lord our God belong mercy and forgiveness

(9 ESV)

the curse and oath ... have been poured out upon us

(11 ESV)

Daniel himself makes no attempt to distance himself from the people's sin even though he was only a child when he was taken into exile. *We are covered with shame*, he says twice (7, 8). Daniel may be praying alone but his outlook is communal before it is personal. We would do well to use 'we' and 'us' even when we pray alone, for we stand before God first and foremost as those who are part of the corporate people for whom Christ died. We cannot pray 'as a freelance'.[5]

Daniel vindicates God's judgment. God has acted in accordance with his word (11–13) and he has acted rightly (14). 'You are right not to hear our prayers,' says Daniel in effect. 'You are right to abandon us.' As Daniel's prayer comes to its climax, he says, *We do not make requests of you because we are righteous, but because of your great mercy* (18).

In verse 16 Daniel speaks of God's *righteous acts*. Verse 15 tells us what these are: they are his saving acts and the supreme act of salvation for the Old Testament people of God which was the exodus from Egypt. God's mercy is not some abstract notion – it is expressed in his saving acts in history. 'So,' says Daniel, 'in keeping with those merciful, righteous, saving, powerful interventions in history – hear my prayer.' Now listen to Paul: 'He who did not spare his own Son, but gave him up for us all – how will he not also, along with him, graciously give us all things?' (Rom. 8:32).

The exodus – and especially the Passover – was a pointer to the giving up by God of his own Son. This is God's greatest *righteous act*. Paul, I suspect, also had Genesis 22 in mind. Abraham stands with Isaac stretched out on the altar before him. He holds up his hand about to strike his beloved son. Then, at the last possible moment, God intervenes. He stops him and Isaac is spared. There is an alternative. But now another Father stands with his Son stretched

---

[5] See K. Barth, *CD* III/3, p. 287; see also pp. 276–283, 288.

out before him. He raises his hand to strike his Son, his only Son, his beloved Son. And there is no intervention. There is no voice from heaven. There is no alternative. Here on the cross God's mercy is written large. Here is God's mercy for all to see. In Romans 1 Paul says of mankind that in his wrath 'God gave them up' (Rom. 1:24, 26, 28 ESV). Now Paul says of the Son that in his wrath God 'gave *him* up for us all'. What else can there be, then, that he will withhold from us? '[Christ] is the one great gift and answer in which all that we can receive and ask is not merely determined but actually given and present and available to us ... Christian petition ... is simply the taking and receiving of the divine gift and answer as it is already present and near to hand in Jesus Christ.'[6]

c. The glory of God

Daniel calls upon God to act *for your sake* (17, 19), as Israel's sins have damaged God's reputation (15). They have made his people an object of scorn (16). Why does Daniel pray? *For your sake* – for God's glory. Why should God respond? *For your sake* – for the sake of his holy name. Daniel talks about the needs of Jerusalem and the needs of the people. But they are *your* city and *your* people. They are the city and people that *bear your Name* (19).

4. The arguments of prayer

We have explored three Old Testament prayers and found three great arguments in prayer. There are many other great Old Testament prayers we could have looked at, but I suggest we would not have found additional arguments in prayer. The promise of God, the mercy of God and the glory of God are the only arguments used by Bible prayers and the only arguments we can use before God. But what a trio! God himself invites us through the Spirit-inspired examples of prayers in the Bible to say, 'Hear our prayer because this is what you have promised. Hear our prayer because you are a merciful God. Hear our prayer because this will bring glory to your name.' Commenting on Daniel 9, Stuart Olyott says, 'Daniel came to God *with strong arguments and with importunity*. Like Moses before him, he gave God convincing reasons why He should hear him, and repeated his requests and reasons with fervour and urgency. This is one of the secrets of those who prevail with God.'[7]

---

[6] Ibid., pp. 271, 274.
[7] Olyott, *Dare to Stand Alone*, p. 121.

In a similar way the Puritan Richard Sibbes says that presenting arguments to God in prayer 'is an excellent thing': 'Study the Scriptures, and ... study all the arguments whereby holy men have prevailed with God ... to see in what cases those arguments were used. They are of use and force to prevail with God ... It is a pitiful thing ... for Christians ... to come to God only with bare, naked petitions ... and have no reason to press God out of his own word.'[8]

a. The promise of God

The people of Nehemiah 9 reminded God of his promise and his faithfulness before urging him to continue his faithfulness. Daniel prayed in response to God's Word. This is an important principle. We are to pray the *promises* of God's Word. We are to use the *language* of God's Word and adopt the *priorities* of his Word. Speaking of Moses' prayer in Exodus 15, Christopher Seitz says, 'It would not be too much to say that God is blackmailed (in a manner of speaking) by Moses, insofar as his suggestion to build a nation out of Moses or send an angel instead of himself is held hostage, Moses insists, to his own prior promises.'[9] As Calvin puts it, 'Nothing is promised to be expected from the Lord, which we are not also bidden to ask of him in prayers. So true is it that we dig up by prayer the treasures that were pointed out by the Lord's gospel, and which our faith has gazed upon.'[10]

George Müller was a pastor in the nineteenth century who became famous for his orphanage in Bristol. He never made requests for financial support – except to God – and many readers will be aware of the rather intimidating stories of his answered prayers. But for many years Müller struggled to pray each morning until he learnt to start not with prayer but with the Scriptures. He read it seeking 'food for my own soul', but found it also provoked him to confession, thanksgiving and intercession. Writing his autobiography some forty years later he said, 'My heart being nourished by the truth, being brought into experimental fellowship with God, I speak to my Father and Friend ... about the things He has brought before me in his precious word.'[11]

The apostle John says, 'This is the confidence we have in approaching God: that if we ask anything according to his will, he hears us' (1 John 5:14). But how do we know what God's will is? Christians sometimes act as if discerning God's will were a

---

[8] Cited by R. Williams, 'Prayer Habits of the Puritans', p. 276.
[9] Seitz, 'Prayer in the Old Testament', p. 16.
[10] Calvin, *Institutes*, 3.20.2.
[11] Cited in Piper, *Desiring God*, p. 128.

mysterious process. It is not. God has revealed his will in the Bible.[12] 'It is a frighteningly simple concept. Praying according to the will of God is finding out from the Scriptures what God has promised and praying for that.'[13]

The promises of God are like moulds into which we pour our prayers like liquid metal. We can pray in accordance with God's purposes because God has revealed his purposes in the Bible. He has not told everything we would like to know. But God has given us, says Peter, 'everything we need for life and godliness' (2 Pet. 1:3). 'What God hath promised, all that he hath promised, and nothing else, are we to pray for; for "secret things belong to the Lord our God" alone [Deut. 29:29], but the declaration of his will and grace belongs unto us, and is our rule.'[14]

There is much talk of listening to God, and prayer as a conversation, that often causes confusion and frustration. While some Christians talk up what they 'hear' from God (Col. 2:18–19), others are left feeling spiritually inadequate. They try to still themselves to hear God's voice but end up thinking only of various tasks that need doing. Prayer is indeed part of a conversation in which God speaks to us, but the way God speaks is through his Son. 'In the past God spoke to our forefathers through the prophets at many times and in various ways, but in these last days he has spoken to us by his Son' (Heb. 1:1–2). The revelation of God through his Son recorded in the Scriptures is in every way adequate: 'The Son is the radiance of God's glory and the exact representation of his being' (Heb. 1:3). We do not have to go back to the *various ways* of the past. To 'listen' to God apart from his Word is to imply that Christ is insufficient. It is to turn from the gospel to mysticism. Through the Spirit, we listen to God as he speaks in his Word. Jim Packer puts it simply: 'The triune God who Christians love and serve communicates, as it were, by letter (the Bible), and we reply, so to speak, by phone (prayer).'[15] Prayer is *not* listening to God, for we hear God's voice in the Bible. Meditation in the Scriptures means simply 'to think about' and its object is God's Word and his ways. Meditation is not about adopting certain postures, turning our palms upwards and emptying our mind: it is filling our minds with God's Word. Quoting a verse of Scripture to a dejected Christian, the Scottish preacher Alexander Whyte said, 'Put it in your tongue and suck it like a sweetie.' So we should pray with an open Bible. How else are we going to know what to pray for? If you pray without a Bible you

---

[12] See Carson, *Jesus and his Friends*, pp. 108–110.
[13] Olyott, *Dare to Stand Alone*, p. 119.
[14] J. Owen, 'Discourse', vol. 4, p. 275.
[15] Jim Packer in Hanes, *My Path of Prayer*, p. 61.

are pitting your wisdom against God's. Instead, for example, try identifying a verse relevant to each prayer request and use it to shape your prayers. Martin Luther, in his book *A Simple Way to Pray* (1535), which he wrote for his barber, outlines an approach to prayer based on reading the Bible. He suggests that in response to a passage of Scripture we should 'fashion a garland of four strands'.[16] We should consider first the *instruction* we find and then turn this successively into *thanksgiving, confession* and *petition.*

The literary quality of Daniel's prayer has led some scholars to doubt its genuineness. In reality Daniel is drawing upon the language and liturgy of the Scriptures with which he is familiar.[17] Charles Hodge says of those who lead public prayer that their 'mind and memory should be well stored with the thoughts and language of Scripture'.[18] Don Carson, describing how Psalm 135 itself is made up of biblical quotations and allusions, says:

> A similar phenomenon was once not uncommon amongst praying evangelicals. As men and women poured out their hearts to the Lord in prayer meetings, both praise and petition were cast in the language of Scripture. Of course, at its worst this sort of thing was a canned recitation of the same half-dozen texts. But at its best, such praise and prayer roamed through ever wider vistas of Scripture, as the people's knowledge of Scripture was itself growing.[19]

b. The mercy of God

Often our prayers focus on our needs. 'We pray for Brian *because he is so ill.*' 'Please help me in this interview *because I need a job.*' In effect we are saying that God should act because our need is great. Or we suggest that God owes us something: 'Why are you doing this to me? Why don't you heal?' We assume that stating our needs is reason enough for God to answer. The whole tenor of the prayers of Nehemiah 9 and Daniel 9 is different. They are full of contrition. Indeed Daniel explains why God has every reason *not* to act. We deserve nothing from God except his wrath. We have no claims on him and no rights before him. Our only recourse is to his mercy. This is why we often add *in Jesus' name* to the end of prayers. We have no claim on God except the mercy he has shown us in Christ (see Luke 18:9–14).

[16] Cited in McGrath, *Christian Spirituality*, p. 87.
[17] See Wallace, *Daniel*, p. 154.
[18] C. Hodge, *Systematic Theology*, vol. 3, p. 708.
[19] Carson, *For the Love of God*, vol. 1 (Crossway, 1998), 4 July.

Anyone who stands before God to pray, in his humility giving glory completely to God, [should] abandon all thought of his own glory, cast off all notion of his own worth, in fine, put away all self-assurance – lest if we claim for ourselves anything, even the least bit, we should become vainly puffed up, and perish at his presence ... The beginning, and even the preparation, of proper prayer is the plea for pardon with a humble and sincere confession of guilt ... believers open for themselves the door to prayer with this key ... Unless they are founded in free mercy, prayers never reach God.[20]

c. The glory of God

The key issue in the confrontation between Hezekiah and Sennacherib was the reputation of the Lord. The focus of Hezekiah's prayer was the glory of God, and not only the glory of God but the glory of God among the nations. Daniel's prayer is prayed *for [God's] sake*. After God has declared that he will strike down the Israelites and build a new nation from Moses, Moses audaciously argues with God: if God strikes down the Israelites the surrounding nations will conclude that 'the LORD was not able to bring these people into the land he promised them on oath' (Num. 14:13–16). In the same way, the glory of God dominates Paul's prayers (Rom. 15:5–6; Eph. 3:20–21; Phil. 1:8; and 2 Thess. 1:12) and the Lord's Prayer begins:

> Our Father in heaven,
> hallowed be your name.
>
> (Matt. 6:9)

The glory of God is to be the chief end of our prayers. All our prayers should head in that direction – not just our praise and thanksgiving but also our requests. We should ask for that which will bring glory to God. This does not mean adding a reference to God's glory as a formulaic conclusion to our prayers. It means every request we make should lead to the glory of God. It helps to determine for what we should pray. We can let the glory of God be our guide. In any situation we can ask ourselves, 'How can God be glorified?' We should be able to say as we make our requests, 'Do this for the sake of your glory.' O. Hallesby describes the time he spent with a godly pastor whose prayers made a deep impression on him. 'He prayed every day for many people and for many things.

---

[20] Calvin, *Institutes*, 3.20.8–9.

But as I listened to these prayers of his I had to say to myself, "After all he prays only one prayer, namely, that the name of God might be glorified." '[21]

What these arguments have in common is *God*. We argue with God on the basis of *his* promises, *his* mercy and *his* glory, not on the basis of our intentions, our needs or our aspirations. Time and again Bible prayers are thoroughly God-centred. They are preoccupied above all with the glory of God's name. What makes this so striking is the contrast with our own prayers. Our prayers are often human-centred. Many of our prayers are all about us and our needs, while Bible prayers are all about God and his glory. Perhaps the key lesson from an examination of Bible prayers is that we should make our prayers God-centred, rather than human-centred. Commenting on Hezekiah's prayer, John Oswalt says, '[The] plea is not based on the righteousness of the petitioner or upon mitigating circumstances. Rather, it is based solely on the character and identity of God ... All too often our well-being is the end and God is only the means to that end. Here Hezekiah demonstrates the opposite: God is the end and deliverance is the means.'[22]

The idea of arguing or persuading raises the question of the relationship between our prayers and God's will. Can God be persuaded to change his mind? Can God be manipulated by our prayers? Bible prayers do not fully explore these questions. But the arguments they offer do not suggest a God who can be outwitted by our reasoning, for the arguments focus on God himself – his faithfulness, his character, his glory. We are not persuading God to act out of character or contrary to his will. Quite the opposite. We are calling on him to be consistent with his word, his character and his intentions. We are calling on him to do what he has said (to keep his promises), to be what he is (to be merciful) and to achieve what he purposes to achieve (to glorify his name).

[21] Hallesby, *Prayer*, p. 100.
[22] Oswalt, *Isaiah*, pp. 653, 655–656.

1 Samuel 1 – 2
8. Praying with Hannah

The book of Judges ends with these words: 'In those days Israel had
no king; everyone did as he saw fit' (Judg. 21:25). A powerful sense
of political and moral crisis runs through the closing chapters of
Judges. Who is going to sort out this crisis? Who is going to put
things right? The next words in the great narrative that runs from
Joshua through to 2 Kings are *There was a certain man from
Ramathaim, a Zuphite from the hill country of Ephraim, whose
name was Elkanah son of Jeroham, the son of Elihu, the son of Tohu,
the son of Zuph, an Ephraimite* (1:1).[1] Reading the narrative in this
way immediately makes us wonder whether Elkanah is the man –
the one who will re-establish God's rule over his people. But
Elkanah cannot even control his own family (1:6–8). Instead we
are thrown into a domestic crisis. The focus switches from Elkanah
to his wife, Hannah, and the pain of her childlessness. 'From his
fathers, Elkanah has a proud past. With his wife, however, he has no
future.'[2] It is a strange opening to the book, and it makes you
wonder whether the writer – and perhaps God himself – has lost the
plot. The crisis of leadership hinted at in the opening narrative (1:3)
will soon be all too clear (2:12–25), but for the moment our
attention is directed away from the pressing issues of the nation to
the problems of one woman.

1. Hannah's prayer: pouring out our souls to the Lord

If we hope to move beyond the superficialities of our culture,
including our religious culture, we must be willing to go down
into the recreating silences, into the inner world of contemplation.

[1] In the Hebrew canon the book of Ruth is not located between Judges and
1 Samuel as it is in our English Bibles, but is part of the Writings.
[2] Brueggemann, *First and Second Samuel*, p. 12.

In their writings all the masters of meditation beckon us to be pioneers in this frontier of the Spirit ... We begin praying for others by first quieting our fleshly activity and listening to the silent thunder of the Lord of hosts. Attuning ourselves to divine breathings is spiritual work, but without it our praying is vain repetition (Matt. 6:7). Listening to the Lord is the first thing, the second thing, and the third thing necessary for successful intercession.[3]

So says Richard Foster in his best-selling book *Celebration of Discipline*. It sounds impressive and profound. I suspect that for many, talk of entering 'the recreating silences', pioneering on the 'frontier of the Spirit' and hearing the 'silent thunder of the Lord of hosts' is intimidating. Prayer, we are told, is about 'quieting our fleshly activity' – disengaging the emotions. It is stilling our passions so that we can be attuned to the 'divine breathings'.

But Hannah's experience of prayer is wholly different. Her anguish is clear. *The LORD had closed her womb*, we are told (1:5). The result is *bitterness of soul* (1:10) and *misery* (1:11). She is *deeply troubled* (1:15) and she talks about her *great anguish and grief* (1:16). The narrator piles up the language of her misery. For many women today childlessness is a source of intense personal anguish. In Hannah's day this was compounded by society's attitudes. Today children often seem to be regarded as another 'consumer choice' and millions of unwanted children are aborted because they do not fit in with people's lifestyles. But in Hannah's culture women found identity and status in childbearing. Children are seen in the Bible as a blessing, and to be childless is seen as a terrible misfortune or even a curse.

The situation for Hannah is made worse by Elkanah's other wife, Peninnah. In contrast to Hannah, Peninnah is all too fertile and likes to let Hannah know it. Verse 2 suggests that Hannah was Elkanah's first wife and it may be that he took Peninnah as his wife because of Hannah's childlessness. She is described as Hannah's *rival: her rival*, we are told, *kept provoking her in order to irritate her* (1:6). The annual festival at Shiloh was a particular occasion for grief. Each year the festive offering was handed out to all Peninnah's children. Verse 5 could mean that Elkanah gave Hannah *a double portion because he loved her*, or it could read *a single portion yet he loved her* – that is, she did not receive extra for her children because she had none. In either case her pain is clear. What should have been an occasion for joy and celebration when the family gave thanks for

---

[3] Foster, *Celebration of Discipline*, pp. 19, 48–49.

God's provision was for Hannah a reminder that God had not provided for her: a reminder that *the LORD had closed her womb* (1:5, 6). *Year after year* they went to sacrifice (1:3) and *year after year* Peninnah goaded Hannah (1:7).

Hannah's response to her misery, to her childlessness and the provocation of Peninnah, is a model of true piety. She does not turn upon Peninnah (as Sarah did in similar circumstances: Gen. 16:4–6). We are not told of any rancour on her part towards Peninnah. Neither does she complain about God's actions or question his love. Agency is clearly ascribed to God by the narrator. Twice we are told that God is the one who has *closed her womb* (1:5, 6). But Hannah's faith remains strong. She does not turn her back on a God who would seem to have turned his back on her. She remains trusting. And indeed she makes the response of faith, which is to pray. 'She addresses Yahweh of hosts, cosmic ruler, sovereign of every and all power, and assumes that the broken heart of a relatively obscure woman in the hill country of Ephraim matters to him.'[4] Prayer is an acknowledgment of our weakness and our need, and an acknowledgment of God's sovereignty and care. Hannah pours out her anguish and bitterness not in aggression to Peninnah but in faith to God.

But notice, too, that she does not simply stoically accept her situation. There are times when we reach the point when we must say, 'Your will be done' (Mark 14:36). But Hannah challenges the will of God in prayer. She implores God to change the status quo. P. T. Forsyth cites 'prayer conceived merely, or chiefly, as submission, resignation, quietism' as an obstacle to deepening our spiritual lives.[5] He continues:

> We say too soon, 'Thy will be done'; and too ready acceptance of a situation as His will often means feebleness or sloth. It may be His will that we surmount His will. It may be His higher will that we resist His lower will. Prayer is an act of will much more than of sentiment, and its triumph is more than acquiescence. Let us submit when we *must*, but let us keep the submission in reserve rather than in action, as a ground tone rather than the sole effort. Prayer with us has largely ceased to be wrestling. But is that not the dominant scriptural idea? ... Resisting His will may be doing His will.[6]

And so Hannah prays with great earnestness: *In bitterness of soul*

[4] Davis, *1 Samuel*, p. 15.
[5] Forsyth, *Soul of Prayer*, p. 82.
[6] Ibid., p. 82.

122

Hannah wept much and prayed to the LORD (1:10). She makes a vow to dedicate the child to God. Indeed so fervent is her praying that Eli, the priest, thinks she is drunk and rebukes her. Her reply is revealing for it expresses the intensity of her praying: *I am a woman who is deeply troubled. I have not been drinking wine or beer; I was pouring out my soul to the* LORD. *Do not take your servant for a wicked woman; I have been praying here out of my great anguish and grief* (1:15–16).

Pouring out my soul is a great description of Christian prayer. Prayer is not the quietening of the soul. It is an expression in faith of the passions of the heart.

In his impressive phenomenological study of prayer, Friedrich Heiler identifies two central traditions of prayer: *mystical* prayer and what he calls *prophetic* prayer. Mystical prayer is the search for communion with God through contemplation. Prophetic prayer, in contrast, is a simple, passionate response to the revelation of God's fatherhood – 'responsive prayer' might be a better phrase. Heiler himself continues to affirm mystical prayer as 'the sublimest kind of prayer',[7] but from a biblical perspective his description is damning. The characteristics of mysticism, he tells us, include a focus upon progressive states of spiritual consciousness, a stilling of the passions, a discouragement of petitions, especially for earthly goods, and a god in whom 'the features of the divine personality begin to fade'.[8]

Heiler himself acknowledges that mysticism is at variance with 'the devotional religion of the Old and New Testaments and of the Reformation'.[9] Whereas mystical prayer focuses on the progressive states of spiritual consciousness, biblical prayer reflects 'unpretentious simplicity and childlike sincerity of heart'.[10] In the mystical tradition union with Christ is attained through spiritual disciplines as the goal of Christian experience. In the biblical tradition union with Christ is given through faith as the foundation of Christian experience. Whereas mystical prayer involves stilling the emotions, biblical prayer arises from 'emotions of great intensity which press for discharge'.[11] Calvin says a 'sweet and perfect repose' is not the characteristic of the spiritually advanced but simply those whose 'affairs are flowing to their liking'. 'For the saints', he continues, 'the occasion that best stimulates them to call upon God is when, distressed by their own need, they are troubled by the greatest

---

[7] Heiler, *Prayer*, p. 225.
[8] Ibid., p. 198.
[9] Ibid., p. 226; see also pp. 130–132.
[10] Ibid., p. 226.
[11] Ibid., p. 230.

unrest, and are almost driven out of their senses, until faith opportunely comes to their relief.'[12] Silence in the prophetic tradition is not the studied contemplation of mysticism that might be interrupted by speech, but rather the failure of language to express the passions of the heart.[13] Even when the emotions are dull, prayer in the prophetic tradition is not stillness but disciplined struggle.

Mystical prayer has always had its proponents within the Christian church.[14] In Colossians Paul has to warn against those who speak of mysteries and visions (Col. 2:2–4, 16–19), and who want to move on from what we have in Christ (Col. 1:15–27; 2:6–10). Paul tells Timothy to refute those who offer a higher knowledge (1 Tim. 6:19) and who want to restrain the passions associated with food and sex (1 Tim. 4:1–5). Mysticism appears impressive, portraying itself as advanced spirituality. But, as Karl Barth says, the beginning of prayer is not an account of 'what a man does when he prays'. Describing the approach of the Reformers, Barth continues, 'the foundation of everything is the certainty that God answers prayers'.[15] In other words, prayer is not the vehicle for human searching after God. 'Spirituality is not demanded; it is offered.'[16] Prayer is simply the cry of the heart in response to the revelation of God. As C. B. Samuel puts it, 'Prayer is not an art. It is a cry. You cannot pretend it or practice it. You can only express it.'[17]

We need to see the distinction between mystical prayer and responsive prayer clearly, for mystical prayer will always have attractions for the devout. For it is through mysticism that we make prayer a supposed achievement on our side. In reality the achievement of prayer is all on God's side. It is the Father who graciously invites us to converse; it is the Son who mediates through his death; and it is the Spirit who awakens within us the desire the pray.

Eli tells Hannah to *Go in peace* (1:17) and this is what she does: *Then she went her way and ate something, and her face was no longer downcast* (1:18). At this point a child has not been conceived, let alone born. We are not told whether her grief is gone because she is confident that God will give her the child she has requested or whether she has a gained a new sense of God's care through prayer, but she is a changed woman. In verse 7 she will not eat. You can

[12] Calvin, *Institutes*, 3.20.11.

[13] Heiler, *Prayer*, p. 239.

[14] For contemporary examples within evangelicalism see Foster, *Celebration of Discipline*; Huggett, *Listening to God*; and Foster, *Prayer*.

[15] K. Barth, *Prayer and Preaching*, p. 16.

[16] Bock, *Luke*, NIVAC, p. 335.

[17] Quoted in Tim Hamilton, *Your Kingdom Come*, p. 4.

imagine her pushing the food round her plate. Now she eats heartily and joins in the family banter. Peninnah's jibes no longer have any effect.

The result is that a son is born and Hannah calls him 'Samuel'. The origin of the word 'Samuel' is disputed. It probably means 'name of God' or 'God is exalted'.[18] But it sounds enough like the Hebrew for 'heard of God' for Hannah to use it as a pun (1:20). Samuel is the answer to Hannah's prayer and she acknowledges this in the name she gives him – God has heard her. After she has weaned him, she dedicates the child to God as she promised by giving him to Eli to serve in the house of the Lord.

Her presentation of Samuel to Eli is a dramatic moment. Her speech in 1:27–28 uses forms of the Hebrew verb *to ask* four times to emphasize her asking.[19] In her first encounter with Eli, when he thinks she is drunk, she does not say what it is for which she has been praying, only that she has been *pouring out [her] soul to the* LORD (1:15). Now she presents the child to Eli, saying, in effect, '*I am the woman* who you thought was drunk and *for this child I prayed*. This is what I was praying for. You thought I was drunk, but here is the proof that I was praying. *The* LORD *has granted me* those prayers which you thought were the babblings of a drunk.'

2. Hannah's praise: our hearts rejoicing in the Lord

Hannah responds to God's activity in her life with a song of praise. The text says that *Hannah prayed* (2:1). But this prayer is all praise and it is in the form of a song. Prayer is not just the *pouring out [the] soul to the* LORD (1:15). It is also *[the] heart rejoic[ing] in the* LORD (2:1). This is an important note for us to remember. We can be so preoccupied with our problems that we focus simply on our petitions. Even when our prayers are answered we all too easily move on to the next request on our mental lists. We can be like the nine lepers whom Jesus healed and who never thought to thank him (Luke 17:11–19). While making requests to God is itself an acknowledgment of his greatness and love, we should not lose sight of the importance of praise in Christian experience. We were made to enjoy God and prayer rightly involves enjoying God and rejoicing in his goodness.

We praise God for who he is and for what he has done – in creation and in salvation. Hannah starts with her experience: *My heart rejoices ... my horn is lifted high ... My mouth boasts ... I*

[18] R. P. Gordon, *I & II Samuel*, p. 76.
[19] Davis, *1 Samuel*, p. 17.

delight (2:1). But her experience is a response to God's intervention: *in the* LORD ... *in the* LORD ... *in your deliverance* (2:1). Her praise begins with the unique being of God: *There is no-one holy like the* LORD; *there is no-one besides you; there is no Rock like our God* (2:2). Hannah lists three ways in which God is beyond compare. First, God's holiness is beyond compare. He alone is pure and righteous. He alone does what is right. He alone rescues his people. Second, God's divinity, as it were, is beyond compare. There is no god to rival him. Hannah's words echo the words of Moses as the people were about to enter the Promised Land.

> Ask now about the former days, long before your time, from the day God created man on the earth; ask from one end of the heavens to the other. Has anything so great as this ever happened, or has anything like it ever been heard of? Has any other people heard the voice of God speaking out of fire, as you have, and lived? Has any god ever tried to take for himself one nation out of another nation, by testings, by miraculous signs and wonders, by war, by a mighty hand and an outstretched arm, or by great and awesome deeds, like all the things the LORD your God did for you in Egypt before your very eyes?
>
> You were shown these things so that you might know that the LORD is God; besides him there is no other ... Acknowledge and take to heart this day that the LORD is God in heaven above and on the earth below. There is no other.
>
> (Deut. 4:32–35, 39)

Finally God is like a rock – a rock like no other. Again Hannah is picking up the language of Moses (Deut. 32:4, 18). The image of God as a rock speaks of his dependability and strength. But it may represent more than that. In Exodus 17, shortly after God has rescued them from Egypt, the people of Israel complain that they are thirsty. The passage speaks of them *testing* God. Their lack of faith in the face of his salvation cries out for judgment. Moses wields the rod of judgment. But instead of dispensing judgment on the people, God tells Moses to use the rod to strike the rock. As Moses does so, water pours forth. It is an evocative picture of God taking judgment on himself vicariously that his people might be spared – and not only spared but richly blessed. This is why Paul can say, 'they drank from the spiritual rock that accompanied them, and that rock was Christ' (1 Cor. 10:4). Striking the rock with the rod of judgment was a pointer to what Christ would do: taking judgment on himself so that living water might flow to God's people. For the Israelites God the Rock was the God who dispensed undeserved blessing.

Hannah also s eaks of God as the one who knows:

> *Do not keep talking so proudly*
> *or let your mouth speak such arrogance,*
> *for the* LORD *is a God who knows,*
> *nd by him deeds are weighed.*

(2:3)

God is not un aring or distant. God has seen the distress of Hannah. He has heard her cries (1:20). He knows our plight. Again Hannah is drawing on the past. Hagar is told to call her son Ishmael, which, akin to the name Samuel, means 'God hears' (Gen. 16:11). Hagar encounters God and 'she gave this name to the LORD who spoke to her: "You are the God who sees me," for she said, "I have now seen the One who sees me"' (Gen. 16:13).

The point is that these great truths about the character of God evoke praise in Hannah. Hannah praises the God who is holy, sovereign, who provides for his people, who protects those who are his, and who knows our plight. But notice, too, that Hannah has a developed doctrine of God. She can draw on biblical language and biblical truths to express her praise. The more we know of God, the more our hearts are tuned to praise him. The route to true heart-felt praise is not evocative music or emotional atmospheres but the truth of God's character and ways. But neither can this truth be allowed to lie cold and dry. It must be lit up into praise so that we cry out with Paul, 'Now to the King eternal, immortal, invisible, the only God, be honour and glory for ever and ever. Amen' (1 Tim. 1:17). We do well to use hymns and songs in our prayers. Time and again Paul draws on early Christian hymns to express himself in his letters. Truth for Paul cannot remain at a cerebral level – it should also move our hearts. Hannah herself draws on the language of the Pentateuch to express her thankfulness.[20] Poetry and music engage our emotions in ways that prose alone cannot.

Hannah not only praises God's character but also his ways in creation and redemption. The song reflects her personal experience. The phrases *My mouth boasts over my enemies, / for I delight in your deliverance* (2:1) and *Do not keep talking so proudly / or let your mouth speak such arrogance* (2:3) suggest her vindication in the face of the taunts of Peninnah. And *She who was barren has borne seven children, / but she who has had many sons pines away* (2:5) evokes the gift of a child to Hannah. But these references are indirect. She is not crowing over Peninnah. Instead she is setting her

[20] See Brueggemann, *First and Second Samuel*, p. 16.

experience in the wider context of God's vindication of his people: *He will guard the feet of his saints* (2:9).

Hannah describes a series of reversals:

> *The bows of the warriors are broken,*
>   *but those who stumbled are armed with strength.*
> *Those who were full hire themselves out for food,*
>   *but those who were hungry hunger no more.*
> *She who was barren has borne seven children,*
>   *but she who has had many sons pines away.*
>
> *The LORD brings death and makes alive;*
>   *he brings down to the grave and raises up.*
> *The LORD sends poverty and wealth;*
>   *he humbles and he exalts.*
> *He raises the poor from the dust*
>   *and lifts the needy from the ash heap;*
> *he seats them with princes*
>   *and has them inherit a throne of honour.*
>
> (2:4–8)

The Lord makes a habit of rescuing the needy and exalting the humble. He opposes those who are proud and mighty. Not only can he bring life where there is no life (as in the case of barrenness). He can even bring life where there is death (2:6). He can perform the ultimate reversal: bringing people back from the grave (2:6). Hannah roots these reversals in creation:

> *For the foundations of the earth are the LORD's;*
>   *upon them he has set the world.*
>
> (2:8)

The God who created the world is radically free. He is not subject to the jurisdiction of princes or bound by the forces of nature. Belief in a Creator relativizes human claims to power, giving Hannah's song a subversive edge. The threats and promises of human leaders are qualified by Hannah's claim that it is the Creator God who raises up and brings to nothing. 'Yahweh presides over the world and therefore can do as Yahweh wills with it ... Yahweh need not bow before, yield to, or defer to any prince or noble. Yahweh need not conform to any legitimated social arrangement. Yahweh is free to reorder the earth and will do so on behalf of the marginal.'[21]

[21] Ibid., p. 19.

The key idea in this song is that Hannah sees what has happened to her against a bigger canvas. Hannah's movement from grief to joy is a sign of the greater movement that God is achieving through his plan of salvation. His kingdom is a kingdom of reversals in which the first shall be last and the last shall be first. Paul writes to the Corinthians:

> Brothers, think of what you were when you were called. Not many of you were wise by human standards; not many were influential; not many were of noble birth. But God chose the foolish things of the world to shame the wise; God chose the weak things of the world to shame the strong. He chose the lowly things of this world and the despised things – and the things that are not – to nullify the things that are, so that no-one may boast before him. It is because of him that you are in Christ Jesus, who has become for us wisdom from God – that is, our righteousness, holiness and redemption. Therefore, as it is written: 'Let him who boasts boast in the Lord.'
>
> (1 Cor. 1:26–31)

God chooses those who are despised by the world to display his grace. We are not saved because of our wisdom, power or nobility; we are saved simply because of God's grace. Those who are proud exclude themselves from his kingdom. *It is not by strength that one prevails*, sings Hannah (2:9). Our only boast is in Christ Jesus. He alone is our 'righteousness, holiness and redemption'.

We see only glimpses of these reversals now. In this life the bows of the warriors are *not* broken. Those who stumble *are* trodden underfoot. The hungry remain hungry. The poor remain in the dust. But what has happened to Hannah is a sign of what is to come. It is part of a trend that will reach beyond our history of injustice and disappointment into an eternity of joy. In the end the meek 'will inherit the earth' (Matt. 5:5).

This is the key to praise. We do not sing the songs of earth that celebrate power and success; we sing the songs of heaven and the new song of God's promise (Rev. 5:9; 14:3). People in difficult situations – those who experience *great anguish and grief* (1:16) – are able to anticipate the future joy of heaven. This is the word the gospel speaks to those who share Hannah's anguish. We may not enjoy the comfort she received in this life but her redemption is a picture of what is to come for all who trust in God. If we only sing of our happiness on earth we shall not have the resources to cope in times of anguish. Sometimes congregational praise can have an element of unreality about it – we sing as if all is good when many in the congregation are hurting. However, we *can* sing with joy not by denying the pain of the present but surmounting it through the gospel with the songs of heaven. We do not deny reality, but we can counter it with the promise of a new reality.

Paul prays for joy – it is not a given. 'May the God of hope', he prays for the Christians in Rome, 'fill you with all joy and peace as you trust in him, so that you may overflow with hope by the power of the Holy Spirit' (Rom. 15:13). He even talks of joy as a decision we can make, as something he can command: 'Be joyful in hope, patient in affliction, faithful in prayer' (Rom. 12:12; see also 2 Cor. 13:11; Phil. 3:1; 4:4; 1 Thess. 5:16). Notice, too, that joy is linked to hope. We can decide for joy by looking heavenward. It was this sense of heavenly joy anticipated now that enabled Paul and Silas to sing in prison (Acts 16:25). It is an idea beautifully captured by the words of the hymn 'How can I keep from singing?'

> My life goes on in endless song
> above earth's lamentations,
> I hear the real, though far-off hymn
> that hails a new creation.
> Through all the tumult and the strife
> I hear its music ringing,
> It sounds an echo in my soul.
> How can I keep from singing?
>
> While though the tempest loudly roars,
> I hear the truth, it liveth.
> And though the darkness round me close,
> songs in the night it giveth.
> No storm can shake my inmost calm,
> while to that rock I'm clinging.
> Since Love is Lord of heaven and earth
> how can I keep from singing?
>
> When tyrants tremble in their fear
> and hear their death knell ringing,
> when friends rejoice both far and near
> how can I keep from singing?
> In prison cell and dungeon vile
> our thoughts to them are winging,
> when friends by shame are undefiled
> how can I keep from singing?[22]

3. Hannah's place in God's purposes: it is not by strength that one prevails

a. Hannah's song and David's song

Does the story of Hannah teach us that God will provide children to childless women who earnestly pray to him? Does it suggest that if we make a vow to God he will be more likely to answer our prayer? The answer to these questions is no. Hannah's story is told not because it is typical but because it is untypical. There were no doubt many childless women in Israel who prayed to God and remained childless. Hannah's prayer is not granted because her prayer was more devout or her anguish more acute or her vow more sincere. Her prayer was answered because of God's grace. Eli says to Hannah, *Go in peace, and may the God of Israel grant you what you have asked of him* (1:17). The answer to her prayer lies in the gift of God. Hannah herself replies, *May your servant find favour in your eyes* (18). The word *favour* or *grace* in Hebrew is ḥēn, and so this is a play on Hannah's name.[23] Hannah's name is a reminder that God acts in his grace.

In his grace God is acting not only in Hannah's life but in the life of the nation. Hannah's story is told because it is part of a bigger story – the story of God's provision of a Saviour. Hannah's son, Samuel, will re-establish the rule of God over the people of God. He will replace the corrupt regime of Hophni and Phinehas (1:3). He will deliver the people from their enemies (1 Sam. 7:2–14). He will judge them with justice (1 Sam. 7:15–17).

Hannah's song ends in an intriguing way:

> *He will give strength to his king*
> *and exalt the horn of his anointed.*
>
> (2:10)

This is Hebrew parallelism. Kings in that day were not crowned but anointed with oil, so *the anointed* One is a reference to the king. It gives us the Hebrew word māšîaḥ, 'messiah', which in Greek is *Christos* (Christ). This is the first reference in the Bible to God's Christ. Yet at this point, as we know from Judges 21:25, Israel has no king. Hannah prays for the strength of God's anointed king, but

---

[22] The song is sometimes described as a traditional Shaker hymn, but is also variously attributed to Susanna Warner (written 1850) or Robert Lowry (1826–99). Lowry wrote a tune to the hymn, so it may be that the words were also attached to his name erroneously.

[23] R. P. Gordon, *I & II Samuel*, p. 76.

there is no king. However, a king is coming and Hannah's son, Samuel, will be the kingmaker. He will be the one who will anoint Israel's first king – Saul – but also declare God's rejection of Saul as king. He it is who will anoint instead Israel's greatest king – David. Through Hannah's son hope is coming – hope of deliverance and the restoration of God's rule.

At the end of the books of Samuel the writer has placed a psalm of David (2 Sam. 22; Ps. 18; see also Ps. 113). It is probably placed there out of chronological order. Together these songs of Hannah and David frame the narrative. They provide 'an interpretative key' by which to understand the history of David's rise to the throne.[24]

David's song of praise begins:

> The LORD is my rock, my fortress and my deliverer;
>   my God is my rock, in whom I take refuge,
>   my shield and the horn of my salvation.
>
> (2 Sam. 22:2–3)

Hannah, too, speaks of God as a rock and her horn (a horn is a symbol of strength). Hannah sings, *there is no-one besides you; / there is no Rock like our God* (1 Sam. 2:2), while David sings, *For who is God besides the LORD? / And who is the Rock except our God* (2 Sam. 22:32). Both songs describe a thunderous coming of God (1 Sam. 2:10; 2 Sam. 22:8–16). Both songs speak of the reversals that God performs. Hannah says of God that *he humbles and he exalts*, while David says, *You save the humble, / but your eyes are on the haughty to bring them low* (1 Sam. 2:7; 2 Sam. 22:28; see also 2 Sam. 22:17–20). They both speak of God protecting those who are faithful (1 Sam. 2:9; 2 Sam. 22:26). David speaks of the way God has rescued him and given him victory over his enemies. Just as Hannah prayed in the temple out of her distress and God heard her, so David says:

> In my distress I called to the LORD;
>   I called out to my God.
> From his temple he heard my voice;
>   my cry came to his ears.
>
> (2 Sam. 22:7)

David's psalm ends with a description of the way in which God has given David victory over his adversaries and rule over the nations

---

[24] Childs, *Old Testament as Scripture*, p. 273. See also VanGemeren, *Progress of Redemption*, p. 206; and Satterthwaite, 'David'.

(2 Sam. 22:38–51). God has shown *unfailing kindness to his anointed* (2 Sam. 22:51). Hannah, too, ends by claiming that

> *those who oppose the LORD will be shattered.*
> *He will thunder against them from heaven;*
> *the LORD will judge the ends of the earth.*

> *He will give strength to his king*
> *and exalt the horn of his anointed.*

> (2:10)

At the heart of Hannah's song is the phrase *It is not by strength that one prevails* (2:9). Hannah's story appears to be an odd opening to the books of Samuel, set as they are against the background of moral and political crisis, because we would not look for the answer to national problems in the desperate prayers of a childless woman. But it is here that they are to be found. God is working through the marginalized, the sad and the troubled. Walter Brueggemann writes:

> In a daring move, back behind 'the great men', the narrator locates the origin of Israel's future and the source of its 'great leaders' in the story of a bereft, barren woman named Hannah (1:2). The story of Israel's waiting that moves from trouble to well-being begins neither in grand theory nor in palace splendour nor in doxological celebration. It begins ... in barrenness wherein is no hint of a future ... in hopelessness.[25]

The narrative of 1 and 2 Samuel reflects this theme of hope from the margins, that God will graciously exalt the humble and topple the mighty. At the beginning of 1 Samuel, Israel is 'a marginal community' under pressure from the Philistines,[26] but by the end of 2 Samuel she is the regional superpower. God defeats the enemies of his people (1 Sam. 7; 11; 14; 15; 17; 2 Sam. 5; 8; 10; 21), but Israel, too, can fall if she trusts in her own strength (1 Sam. 4; 31). David himself is the shepherd boy who brings down the giant Goliath because he comes 'in the name of the LORD Almighty', and the Lord hands Goliath over to David, demonstrating that 'it is not by sword or spear that the LORD saves' (1 Sam. 17:45–47). David is portrayed as the king who will not seize power 'by sword or spear' (1 Sam. 24; 26). David will not oppose 'God's anointed One' even when he has been anointed as Saul's successor. Instead he spends much of the

---

[25] Brueggemann, *First and Second Samuel*, p. 11.
[26] Ibid., p. 10.

narrative on the margins, as a fugitive on the run from Saul. David trusts in the promise of God. God will build his kingdom. God will make his king rule over his people. It is David's humble trust in the God who humbles and exalts (2:7), not some inherent kingly dignity, that leads to true honour (2 Sam. 6:20–22). Hannah's song begins and ends with the same themes:

> *My heart rejoices in the LORD;*
> *in the LORD my horn is lifted high.*
>
> (2:1)

> *He will give strength to his king*
> *and exalt the horn of his anointed.*
>
> (2:10)

It is God who gives strength. It is God who exalts.

When the people of Israel are tempted to trust in military and economic power, or when they are afraid of their enemies, the message of 1 and 2 Samuel is that *it is not by strength that one prevails* (2:9). The story of Hannah is a reminder that God works his purposes out through the weakness of human beings. At each point in the story God is the central actor:

> *the LORD had closed her womb*
>
> (1:5–6)

> *may the God of Israel grant you what you have asked of him*
> (1:17)

> *the LORD remembered her*
>
> (1:19)

> *the LORD has granted me what I asked of him*
>
> (1:27)

Walter Brueggemann comments, 'Israel's new life emerges out of barrenness by the power of God.'[27] We need not fear the power of people; nor should we rely on our own power. At this point in the story of salvation God achieved his purposes through the desperate prayers of a childless woman.

We can overrate strategy in Christian work. Perhaps we should leave the strategy to God and instead offer ourselves to his service.

---

[27] Ibid., p. 15.

We should get on with being faithful to him in the situation in which we find ourselves. It may be that God will use us to achieve great things. It may be that he calls us simply to be faithful. It may be that in the topsy-turvy economy of God's reign what we think of as great and significant has little eternal weight and it is the unnoticed acts and the anguished prayers of humble servants that bear fruit for all eternity.

b. Hannah's song and Mary's song

Hannah is not the first barren woman in the story of salvation; nor is she the last. The promise of salvation first came to Abraham. God promised that through his offspring salvation would come to all nations. But Abraham did not have any offspring. Sarah, his wife, was not only barren but well past the age of childbearing. It seemed as if God had made a mistake, as if he had picked the wrong person. And like Hannah, Sarah had a rival, Hagar, through whom Abraham had a child and who began to despise Sarah. But God had not made a mistake. He can fulfil his promises even if it means giving a son to a barren, old woman. God's plans do not depend upon Abraham, nor his family, nor the people of Israel, nor upon us – they depend solely upon his grace and power. As if to emphasize the point, Sarah's daughter-in-law was also barren and once again God gave her children in answer to prayer (Gen. 25:21). The judge before Samuel, Samson, had also been born to a barren woman (Judg. 13:2–3). And now he makes the point again as Samuel the king-maker is born to Hannah, whose *womb is closed*.

Where are God's plans and promises going? What is their climax? Who is the key player to whom all the others point? The answer, of course, is Jesus Christ. And he is born not to a barren woman nor to a woman past the age of childbearing, but to a virgin. God, as it were, goes one better this time. Now there can be no mistake that this is his doing. 'How will this be?' asks Mary. And the angel replies, 'nothing is impossible for God' (Luke 1:34, 37). Whereas Hannah prays, *O LORD Almighty, if you will only look upon your servant's misery and remember me, and not forget your servant but give her a son* (1 Sam. 1:11), in Luke, Mary sings:

> my spirit rejoices in God my Saviour,
> for he has been mindful
> of the humble state of his servant.
>
> (Luke 1:47–48)

Whereas Hannah prays for God to look upon and remember his

maidservant, Mary says that God has indeed looked and remembered. It is as if what has happened to Mary is an answer to the prayer of Hannah. At the heart of what God is doing in salvation is not our worth or what we contribute but his grace and his power.

Both Hannah and Mary realize this. They both realize that it is characteristic of God to choose the lowly, the sinful, the barren, the insignificant, the poor and make them part of his purposes. As Mary sings in celebration of the child within her womb, she draws upon the language of Hannah's song. Hannah's begins, *My heart rejoices in the LORD; / in the LORD my horn is lifted high* (1 Sam. 2:1), while Mary begins, 'My soul glorifies the Lord / and my spirit rejoices in God my Saviour' (Luke 1:46–47). But the similarity is far more significant than that. Both songs reflect the same understanding. Hannah's song is so much more than 'Thank you for my baby.' It moves way beyond Hannah's personal experience, because Hannah understands that her experience is typical of the way God works. Her experience illustrates a broader principle, which is that *God chooses the humble and helpless to demonstrate his holiness and power*. The prominence of barren women in the story of God's purposes reminds us that God's people 'begin with nothing'.[28]

Mary and Hannah are blessed because of what God has done (Luke 1:49). They boast in his deliverance (2:1). Both see what has happened to them as a demonstration of the holiness of God (1 Sam. 2:2; Luke 1:49). Whom are the ones God chooses? Whom does he save and whom does he use? The answer is, those who recognize that he alone is holy and mighty. We are not holy enough or strong enough apart from God to be used by him. Salvation and service are all of his grace. And so both Hannah and Mary go on to speak about a series of reversals. Those who are proud and powerful are brought low, while those who are weak are lifted up (1 Sam. 2:3–4; Luke 1:51–52). Those who have plenty are sent away empty, while those with nothing are filled (1 Sam. 2:5, 7–8; Luke 1:53).

This is a foundational truth for prayer: it is not by might that one prevails. It is only as we feel the truth of this for ourselves that we pray with the passion with which Hannah prayed. If we think we can prevail by our strength, then we shall pour our energy into activity. If we grasp the fact that we can prevail only through God's strength, then we shall pour energy into prayer as well.

4. Conclusion

In 1 Samuel 1 – 2 we have two stories: the story of Hannah and the

---

[28] Davis, *1 Samuel*, p. 13.

story of God. Or rather we have a story within a story, an episode in God's great story of salvation. We have the story of a woman whose anguished prayers for a child are wonderfully answered. And we have the story of how God moves forward his great plan of salvation, showing us once again that he chooses the humble and helpless to demonstrate his holiness and power. It is at once domestic and historic.

Hannah's faithful and passionate prayer is a model for us because we, too, are part of the same story. We look to the same God and we look to the coming of his anointed One. God *will give strength to his king / and exalt the horn of his anointed*, says Hannah (1 Sam. 2:10), and her son anoints King David. But King David is a pointer to God's ultimate anointed One – his Christ – the son born of the virgin. We find provision and protection in Jesus Christ. He is the one who re-establishes God's rule, who lifts up the needy and provides for the poor. Hannah says:

> The LORD *brings death and makes alive;*
>   *he brings down to the grave and raises up.*
> The LORD *sends poverty and wealth;*
>   *he humbles and he exalts.*
>
> (2:6–7)

The truth is that God makes us alive by bringing death to his Christ. He raises us up by bringing his Christ down to the grave. He exalts and enriches us by humbling his son. 'For you know the grace of our Lord Jesus Christ, that though he was rich, yet for your sakes he became poor, so that you through his poverty might become rich' (2 Cor. 8:9).

Psalm 2 and Acts 4
9. Praying with the psalmist

It is common for people to commend the psalms as a model for prayer. They express such a variety of human emotion and such a rich experience of God. For many people the psalter is part of the daily routine of prayer. The problem is that for most of us this is a selective process. More recent editions of the psalter acknowledge this with sections in brackets that may be omitted in congregational worship. This has the merit of honesty, but it must leave evangelicals uneasy. Can we edit the Scriptures to suit the sensibilities of our day? Surely our sensibilities should be shaped by the reading – and the praying – of God's Word. Yet what are we to do when the psalter says:

> O Daughter of Babylon, doomed to destruction,
>   happy is he who repays you
>   for what you have done to us –
> he who seizes your infants
>   and dashes them against the rocks?
>
> (Ps. 137:8–9)

While this language of violence and vengeance is by no means the dominant theme of Psalms, neither is it an aberration. Nor is it just the so-called imprecatory psalms that cause us to hesitate as we pray the psalms. We are also troubled by declarations of righteousness:

> Vindicate me, O LORD,
>   for I have led a blameless life;
> I have trusted in the LORD
>   without wavering.
>
> (Ps. 26:1)

That the author of these words turned out to be an adulterer and murderer may comfort those of us who do not feel we have led a blameless life, but it also lays them open to the charge of hypocrisy. At times these claims to righteousness are linked to specific right-eous acts such as David's refusal to take Saul's life (Ps. 18:1 [superscription], 20–21), yet at others times they are sweeping. It is surely as hard for the sensitive believer to say, 'I keep your precepts with all my heart' (Ps. 119:69) as it is to say:

> May no-one extend kindness to him
> or take pity on his fatherless children.
>
> (Ps. 109:12)

While many people love the psalms because of the range of emotions they express, we baulk at the extremes. Praying with the psalmist is not straightforward.

1. Psalm 2 in the psalter

Psalm 2 may at first seem an odd choice of a psalm to explore something of what it means to pray with the psalmist, not least because it is not in the form of a prayer. But two things make it a good starting point. First, it formed the heart of the prayer of the early church in Acts 4. After the Sanhedrin had told Peter and John to stop proclaiming the name of Jesus, the two apostles reported this to the church, who then joined together in prayer. Luke provides us with a record of that prayer and it is shaped by Psalm 2. So if we want to understand how the early church used the psalms in prayer – and that is our concern – then Psalm 2 is a good place to start. Indeed Acts 4 offers the most extensive use in the New Testament of a psalm in the context of prayer. At the beginning of the church and its mission Psalm 2 played a key role in shaping their identity and their praying.

Second, Psalm 2 also plays a significant role in the psalter. Along with Psalm 1 it offers an interpretative key for what follows. The psalter is divided into five books and Psalms 1 and 2 are the only psalms in Book 1 (Pss. 1 – 41) without a heading, which suggests they belong to the psalter as a whole. Psalms 1 and 2 have been placed at the head of the psalter to guide the readers' – and that means the prayers' – approach to the psalms.

Psalm 1 proclaims that blessed is he who delights in the law of the Lord. The prayers of Israel are a response to God's Word. Prayer is not the vehicle for a spiritual journey or a search for God but a response to the God who has come down and revealed himself to his people. It is premised on God's redemptive acts in history and God's promise to his people. For the psalmist these were encapsulated in the Law (the Torah) – the first five books of the Bible. True spirituality – the spirituality of the psalms – is a response to God's word of promise. And it is as a God-inspired response to God's Word that the psalms in turn become God's Word for us. They model prayer in the context of the covenant promises. The psalms show us communities and individuals responding both to the varied circumstances of life and the promises of God – and often to the tension between the two; between what is and what is promised in the law of God. Psalm 1 may also have had a royal connection, for it was a basic requirement of the king that he delight in the law of God, and the law was given to the king at his enthronement (Deut. 17:18–20).

The psalms not only look back to the exodus and Sinai; they also look forward. God not only rules through his word. He is going to re-establish his rule through his anointed king who will mediate the rule of God on earth. This is the theme of Psalm 2. Psalm 2 introduces us to the main characters of the psalter: the nations, the Lord, the Lord's anointed king and those who are blessed by his reign. So Psalm 2 gives us a window on to the rest of the psalter.

2. Psalm 2 in the history of Israel

One of the most significant figures in the twentieth-century scholarship of Psalms is Hermann Gunkel. Gunkel categorized the psalms not so much by their content as their form. He identified five main genres in the psalms, including a group of 'royal psalms'. It was in this category that he placed Psalm 2 (see also Pss. 18; 20; 21; 45; 72; 101; 132; 144). Sigmund Mowinckel extended this by suggesting an annual re-enthronement ceremony for which these psalms were composed and in which a cosmic drama was re-enacted by the king.[1] There is, however, little evidence for such a ritual – it owes more to the study of comparative anthropology than to the biblical text itself.[2] It is more likely that Psalm 2 started life as a coronation psalm or commemorated the coronation without being tied to a specific annual ceremony.

The psalm, which has four sections (each with three verses) and four voices, is like a play in which the actors involved speak in turn:[3]

[1] Mowinckel, *Psalms in Israel's Worship.*
[2] Kidner, *Psalms 1 – 72*, pp. 11–12.
[3] Craigie, *Psalms 1 – 50*, pp. 64–65.

1. the rulers of the earth (1–3)
2. the Lord (4–6)
3. his anointed king (7–9)
4. the psalmist himself (10–12)

a. The rebellion of mankind (1–3)

The nations that surround Israel have risen in rebellion. It is tempting to look for a historical event or events to which these verses refer, but the paradigmatic status of this psalm suggests that we should see this rebellion as typical of the nations' attitude towards God's anointed. Indeed opposition to God's anointed, as the title of the following psalm makes clear, could be internal as well as external. The world, typified by its rulers, wants to break free of the chains that God and his anointed have put on them. Each new coronation was a reminder that Israel's king had to reign precariously among hostile nations. 'The ideal was that of a world in which all nations and kings recognized the kingship of God and his appointed sovereign; the reality was seen anew in each coronation, that such was not the case. Foreign nations would act violently against Israel's king and in so doing would be rebelling against divine rule.'[4]

The psalmist states this reality as a question. Rebellion against God may be normal, but it is not reasonable. 'Why do they do it?' asks the psalmist. Why do the nations rage against the One whose rule is freedom and blessing?

b. The sovereignty of God (4–6)

The action moves from earth to heaven, from an enthronement on earth to the eternal throne of heaven. God is not worried by the raging of the nations. The Lord is not cowering behind the furniture as mankind bangs on the palace doors. No, he is laughing. The rebellion is ridiculous and the Lord is undisturbed. Nor does the rebellion of the nations alter his plan. The nations may rage against God's anointed, but God will install him as king.

c. The enthronement of God's anointed (7–9)

In verses 7–9 it is the king who speaks, reporting what the Lord has said to him. God has given him rule over all things. God described the nation of Israel as his son when he told Moses to confront Pharaoh (Exod. 4:21–23). Now this filial choice is focused on the

[4] Ibid., p. 66.

king (7). In his covenant with David God said of the Davidic king, 'I will be his father, and he shall be my son' (2 Sam. 7:14). In the coronation, or the remembrance of the coronation, this covenant is renewed and its promises recalled. The king is God's son ruling on God's behalf. He rules the nations from one end of the earth to the other (8) and he will defeat their rebellion (9). There is no hiding from the violent imagery of an iron bar smashing into a brittle piece of pottery (9).

d. The proclamation of God's people (10–12)

Until now the psalmist has been narrating what others have said; now he himself addresses the nations. He represents the response of all God's people. The psalmist draws conclusions from what has been said. This is his advice: be wise – submit to God – get right with his son. To kiss the son was a sign of homage, much as later European rulers would expect homage to be paid by the kissing of their ring. Continued rebellion will lead to disaster and judgment, but submission will lead to safety and security.

3. Psalm 2 in the history of redemption

While Psalm 2 started life as a celebration of Israel's king, it must always have looked to the future. At no time in David's reign was his dominion anything like that pictured in the psalm. Nor was this so in Solomon's reign, nor under any of the following kings. Rather the power of Israel steadily diminished as the kingdom was divided and ultimately overrun. Israel's kings were supposed to rule on God's behalf, but time and again they failed. As the Old Testament progresses there is an increasing expectation that God will send another king to rule perfectly on his behalf – a king like David and yet greater than David. Brevard Childs says, 'Although the royal Psalms arose originally in a peculiar historical setting of ancient Israel ... they were treasured in the Psalter ... as a witness to the messianic hope which looked for the consummation of God's kingship through his Anointed One.'[5]

So the psalm points beyond the Old Testament kings of Israel to God's Messiah who will be the king of the Jews and the king of the world. It points, in other words, to Jesus Christ. Indeed this psalm is one of the Old Testament passages to which the New Testament most frequently alludes, second only to Psalm 110. It was to Psalms 2 and 110 that the early church turned first to demonstrate that Jesus

[5] Childs, *Old Testament as Scripture*, p. 517.

was the Christ promised in the Scriptures. And it was to Psalm 2 that the early church turned in Acts to shape their prayer.

a. The rebellion of mankind

The first stanza of Psalm 2 speaks of the rebellion of mankind (1–3). This is the portion of the psalm that is quoted in the prayer recorded in Acts 4:

> *You spoke by the Holy Spirit through the mouth of your servant, our father David:*
>
> > *'Why do the nations rage*
> > *and the peoples plot in vain?*
> > *The kings of the earth take their stand*
> > *and the rulers gather together*
> > *against the Lord*
> > *and against his Anointed One.'*
>
> *Indeed Herod and Pontius Pilate met together with the Gentiles and the people of Israel in this city to conspire against your holy servant Jesus, whom you anointed.*
>
> (Acts 4:25–27)

The early church recognized that the rebellion of the nations against the rule of God was not a historical aberration. This is the one unifying factor in human behaviour – the desire to rebel against God. The psalm itself recognizes that the nations rise up in rebellion not only against Israel's king but ultimately against Israel's God.[6] This rebellion, common to all human societies, is the thread that runs through history. 'There is scarcely a commercial or intellectual or cultural interest anywhere on earth which would not resent his claims on it.'[7] The peoples of the world argue that the rule of God is restrictive and unpleasant (3). That has been the lie of Satan from the garden of Eden onwards.

But more than this, the early church recognized that this rebellion had been focused in the death of Jesus. The cross is the climax of human rebellion against God. The psalm says that, given the opportunity, we shall murder our Creator and that is exactly what we did. As Jesus foretold in the parable of the tenants, when we see the Son we say, 'This is the heir. Come, let's kill him and take his inheritance' (Matt. 21:38).

6 See Weiser, *Psalms*, p. 111.
7 Wilcock, *Psalms 1 – 72*, p. 23.

But notice the context in which this prayer is prayed. Peter and John have been seized by the temple guard, put in jail overnight, hauled before the Jewish leaders and ordered with unspecified threats to stop proclaiming the name of Jesus. This psalm and prayer are apposite for this occasion because the early church saw that the rebellion of mankind against God, which had come to a climax in the cross of Jesus, now continued in the opposition to the proclamation of his name. Psalm 2 spoke of *their* experience. As the psalms speak of Christ, so they speak of those who are in Christ. As the psalms speak of the suffering of God's Messiah, so they speak of the suffering of God's messianic people.

b. The sovereignty of God

Jesus commissioned the apostles to witness to him from Jerusalem to the ends of the earth (Acts 1:8). Yet now, before the gospel has even left Jerusalem, it all seems to be going wrong. The leaders of 'Israel' have told them to stop the process – to put it into reverse. This is a significant moment in the history of the church for this is the first time it has faced persecution. Has God lost control? Are his purposes to be frustrated?

The second stanza (4–6) affirms that God is not thwarted by the rebellion of mankind. He is enthroned in heaven. Psalm 2 enabled the early church to recognize that even the climax of human rebellion – the cross – was part of God's sovereign plan: *They did what your power and will had decided beforehand should happen* (Acts 4:28). This prayer is addressed to the *Sovereign Lord* who *made the heaven and the earth and the sea, and everything in them* (Acts 4:24). In this moment of crisis the early Christians appealed to the sovereignty of God who accomplishes his purposes even through the greatest act of rebellion against him. The psalm enabled them to approach the opposition they were facing with confidence in the sovereignty of God. It enabled them to draw comfort from the throne of heaven.

This is the basis of their prayer for boldness (29). As if to confirm their confidence in his purposes, God gave them a Pentecost-like experience. The place where they were meeting was shaken and they were filled with the Holy Spirit and *spoke the word of God boldly* (31).

c. The enthronement of God's anointed

The one against whom both Gentiles and Jews conspired is *Jesus, whom [God] anointed* (27). In the third stanza (7–9) God's anointed king speaks, proclaiming that God has designated him as his son, promised him rule over the nations and the defeat of God's enemies. In the prayer of Acts 4 the early church identified the promised messianic king as Jesus of Nazareth. To the writer to the Hebrews it is self-evident that the designation of the king as God's son is a description of Jesus (Heb. 1:5; 5:5). Likewise, the voice from heaven saying 'This is my Son' at the baptism and transfiguration of Jesus should be understood not just as fatherly affirmation, but in the light of Psalm 2 as a declaration of the kingship of Jesus (Matt. 3:17; 17:5). In his preaching in the synagogue of Pisidian Antioch Paul said that the resurrection of Jesus was the fulfilment of this declaration of sonship (Acts 13:32–33). Jesus himself tells us that all authority has been given to him (Matt. 28:18). He shall reign and he shall destroy all that is evil. Again the beleaguered group of believers in Jerusalem were encouraged to pray for boldness by what this psalm says about the rule of Christ.

Psalm 2 has a lot to teach us about mankind, sin, God, Christ, mission and conversion. But we must remember that it is a psalm – a song of praise. It is not a treatise, but a celebration of the sovereignty of God and the reign of his son. The raging of the nations, in whatever form it takes for us, can seem overwhelming. But celebrating the kingdom of God helps us put the din of the nations in perspective, just as John's vision of the throne of heaven in the book of Revelation comforted the suffering church to whom he wrote.

d. The proclamation of God's people

In the final stanza (10–12) the psalmist proclaims the coming of the king, calling upon the nations to submit to him or face his wrath. And this is the task of the missionary church. We proclaim the coming of the king, which is what it means to preach the kingdom of God. We call on men and women to submit to Christ and find refuge in him. The early church certainly seemed to have understood that Psalm 2 spoke of the proclamation of the gospel. The petition of the prayer of Acts 4 is a request for missionary advance: *enable your servants to speak your word with great boldness. Stretch out your hand to heal and perform miraculous signs and wonders through the name of your holy servant Jesus* (Acts 4:29–30).

It is because all authority has been given to him that Jesus sends us to all the nations (Matt. 28:18–19). It is through the preaching of the gospel that Jesus is wielding his sceptre in the world. Even now he exercises his rule through the preaching of the gospel. To tell people the gospel is to announce the kingdom or kingship of God and his Christ. We are ambassadors for Christ bringing an

THE MESSAGE OF PRAYER

authoritative pronouncement from the king. When we preach the gospel we are heralds of a coming king. We go to the citizens of a country and say that a king is coming who rightly claims their allegiance. Those who currently rule them are usurpers and tyrants. If they acknowledge his lordship, they will experience his rule as blessing, life and salvation. If they reject him, they will experience him as their conqueror and judge.

There will come a day when men and women will cry to the very rocks to hide them from the wrath of God. The only refuge on that day will be in the Son (12). The refuge he provides is a refuge from his own wrath. The one who is our dreadful enemy is the one who provides a refuge for us. This is a gracious enemy who does not come by stealth, but announces his coming through his people so that men and women have the opportunity to escape his judgment.

e. Conclusion

Some people are natural evangelists, but most of us speak of Christ only when the opportunity is so obvious that we cannot get out of the way in time. Our problem is not that we lack the wisdom – we know that God can use whatever we say. Our problem is a lack of nerve. We are concerned about how we shall be perceived. We do not want to jeopardize our friendships. The early church faced such challenges, but in a far more acute form. For them the fear was persecution and imprisonment. Yet the apostles preached publicly in the temple after they have been imprisoned for preaching (Acts 5:17–21). Stephen did not hesitate to preach even when it cost him his life (Acts 6:8 – 7:53). Ordinary believers were scattered by persecution, taking the gospel with them as they went (Acts 8:1–4). This boldness was surely the answer to the prayer of Acts 4.

4. The psalms and the prayers of Christians

Dietrich Bonhoeffer encouraged the community of Christian students, set up in defiance of the Nazis, to pray the psalms as the prayers of Christ: 'The *Man* Jesus Christ, to whom no affliction, no ill, no suffering is alien and who yet was the wholly innocent and righteous one, is praying in the Psalter through the mouth of his Church. The Psalter is the prayer book of Jesus Christ in the truest sense of the word. He prayed for the Psalter and now it has become his prayer for all time ... The Psalter is the vicarious prayer of Christ for his Church.'[8]

[8] Bonhoeffer, *Life Together*, pp. 31–32.

146

Bonhoeffer described this as 'the secret of the Psalter'.[9] In conclusion I want to highlight two ways in which Psalm 2 and its use in Acts 4 enable us to read and pray the psalter in a Christological way.

a. In Psalms we understand our experience as those who are in Christ

As I have already suggested, the position of Psalm 2 at the head of the psalter suggests that, whatever its original cultic setting, it was intended by the compilers of the psalter to provide a commentary on Psalms as a whole. This messianic hermeneutic extends beyond the so-called royal psalms and beyond those psalms traditionally thought of as messianic psalms in a predictive sense. When we read the words of God's anointed we should read these as the words of the Christ – Jesus of Nazareth – and therefore as the prayer of those who are in Christ. In Bonhoeffer's words, the psalter is the prayer book of Jesus Christ.

It is in Jesus that the psalms are fulfilled and it is in Jesus that the psalms become the experience of God's people. Psalm 2 describes our experience – just as it described the experience of the early church – because we are those who are *in Christ*. The psalms that describe the afflictions of David do not speak of a universal human experience. They speak of the real historical experience of God's anointed. David was God's anointed and it was as God's anointed that the psalms speak of him. As well as looking at 'royal psalms' we need also to recognize a far greater category, which we might call 'Davidic psalms' – psalms that are by or about king David. David speaks as God's anointed and the psalms give content to what it means – and what it would mean – to be God's anointed.

In Luke 24 Jesus told his disciples that the meaning of Psalms, along with the Law and Prophets, is that 'The Christ will suffer and rise from the dead on the third day' (Luke 24:44–46). Any interpretation of the psalms that claims to be Christian must start with this statement by Jesus that Psalms as a whole speaks of his suffering. When the early church wanted to demonstrate that the Christ must suffer – a key issue in dialogue with Judaism – they did so by turning to the psalms that speak of the suffering of God's anointed. David's experience of suffering – whether at the hand of Saul, rebellious nations or rebellious sons – points to the Messiah whose kingship is built on his suffering and death.

And so by extension the psalms speak of our experience as

[9] Ibid., p. 31.

Christ's messianic people who suffer as we extend his kingdom. Psalm 23 offers me hope in the valley of death not because I am the subject of the psalm but because the Christ is the subject of the psalm. It is because God rescued the Christ from death that I, as someone who is in Christ, can know comfort. My confidence is built not on a common human experience of escape from death but on the suffering and resurrection of the Christ. Psalm 23 gives me words to articulate that confidence.

It is not only the sufferings of the Messiah, however, of which the psalms speak. In Luke 24 Jesus goes on to say that the psalms speak of how 'repentance and forgiveness of sins will be preached in his name to all nations, beginning at Jerusalem' (Luke 24:47). The psalms speak of the advance of the Messiah's kingdom and the proclamation of his name to the nations. In the prayer of Acts 4 the early church recognized that Psalm 2 spoke of the missionary task of Christian believers as we declare the rule of God's anointed king.

b. In Psalms we understand our experience in the context of Christ's redemptive reign

Not all the psalms are about God's anointed. We cannot pray every psalm as if it were a prayer of Jesus addressed to the Father. Some psalms describe the experience of a faithful individual or the people of God as a community. Yet, as Jesus suggests in Luke 24, we must still look to find the meaning for us of these psalms in Christ and his redemption.

Walter Brueggemann suggests a categorization of the psalms that is based not so much on their poetic form or their cultic setting as on their content.[10] Some psalms speak of being securely *oriented*: they celebrate life in the world as God created it – ordered and good. More often psalms speak of being painfully *disoriented*: they lament life in a disordered world with experiences that provoke bewilderment, sorrow or rage. A third category of psalms speak of being surprisingly *reoriented*: they point to the promised redemptive intervention of God. This recognition of disorientation and yearning for reorientation gives the psalter a subversive quality, for it challenges the settled orientation of those who defend the status quo.

Psalm 2 suggests that any psalm can be viewed in the context of a wider movement, from orientation through disorientation to redemptive reorientation – a movement focused on the coming reign of God's anointed king. This movement, particularly that from

---

[10] Brueggemann, *Praying the Psalms*, p. 14. See also Brueggemann, *Message of the Psalms*.

disorientation to reorientation, can occur within a single psalm with a suddenness that troubles interpreters (see e.g. Ps. 22:1–21, 22–31).[11] And this movement from disorientation to reorientation is reflected in the shape of the psalter itself. Psalms 3 – 7 are psalms of lament, and fifty-two of the first eighty-nine psalms (books one and two of the psalter) are laments. In contrast Psalms 144 – 150 are all psalms of praise, and thirty-seven of the last sixty-one psalms (books four and five of the psalter) are psalms of praise. 'The Psalter', it has been said, 'begins in lament and ends in praise.'[12]

Brueggemann himself refuses to see a wider movement from disorientation to reorientation focused on the coming of God's king, because ultimately he divorces the psalms from the Christian gospel. He resists treating the psalms as 'claims about Jesus Christ', because he will not say to Jews, as Peter did in Acts 4, that there is no other name except that of Jesus Christ of Nazareth given to men by which we must be saved (Acts 4:10–12). 'We will be helped to a more genuine piety and a more authentic faith', he argues, 'if we engage the psalms as poetry about our common, particular humanness.'[13]

But the use of Psalms by the early church – a church that was predominately Jewish, but which now saw its identity in Christ – suggests that the orientation, disorientation and reorientation of which the psalms speak are part of a cosmic movement focused on Jesus Christ. We do not simply find in the psalms that someone has undergone a similar experience to us. We find Christ reordering this disordered world through his redemptive reign. So, for example, psalms such as Psalm 73, which express confidence in God despite the prosperity of the wicked, need to be seen in the wider context of the promised re-establishment of God's righteous rule through his anointed king. They wrestle with the tension between what is and what is promised, and resolve that tension by looking forward to the coming of God's rule.

Psalm 51, to take another example, is a psalm of David, but it is David the sinner who speaks. There is hope in Psalm 51, not because David is the Christ, but – as the experience that prompts the psalm graphically reveals – precisely because ultimately he was not *the* Christ. There is hope because a greater son of David is coming. David prays Psalm 51 as a 'Christ' – an anointed one – who has failed as a 'Christ'. We, too, pray Psalm 51 as *Christ*ians – anointed ones (1 John 2:18–20) – who have failed as Christians, and the psalm

[11] See also Jung, 'Prayer in the Psalms', pp. 52–53; and Childs, *Old Testament as Scripture*, p. 518.

[12] Woodhouse, *Preaching Christ*, tape 1.

[13] Brueggemann, *Praying the Psalms*, pp. 44–45.

expresses the real pain we feel in that failure. But as Christians we can pray the psalm trusting in the forgiveness that comes through the Christ who was without sin, but who was made sin for us.

5. Conclusion

This Christological approach to Psalms means we can pray without shame the psalms that speak of the praying person's righteousness before God, for we *are* righteous before God. The psalms remind us that only the righteous can come before God:

> LORD, who may dwell in your sanctuary?
>   Who may live on your holy hill?
>
> He whose walk is blameless
>   and who does what is righteous.
>
> (Ps. 15:1–2)

> Who may ascend the hill of the LORD?
>   Who may stand in his holy place?
> He who has clean hands and a pure heart,
>   who does not lift up his soul to an idol
>   or swear by what is false.
>
> (Ps. 24:3–4)

The righteousness that qualifies us for the holy presence of God is not ours, however, but a righteousness that has become ours in Christ. We are not proclaiming our inherent goodness but laying claim to the perfection of Christ on our behalf.

Seeing the psalms as the prayers of Christ does not perhaps 'solve' the problem of the language of violence, but it moves the problem elsewhere. It is not just that the people of the Bible call for violent retribution; they do so because the God of the Bible promises violent retribution. The calls for vengeance in Psalms point us to the final judgment of God. Psalm 2 is quoted by the apostle John as he describes the Christ riding out to trample the nations underfoot: 'Out of his mouth comes a sharp sword with which to strike down the nations. "He will rule them with an iron sceptre." He treads the winepress of the fury of the wrath of God Almighty' (Rev. 19:15).

This, then, is where our instinct for revenge belongs: in prayer. It is legitimate for Christians to cry out for vindication in the face of injustice. If your spirituality does not allow you to express indignation before God, then it will find expression in other, less righteous, ways. In prayer we acknowledge that God is the judge and that, however painful injustice may be now, one day God will reimpose moral order on the universe. When Paul encourages us to do good to our enemies he does so not because retribution is wrong but because vengeance belongs to God (Rom. 12:19–21). Any violence other than the righteous violence of God perpetuates further injustice. Also, when psalms call for infants to be dashed against rocks, a Christological focus reminds us that God himself dashed his own Son against his justice that we might escape his vengeance.

Psalm 2 enabled the church in Acts 4 to understand their experience as part of Christ's suffering and triumph, and to pray in the light of that understanding for the boldness to proclaim his name in the face of opposition. As we use the psalms in prayer we set our human experience before God in the context of Christ's redemptive reorientation of all things.

When faced with the extremes of human experience, we find in the psalms more than an echo of our experience – we can find renewed confidence in the coming reign of Christ. Saying that the psalms do not speak of universal human experience need not disenfranchise the Christian believer from them: it is right for Christians to use the psalms to articulate our feelings and desires in prayer. A Christ-centred hermeneutic does not invalidate this. Rather it provides a theological foundation for a Christian use of these ancient Israelite poems. It shows how we can use *all* the psalms as our own – even those that express an experience alien to us.

A Christological focus restores the psalms to us in their redemptive context. In dark moments we find in the psalms not simply that someone else has undergone a similar experience. We find that the Christ has suffered and, more than that, is reorienting this disordered world through the coming of his reign. They articulate for us the often painful tension between our reality and God's Word – between what is and what is said to be. But they also enable us to turn that tension into trusting prayer as we view it in the light of the coming rule of God's king. They provide us with words as we long for God's rule, as we celebrate its re-establishment through Christ and as we commend to God our part in the advance of his rule through suffering and proclamation.

Matthew 6
10. Praying as Jesus taught us

'During the days of Jesus' life on earth,' says the writer of Hebrews, 'he offered up prayers and petitions with loud cries and tears to the one who could save him from death, and he was heard because of his reverent submission' (Heb. 5:7). At key moments in his ministry (such as when the crowds threatened his preaching ministry and in the garden of Gethsemane) Jesus withdrew to spend time in prayer with his Father (Mark 1:35; 14:32–42 par. Matt. 26:36–46; Luke 22:39–46). Luke's Gospel also sets the choosing of the Twelve and the transfiguration in the context of Jesus at prayer (Luke 6:12; 9:28). Indeed Luke presents withdrawal by Jesus to pray as a habitual activity: 'Jesus often withdrew to lonely places and prayed' (Luke 5:16; see also 9:18; 22:39). Jesus also desired to pray with others (Mark 14:32–42; Luke 9:28). Though he was the incarnate Word of God, Jesus felt the importance of prayer. As in all things, he sets us an example in prayer that we should follow. Calvin says, 'no-one will learn to pray aright whose lips and heart are not schooled by the heavenly Teacher'.[1] In the Sermon on the Mount Jesus teaches his disciples about prayer. He tells us both how not to pray (5–8) and shows us how we should in what has become known as the Lord's Prayer (9–13).

1. When you pray, do not ... (5–8)

In these verses Jesus gives us two warnings, each with a lovely promise attached.

---

[1] Calvin, *Gospels*, vol. 1, p. 205.

a. Warning: do not pray to be seen (5–6)

When we pray, says Jesus, we are to do it in private with the door closed. This does not mean we are to be furtive in our praying or diffident in prayer meetings. That would be to misunderstand both the wider biblical context and the immediate context of Jesus' words. Calvin says, 'we must not press the words ... as though [Jesus] told men to hide away, and say that we cannot pray aright unless without witness'.[2] It is sometimes said that good private prayer is the foundation of good corporate prayer, but it may be more biblical to say that corporate prayer is the foundation of private prayer. Our experience of God in Christ is corporate. Western individualism has made the individual alone with God the centre of spirituality. For the people of the Bible it is the relationship between God and his people that is central. Personal prayer revolves around this common experience – not the other way round.

Here in Matthew 6 Jesus is opposing prayer *to be seen by men* (5). He is not opposing public prayer, but he is opposing prayer *to* the public; that is, prayer directed at other people to impress them. Indeed it is possible to 'slip' away to private prayer in an ostentatious way.[3] In Jesus' day, prayers would be led each sabbath by a man standing at the front in the synagogue. It is easy to imagine someone revelling in the attention or trying to display his eloquence and spirituality. On feast days a trumpet would sound, inviting people to pray. So the Pharisee would stop where he was *on the street corner* and with a self-conscious display of piety pray towards the temple.[4] The form of the word 'to stand' (*hestōtes*) 'has the nuance of having taken a position and continuing to stand in it, and this implies the enjoyment of public attention'.[5] Sadly, we do not have much of a problem imagining what it might have been like – we have been there ourselves, looking for the right clichés, the polished turn of phrase, the clever idea or biblical connection, the dramatic tone of voice, the covert teaching, the display of eloquence. Dietrich Bonhoeffer warns us that even when we pray alone we can pray in this way: 'It is even more pernicious if I turn myself into a spectator of my own prayer performance, if I am giving a show for my own benefit ... The publicity which I am looking for is then provided by the fact that I am the one who at the same time prays and looks on.'[6]

[2] Ibid., p. 203.
[3] Lloyd-Jones, *Sermon on the Mount*, vol. 2, p. 26.
[4] See Carson, *Sermon on the Mount*, p. 58.
[5] Hagner, *Matthew 1 – 13*, p. 142.
[6] Bonhoeffer, *Cost of Discipleship*, p. 146.

If your intent in prayer is to impress others, says Jesus, then you will be rewarded. People will be impressed. But that is it – that is all the reward you will get. *They have received their reward* in full (5). Don Carson recalls the story of a minister who described an elaborate and polished prayer as 'the most eloquent prayer ever offered to a Boston audience'. Carson adds, somewhat caustically, 'Just so.'[7] The prayer was offered to a Boston audience, not a heavenly one. It is easy for us to start applying this teaching to others, but coming soon in the Sermon on the Mount are the words 'Do not judge, or you too will be judged' (Matt. 7:1).

b. Promise: you are seen by God (6)

Jesus warns us not to pray in order to be seen by others, but with this warning gives a lovely promise. We are seen by God (6). God hears us when we pray and he rewards (see Pss. 6:9; 34:4, 17–18; 40:1–3).

This section on prayer comes in a wider section about 'acts of righteousness' (6) covering giving, praying and fasting. *Do not be like the hypocrites* is the theme in each case (2, 5, 16). It is a sobering thought that sin is such an incipient thing that it can follow us into the presence of God.[8] Even fasting, which is supposed to be a sign of humility, can become a sign of self-righteousness. Similar wording is used in each case:

when you give ... do not ... [do] as the hypocrites do ... to be honoured by men. I tell you the truth, they have received their reward in full ... your Father, who sees what is done in secret, will reward you.

when you pray, do not be like the hypocrites ... to be seen by men. I tell you the truth, they have received their reward in full ... your Father, who sees what is done in secret, will reward you.

when you fast, do not [do] as the hypocrites do ... to show men they are fasting. I tell you the truth, they have received their reward in full ... your Father, who sees what is done in secret, will reward you.

(2, 4, 5, 6, 16, 18)

[7] Carson, *Sermon on the Mount*, p. 59.
[8] Lloyd-Jones, *Sermon on the Mount*, vol. 2, p. 21.

The pattern is the same in each case:

A. A warning not to be like hypocrites
   B. The measures the hypocrites take so as to be seen
      C. The hypocrites receive their reward – the praise of people
   B'. The measures we are to take so as *not* to be seen
      C'. We receive our reward – from the Father who sees what is done in secret

This pattern highlights the choice Jesus gives us. We can choose to be rewarded here on earth or be rewarded by our heavenly Father. We can choose between human praise and divine glory. Our 'acts of righteousness' are to be done to God so that it matters nothing to us whether they are seen by others or not (see Col. 3:22–24).

c. Warning: do not babble (7)

'Prayers', it has been said, 'are not measured, but weighed.' We do not have to explain the situation to God – he already knows more than us. We do not have to tell him what to do – he knows what is best. We cannot nag God into doing what we want.

> The faithful do not pray to tell God what He does not know, or urge Him to His duties, or hurry Him on when He delays, but rather to alert themselves to seek Him, to exercise their faith by meditating upon His promises, unburdening their cares by lifting themselves in His bosom, and finally to testify that from Him alone, all good for themselves and for others is hoped and asked. As for Himself, what He determined to give, of His own free will and even before He is asked, He promises to give all the same, in response to our prayers. Keep hold of both points, then: our prayers are anticipated by Him in His freedom, yet, what we ask we gain by prayer.[9]

Jesus, of course, is not saying that we should only pray for short periods, still less that short prayers are the best way to twist God's arm. Elsewhere Jesus commends perseverance in prayer (Luke 18:1–8). John Stott says, 'what Jesus forbids his people is any kind of prayer with the mouth when the mind is not engaged',[10] while D. L. Moody is reputed to have said, 'some people's prayers need to be cut

---

[9] Calvin, *Gospels*, vol. 1, p. 204.
[10] Stott, *Sermon on the Mount*, p. 144.

off at both ends and set fire to in the middle'.[11] The problem is any image of prayer that sees it as a mechanism to make things happen. We should not think that through 'good' prayer God can be made to do something for us as if we could wrest favours from him by the sheer volume of our praying. To babble on is to pray *like pagans* (7). Pagan religion believes the gods can be manipulated or appeased through sacrifices, rituals and supplications. The prophets of Baal on Mount Carmel spent the day in an ecstatic state, mutilating their bodies and frantically prophesying in order to attract Baal's attention (1 Kgs. 18:26–29). Yet, as the writer of Kings so poignantly puts it, 'there was no response, no-one answered, no-one paid attention' (1 Kgs. 18:29). Then with a few words of prayer Elijah calls down fire from heaven to ignite a watery altar (1 Kgs. 18:36–38). 'God is in heaven / and you are on earth,' says the Preacher of Ecclesiastes, 'so let your words be few' (Eccles. 5:2).

True prayer is an unburdening of the heart. Calvin says, 'When we come to pray with serious intention, the tongue does not outrun the heart, nor is God's favour secured by an empty flow of words, but rather, the longings which the devout heart sends out like arrowshots are those that reach heaven.'[12]

Prayer is complete not when the clock has ticked through some allotted period but when the heart has been emptied of its concerns and filled instead with renewed confidence in God.

d. Promise: you are known by God (8)

Along with the warning not to babble, Jesus gives us another promise: we are known by God. We address God as our Father (9). God knows us and understands our problems. In Isaiah 65 God promises that in the last days – the days Jesus is now inaugurating –

> Before they call I will answer;
>   while they are still speaking I will hear.
>
> (Is. 65:24)

Martin Luther once said, 'By our praying we are instructing ourselves more than we are him.'[13] God knows better than we do what we need.

Hypocrites are those who say one thing, but do another. Their actions or attitudes do not match their words. Hypocritical prayers claim to be seeking something from God, but are really seeking

[11] Cited in Bewes, *Talking about Prayer*, p. 46.
[12] Calvin, *Gospels*, vol. 1, p. 203; see also Calvin, *Institutes*, 3.20.29.
[13] Cited in Stott, *Sermon on the Mount*, p. 145.

something from other people. They make their requests to God, but are really after the praise of men. The tragedy is, they get that which they seek, but nothing more. Hypocritical prayers look to the sovereign power of God, but believe they can manipulate God with their lengthy prayers. They render impotent the god to whom they look for power, for a god who can be manipulated is not the God who can help in time of need. Those who approach God in prayer must do so with sincerity. We must make our requests, believing that God and God alone can help. In 1–18 Jesus calls God 'Father' ten times. The problem with the hypocrites is that they do not know God as Father. True prayer arises as we recognize our utter dependence on God and approach him as humble subjects coming before their king. There can be no thought of bending God's arm. We can only remind him of his promises, his mercy and his glory.

According to the mnemonic 'ACTS', prayer should contain *Adoration*, *Confession*, *Thanksgiving* and *Supplication* – their initial letters forming the mnemonic. This has undoubtedly helped many Christians to pray in a more rounded way. But it is somewhat artificial because to come sincerely before God with our supplications is an act of adoration. We praise God when we make our requests to him because in so doing we acknowledge his power, goodness and wisdom. When we babble we impugn either God's power (we babble because God can be manipulated), his wisdom (we babble because God needs our advice) or his goodness (we babble because God's reluctance must be overcome by our persistence). But when we pray with sincerity we glorify his gracious power and his fatherly wisdom.

2. This is how you should pray (9–13)

The word 'you' in verse 9 is emphatic. The disciples are to pray in a way that contrasts with that of the hypocrites. Jesus is not giving words to be repeated verbatim, but a model to shape all our praying. 'This is how you should pray' is literally 'Pray in this manner' and implies an example to adapt rather than a mechanical formula.[14] While repeating the words of the Lord's Prayer is not to be discouraged, the more important thing is that Christians pray in this kind of way. Whatever it is for which we pray, we should pray with these priorities. Luther said 'a Christian has prayed abundantly who has rightly prayed the Lord's Prayer'.[15] Jim Packer commends going through the Lord's Prayer 'amplifying and specifying each

[14] Davies and Allison, *Matthew*, p. 599.
[15] Cited in Heiler, *Prayer*, p. 283.

clause (what the Puritans described as "branching", and C. S. Lewis called "festooning")'.[16] This is a model prayer, a prayer upon which to base our praying. It is like the headings of talk waiting to be filled by us with personal application.

One naturally hesitates to write about a prayer that is so deeply part of Christian spirituality. The Lord's Prayer became part of the 'liturgy' of the early church, at least in the sense of being taught as a model for prayer. Matthew's version, which is longer than the parallel version in Luke (Luke 11:1–4),[17] may represent a fuller liturgical version, although it is equally possible that Jesus presented the prayer in different forms during the course of his teaching ministry. The line 'for the kingdom, the power, and the glory are yours now and for ever' was an early addition. A version in the *Didache*, written in the first half of the second century AD, ends, 'for yours is the power and the glory forever'. But the line is in neither Gospel account of the prayer, even though its later liturgical use has led to its incorporation in some translations, most notably the AV.

3. A prayer for the future

In the Lord's Prayer Jesus invites us to pray for the coming intervention of God in its different dimensions. Every line of the prayer is steeped in the Old Testament, but each time it is the expectation of the Old Testament to which Jesus refers. It is a thoroughly eschatological prayer just as Jesus is an eschatological figure and the gospel is an eschatological word of promise.

> The Lord's Prayer is the 'true Exodus' prayer of God's people. Set originally in a thoroughgoing eschatological context, its every clause resonates with Jesus' announcement that God's kingdom is breaking into the story of Israel and the world, opening up God's long-promised new world and summoning people to share it. If this context is marginalized ... the prayer loses its peculiar force and falls back into a generalized petition for things to improve.[18]

The Sermon on the Mount, in which Matthew's account of the Lord's Prayer is set, is the first of five blocks of teaching by Jesus in

[16] In Hanes, *My Path of Prayer*, p. 60.

[17] On the sources of the Lord's Prayer and the relationship between Matthew and Luke's accounts see Carson, *Matthew*, pp. 167–168; and Davies and Allison, *Matthew*, pp. 590–593.

[18] N. T. Wright, 'Lord's Prayer', p. 133.

the Gospel. Matthew may be drawing a parallel with the five books of the Torah (the Pentateuch). The fact that the first is given on a mountain suggests Matthew intends us to see Jesus as a new Moses, and in Matthew 5:17–48 Jesus presents himself as the new lawgiver. Jesus gives a new law for a new age. The Beatitudes, too, with which the sermon begins, are explicitly eschatological. They resonate strongly with Old Testament spirituality, but Jesus sets this in a framework of promised future blessing. The context, then, of the Lord's Prayer is one of eschatological expectation.

a. Our Father in heaven

The Father whom we address is the God and Father of our Lord Jesus Christ. God's fatherhood is based not on a common biology, but upon his gracious initiative in Christ. As we are united to Christ we share in the trinitarian community. Our current experience of God as Father anticipates our full inclusion into the trinitarian relationship (1 John 3:2). Addressing God as Father directs our attention beyond our present experience of his fatherhood. In the Old Testament Israel is called the son of God. The first occurrence of this is when Moses is sent to Pharaoh to demand that God's people should be freed from slavery. Now, in the context of giving a new law on a new mountain, Jesus invites his disciples to call God *Father*. He is identifying them as the new people of God. He is telling them to address the liberating Father. He is inviting them to seek a new exodus – one that will liberate them from the ultimate enemies of sin and death.

The Father to whom we pray is also *in heaven* (see also Matt. 5:48; 6:26, 32; 15:13; 18:35; 23:9). Although God is our Father, it remains true that our Father is God – the mighty Creator and Sovereign. He has not become some domestic deity. As our Father he delights to hear our concerns, and as the Father in heaven he is able to respond in power and wisdom. The word 'heaven' is used in a number of ways in the Scriptures:

1. The sky together with the stars, moon and planets.
2. A dimension woven into the fabric of the universe, which is inhabited by the spiritual world – both good and evil.
3. The unmediated presence of God.
4. The place from whence the future comes.

In the apostle John's vision the new Jerusalem comes down from heaven. Heaven is a spatial metaphor for a future event. 'Heaven', says Tom Wright, 'is God's space, where God's writ runs and God's future purposes are waiting in the wings.'[19] The Father in heaven is the coming Father. The God of heaven is the One 'who is, and who was, and who is to come' (Rev. 1:4). Notice that he is not said to be the One 'who will be' as would be required for a consistent grammatical form. Rather he is the One who is coming to bring a new future. To call on our Father in heaven is to look forward to the climax of our liberation and our inclusion into the trinitarian community.

b. Hallowed be your name

To 'hallow' God's name is to recognize that his name is holy. It is for God's name to be glorified. People's names in Hebraic thought often represented the people themselves. So we are asking God to intervene in history to establish his honour and vindicate his reputation.

The phrase *hallowed be your name* is rooted in the Old Testament where God vindicates his name as he acts to counter the taunts of Israel's enemies and prove himself faithful to his promise. In Ezekiel, to take one example, the refrain 'then they will know that I am the LORD' is repeated more than sixty times. This is Ezekiel's central theme – God will intervene in history 'for the sake of my holy name' (Ezek. 36:22). Israel brought God's name into disrepute. She was supposed to be a light to the nations, but instead profaned God's name. So by judging Israel God honours his name: he will not be associated with the sin of his people. But after he has judged his people, God's name is again brought into disrepute. Now the nations suppose Yahweh is impotent to save his people. Now God's people claim he has abandoned his covenant. So Ezekiel promises that God will honour his name by saving his people, establishing his rule and fulfilling his purposes. Whether in judgment (Ezek. 6:10, 13, 14; 7:4, 27; 33:27–29) or in salvation (Ezek. 34:30; 36:11, 37–38; 37:13–14, 28; 39:27–28), God acts so 'that they will know that I am the LORD'. Beyond judgment and salvation is a greater purpose of God, namely to bring glory to his name.

> This is what the Sovereign LORD says: It is not for your sake, O house of Israel, that I am going to do these things, but for the sake of my holy name, which you have profaned among the nations where you have gone. I will show the holiness of my great name, which has been profaned among the nations, the name you have profaned among them. Then the nations will know that I am the

[19] N. T. Wright, *Lord and his Prayer*, p. 25.

LORD, declares the Sovereign LORD, when I show myself holy through you before their eyes.

(Ezek. 36:22–23)

We are to pray that God will intervene in history to vindicate his name, by establishing his rule and his will. In other words, the first three petitions of the Lord's Prayer overlap. They do not refer to some existential or ethical event in the life of the praying individual. Rather they refer to an eschatological event, to the promised divine intervention in history in salvation and judgment. 'All three [requests] are primarily a plea that God will act so decisively in judgment and salvation that his glory will be unveiled, and all (as a result) be enabled to see him as the holy, almighty King he truly is. It is thus a prayer for the End, for the consummation of the kingdom of God, and for the bringing into being of the new earth and the heavens that the End entails.'[20]

c. Your kingdom come, your will be done on earth as it is in heaven

In Matthew 4 Jesus arrives on the scene announcing the coming of God's kingdom and calling upon people to repent. God created Adam and Eve to live under his rule – a rule characterized by blessing, freedom, life and love. But mankind rebelled against God's rule. Satan caused Adam and Eve to doubt the word by which God ruled. But God remains King. He begins to re-establish his rule through his word of promise. As the kings of Israel fail to mediate God's rule, God promises a coming King who will re-establish God's rule forever.

The Jews of Jesus' day expected a messianic King who would usher in God's rule, sweeping away God's enemies and vindicating his people. But Jesus is opposed and rejected. How can this be the coming of God's kingdom? In Matthew 13 Jesus tells a series of parables about the kingdom. They speak of the kingdom coming secretly like seed sown in the ground; like a small mustard seed; like yeast in the dough. But they also speak of a day of harvest; of a seed grown to be the largest tree; of yeast throughout the dough. The Jewish expectation was right. The kingdom of God will come in power and glory. There will be a harvest, a sorting, a judgment. But first the kingdom comes in a hidden, gracious way. The Lord's Prayer directs those who know the secrets of the kingdom (Matt. 13:11), who have experienced the gracious coming to the kingdom,

[20] Turner, 'Prayer in the Gospels and Acts', p. 65.

to pray for its coming in glory. Donald Hagner translates this phrase 'bring in your eschatological kingdom'. He goes on:

> This refers to the eschatological rule of God expected and longed for by the Jewish people. It involves the consummation of God's purposes in history, the fulfilment of the prophetic pictures of future bliss. The gospel is itself, above all, the announcement that God's promised rule has now begun in and through the work of Jesus the Messiah, so the disciples are thus encouraged to pray that what has begun in the ministry of Jesus, what they have now begun to participate in, may be experienced in all fullness.[21]

The Lord's Prayer is an eschatological prayer – even an apocalyptic prayer. We are praying for the coming of God's kingdom in glory, and to pray for the coming of God's kingdom is to pray for Christ's return, for Christ is God's King. Tim Bradshaw says, '"Your kingdom come" calls upon God to act in a decisive fashion to end the ambiguity of the world's sin and confusion ... This is not a request to God to *help us* to implement the kingdom, but plainly asks for the coming of the kingdom that only God can bring.'[22]

To pray 'your will be done on earth as it is in heaven' is to pray that earth and heaven will be brought into conformity, and ultimately this takes place as described in Revelation 21 when heaven comes down to earth and God dwells with his people (Rev. 21:1–4). On that day, as Tom Wright puts it, 'God's space and ours are finally married, integrated at last.'[23] Elsewhere Wright says that this is 'to pray not merely that certain things might occur within the earthly realm that would coincide with plans that God had made in the heavenly realm, but that a fresh integration of heaven and earth would take place'.[24]

d. Give us today our daily bread

If the first three requests of the Lord's Prayer are for the coming of the kingdom, the second three are for our participation in the kingdom. The word translated *daily* (*epiousios*) in most modern translations is better translated 'tomorrow' or 'coming day'.[25] Some see the coming day as a reference to the needs of the next day, but it

[21] Hagner, *Matthew 1 – 13*, p. 148.
[22] Bradshaw, *Praying as Believing*, p. 78.
[23] N. T. Wright, *Lord and his Prayer*, p. 25.
[24] N. T. Wright, 'Lord's Prayer', p. 142.
[25] Hagner, *Matthew 1 – 13*, pp. 149–150; and Davies and Allison, *Matthew*, pp. 608–610.

is not clear why we pray to have this *today*.[26] Instead, in common with the rest of the prayer, this petition is eschatological in orientation. We are praying for the bread of the coming day or age.

Jesus uses the image of a banquet to describe the blessings of the coming age (Matt. 8:10–12; Luke 14:15–24; 22:29–30; see also Is. 25:6–8). At the Last Supper Jesus says he will not drink again of the fruit of the vine until he does so in the kingdom of God (Luke 22:18). The Gospel writers portray Jesus' table fellowship as an anticipation of the great messianic banquet (Luke 14:12–24). 'For the disciples of Jesus, every meal, and not just the last one, had deep eschatological significance. Every meal with Jesus was a salvation meal, an anticipation of the final feast.'[27] Ernst Lohmeyer concludes, 'all Jesus' sayings about eating and drinking, being hungry and thirsty, and giving feasts, have a sense of eschatological fulfilment'.[28] The bread also recalls the provision of manna (Exod. 16). On the day before the sabbath the people were to gather twice as much so that they had no need to gather on the day of rest (Exod. 16:21–30). They received, as it were, bread for tomorrow. Now Jesus is inviting us to pray that we might have bread in the eschatological rest to which the sabbath points (Heb. 4:1–11). We pray that we might share in the future feast and have a foretaste of it *today*.

This reading of the prayer feels odd to those of us familiar with 'give us this day our daily bread'. And perhaps we should not draw the distinction too sharply, for present provision is a foretaste of the eternal provision. But if it seems too much to imagine that the disciples would have understood this as a reference to the messianic banquet rather than to the next meal, then we need to remember the context in which it was originally spoken. Jesus was portraying himself as an eschatological figure. He was making connections between his table fellowship and God's coming kingdom. In the Sermon on the Mount he has spoken of those who hunger for justice being filled when the kingdom comes. The first half of the prayer directs attention to the future. In this context a reference to 'the bread of tomorrow' is going to bristle with eschatological overtones.

So to pray the Lord's Prayer is to pray that we might enjoy the blessings of the coming age pictured as a messianic banquet. It is both to pray for the messianic banquet to come soon (*today*) and to see in today's provisions anticipations of the eschatological provision and security promised us in the gospel.[29]

---

[26] Hagner, *Matthew 1 – 13*, p. 149.
[27] J. Jeremias, cited in Davies and Allison, *Matthew*, p. 610.
[28] Lohmeyer, *Lord's Prayer*, p. 150.
[29] Hagner, *Matthew 1 – 13*, p. 150.

e. Forgive us our debts

When Jesus expands upon this phrase in verses 14–15 he uses the word 'transgressions'. But here the word is 'debts' (*opheilēmata*) – one of a number of pictures the Bible uses to describe our sin. We have an obligation of honour, obedience and love towards God as our Creator and Ruler, for he has been constant in his love towards us (Matt. 5:45). The proper response we should make was summed up in the law and reiterated by Jesus: 'Love the Lord your God with all your heart and with all your soul and with all your mind' (Matt. 22:37). But we have failed to meet our obligation and the arrears have amounted to a huge debt. We have no resources with which to repay what we owe. All that we could give to God is already part of what we owe. Our only hope is mercy. The only way the debt can be removed is if God graciously cancels it. One day we shall all stand in the debtors' court, where our arrears will be revealed, our bank balance be examined. Our only hope is the mercy of our Creditor.

Jesus invites us to pray that God will forgive us on the final day of reckoning. Again, the focus is eschatological. Verses 14–15 speak of God forgiving us in the future. We can talk of being forgiven by God now, but the test of that forgiveness will be when our case comes to court. The gospel is the promise – the certain promise grounded in the Word of God, the sufficient death of his Son and the guarantee of the Holy Spirit – that when that day comes the debt will have been wiped clear. The account book will say, 'Paid in full by the precious blood of Jesus' (Col. 2:13–14).

f. Lead us not into temptation, but deliver us from the evil one

The word translated in the NIV 'temptation' (*peirasmos*) can be 'temptation' or 'testing'. Since God does not tempt us (Jas. 1:13), it is better to see it as testing. Jesus is talking not about the 'ordinary' testing of daily life, but the eschatological testing that precedes the return of Christ – what are sometimes called 'the messianic woes'. In Revelation 3 the risen Christ promises the church at Philadelphia, 'I will also keep you from the hour of trial that is going to come upon the whole world to test those who live on the earth' (Rev 3:10). ' "Do not put us to the test" refers to the coming time of trouble, to the "messianic woes". *peirasmon* does not so much refer to the trials or temptations of everyday life as to the final time of tribulation which will precede the renewal: one prays for preservation from evil or apostasy in the great tribulation.'[30]

[30] Davies and Allison, *Matthew*, p. 594.

In Matthew 24 Jesus describes such testings as 'the beginning of birth-pains' of the new age (Matt. 24:8). The disciples have asked 'what will be the sign of your coming and of the end of the age?' (Matt. 24:3). Jesus responds in 24:4–28 by describing the signs of the last days. The last days will be characterized by times of tribulation – the birth-pains of the new age. Some of these are general troubles that will afflict a world convulsing between two ages: wars, rumours of war, famine and earthquakes (Matt. 24:6–8). Some are particular to the people of God in this time of crisis: false messiahs and persecution (Matt. 24:5, 9–13, 23–28). The destruction of the temple that took place in AD 70 is part of these end-time tribulations (Matt. 24:15–21). Indeed it is a picture of the tribulations that will characterize the entire end times. Through it all the gospel will be proclaimed to all nations (Matt. 24:14). And one day God will bring this time to an end as a mercy to his people (Matt. 24:21).

When the birth-pains are complete – that is, 'immediately after the distress of those days' (Matt. 24:29) – Christ will return in glory and gather his elect from throughout the world (Matt. 24:29–31). Jesus summarizes with a lesson from the fig tree (Matt. 24:32–35). Just as the fig tree breaks into leaf when summer is coming, so these terrible distresses are an assurance that Jesus is coming again in glory. The tribulations of the last days are to strengthen our confidence in the enduring words of Jesus. Finally, while the signs of the last days remind us that Jesus is coming (Matt. 24:29–35), they do not allow us to predict the exact date of his return. That is known only to the Father and so we must be ready at all times (Matt. 24:36–51).

In the Lord's Prayer Jesus invites us to pray that we shall be spared such testing as might bring a crisis of faith (1 Cor. 10:12–13). Indeed Tom Wright suggests that we are praying not that God would not test us, but that we would not test God as Israel did in Exodus 17:7 through their unbelief.[31] In 1 Corinthians 10 Paul alludes to the events described in Exodus 17, describing them as a warning to us before assuring us that there is no 'temptation' (*peirasmos* – the same word as that in Matt. 6:13) from which God cannot deliver us (1 Cor. 10:1–13). Our prayer is that we shall not test God, but that instead he will keep us from responding to the eschatological tribulations with unbelief.

In the Lord's Prayer we turn Matthew 24:10–14 into prayer. During the testing of the end times

---

[31] N. T. Wright, 'Lord's Prayer', pp. 144–147.

- 'many will turn away from the faith and will betray and hate each other' (24:10), and so we pray that we shall not turn from the faith or betray each other;
- 'many false prophets will appear and deceive many people' (24:11), and so we pray that we shall not be deceived;
- 'the love of most will grow cold' (24:12), and so we pray that our love will not grow cold;
- 'but he who stands firm to the end will be saved' (13), and so we pray that we shall stand firm to the end;
- And through it all we pray that 'this gospel of the kingdom will be preached in the whole world as a testimony to all nations' (24:14).

While we pray to be kept during the trials and evils of the time of testing, this prayer also looks ahead to the ultimate deliverance from evil and the end of testing. 'The final deliverance from evil comes with the *eschaton*, the reign of God, the judgment and vindication.'[32] To pray this prayer is to join with the martyred souls of John's vision who cry out, 'How long, Sovereign Lord, holy and true, until you judge the inhabitants of the earth and avenge our blood?' (Rev. 6:10).

4. A prayer in the present

The Lord's Prayer is a prayer *for* the future. But it is a prayer we pray *in* the present. The future orientation of the prayer is not escapism. It radically affects our actions in the present. 'If one sincerely prays for the realization of certain eschatological hopes, the present cannot but be implicated: one must live in accordance with that ideal future for which one prays and prepare oneself and others for it.'[33] As we pray the Lord's Prayer in the present, we reorient ourselves to God's promised future and live afresh in the light of Christ's coming (Col. 3:1–2; Heb. 12:1–3). It is not just that we pray for both the future kingdom and the present kingdom. Rather the Lord's Prayer is directed first and foremost to the future. But, by directing us to God's radical future, the Lord's Prayer radicalizes our walk with God in the present. By making the Lord's Prayer our own, we understand Jesus and what it means to follow him. The Lord's Prayer gives us a window on to the priorities of Jesus and so on to the priorities we should have. 'This prayer serves as a lens through which to see Jesus himself, and to

[32] Bradshaw, *Praying as Believing*, p. 187.
[33] Davies and Allison, *Matthew*, p. 607.

discover something of what he was about. When Jesus gave his disciples this prayer, he was giving them part of his own breath, his own life, his own prayer. This prayer is actually a distillation of his own sense of vocation, his own understanding of his Father's purposes.'[34]

a. Our Father in heaven

The Lord's Prayer is oriented to the future, but it is oriented to *God's* future. It is a vision of the future that is thoroughly God-centred, and it thus stands in contrast to any form of man-centred religion. The focus of our prayers should be upon God, upon his holiness and upon his glory. It is appropriate, of course, that we bring our needs to God. In inviting us to call on God as Father, Jesus invites us to see prayer as the expression of a father–child relationship. But even then the focus is upon God's grace, love and wisdom. If our prayers are God-centred they will be characterized by a desire to reflect his glory in our lives. Our supplications for present needs will be directed to the honour of God's name.

b. Hallowed be your name, your kingdom come, your will be done

To look to the coming of God and his kingdom has profound implications for us in the present because mission is to announce the coming of the King. The kingdom is advanced through the proclamation of the gospel. The basis for the Great Commission is the fact that all authority has been given to the Son (Matt. 28:18–20), and mission is to call on people to submit to his authority. This is our message: if you continue to defy God, then you will experience his coming rule as judgment and destruction; but if you submit to him now you will experience his coming rule as life, freedom and blessing. That is the good news of the kingdom of God. Our missionary task is to announce the coming of the King and command all people everywhere to repent. To pray for the coming of God's kingdom will direct our attention and our prayers to mission.

c. Give us today our daily bread

This petition of the Lord's Prayer directs our attention to the messianic banquet. The parties in which Jesus participated were

[34] N. T. Wright, *Lord and his Prayer*, p. 2.

pictures of this coming banquet. They celebrated the promise of God's eschatological provision. The Jews of Jesus' day shared this expectation, but they had a problem with Jesus' guest list. Jesus had come to rescue sinners (Mark 2:17) and his table fellowship was a model of God's grace. But Jesus went further. In Luke 14 he says that when we hold a party we are to 'invite the poor, the crippled, the lame, the blind' (Luke 14:13). Why? Because God is inviting 'the poor, the crippled, the blind and the lame' (Luke 14:21) to the great banquet he is preparing. Our attitude to the poor is to reflect God's grace towards us. To pray this prayer is to remember our responsibility to those in need. The more we realize God's gracious blessing to us, the more we shall want to reflect that grace by blessing others. Tim Bradshaw says:

> Praying for the kingdom to come means praying for the final climax of the kingdom, the unambiguous rule of God. But praying in the name of Jesus, given the attitude of Jesus to the poor in every sense, means that such a petition cannot be offered from the stance of a ghetto walled off from concern for the world and its confusion and misery. Prayer for the final kingdom, the unqualified rule of God, feeds back into our prayer life, fuelling prayer for the world.[35]

d. Forgive us our debts, as we also have forgiven our debtors

It is in this petition that Jesus himself most clearly spells out the implications for the present and develops them in the comment that follows the prayer: *For if you forgive men when they sin against you, your heavenly Father will also forgive you. But if you do not forgive men their sins, your Father will not forgive your sins* (Matt. 6:14–15).

God forgiving us in the future is linked to us forgiving others in the present. It is not that God's forgiveness is dependent on our forgiveness as if we could earn forgiveness by being forgiving. It is rather that our experience of God's great mercy should make us gracious, merciful people (1 John 3:16–17). The best commentary on this phrase is Matthew 18:21–35 where in response to Peter's question about how often he should forgive someone, Jesus tells a parable of man who is forgiven a vast sum by his master. The forgiven servant then hounds a fellow servant who owed him a small amount. Perhaps the key to the parable is the reaction of the other servants to this. They are 'greatly distressed' (Matt. 18:31). An unmerciful act from one who has received such great mercy is

---

[35] Bradshaw, *Praying as Believing*, p. 95.

utterly incongruous, outrageous and distressing. So when the master is informed he punishes the debtor whom he originally forgave. We have been forgiven a vast sum – the huge obligation that we have failed to pay to God. If this means anything to us, then we shall be merciful people. If we are not forgiving, then we demonstrate that we have not understood the forgiveness God offers to us in Christ.

It is not just about interpersonal conflict; it is about how we treat other people. As already mentioned, Matthew uses the word 'debts' (*opheilēmata*) here. We are forgiven our debts as we forgive our debtors. Our acts of mercy include not only the forgiving of wrongs done to us, but economic generosity. In Luke's account the economic dimension is even clearer. In Luke 11 the debts we forgive cannot be read simply as sins against us, since Luke (11:4) uses the word 'sin' (*hamartia*) for that which God forgives us. If Luke had meant sins alone he would have used the word for 'sin' in both cases. Instead, while God forgives our sins, we forgive our debtors.

John Howard Yoder argues that in proclaiming 'the year of the Lord's favour' (Luke 4:19) Jesus was announcing an eschatological jubilee.[36] Seen in this light, the Lord's Prayer 'is genuinely a jubilary prayer'.[37] In the Year of Jubilee debts were forgiven and slaves set free as the people celebrated God's provision of atonement (see Lev. 25; Deut. 15). Now the promise of atonement is about to be fulfilled in the sacrifice of the Lamb who takes away the sins of the world. In the light of this forgiveness, a new era of economic and social relations is inaugurated among those thus forgiven and set free.[38] The followers of Jesus are to live as both recipients of, and participants in, a permanent jubilee. It ties in with the previous line of the prayer. As we have been welcomed to God's eschatological banquet, so we are to be welcoming people. And as we have been shown mercy, so we are to be people who show mercy (see Matt. 5:7).

The qualification of this prayer for forgiveness is part of a wider pattern of prayer that God says he will not hear. In Isaiah 58 the people earnestly seek God in prayer and fasting, but he will not hear them because they oppress their workers. In the same way in Isaiah 1 God says he will not listen to the people's prayers until they stop doing wrong and instead seek justice and encourage the oppressed (Is. 1:15–17). Previously in the Sermon on the Mount Jesus has told his followers to be reconciled with people before they offer their gift before God (Matt. 5:23–24) and Peter says that husbands can

[36] See Yoder, *Politics of Jesus*, pp. 34–39, 64–77.
[37] Ibid., p. 67.
[38] N. T. Wright, *Lord and his Prayer*, pp. 51–56.

hinder their prayers if they are inconsiderate towards their wives (1 Pet. 3:7).

What these passages have in common is broken relationships. We need to see prayer in relational terms. Sin of itself need not hinder our prayers, since Christ has atoned for sin. We do not have to reach a certain standard of holiness for our prayers to be effective, as our prayers are effective through the mediatorial work of Christ. What hinders our prayers is broken relationships. We cannot pray to God when our relationship with him is not right. If we cherish sin in our hearts we cannot come to him, ignoring the sin and blithely praying about other issues (Ps. 66:18–19). The sin must be confessed. But when we confess our sins in this way God is faithful and just to forgive us our sins (1 John 1:9). The relationship thus restored, we are able to pray freely. This is why sin per se need not hinder our prayers.

But all these passages speak of broken relationships *with other people*. We cannot come before God with unhealthy relationships with others. But neither can we resolve those relationships with God alone. When we come before God we can make things right with him through confession. But we cannot make things right with others while we are praying to God. God says he will not hear prayer where there is no intent to right the wrong we have done to our neighbours, our fellow believers, our wives or the poor.

What these passages highlight is the corporate nature of our relationship with God. We do not pray alone. Even when other people are not present with me, I pray as part of a wider community. The notion of me and my God in my private place of prayer does not fit the biblical theology of salvation and ecclesiology. Love for God is expressed through love for my neighbour and prayer to God cannot ignore my relationships with my neighbours.

e. And lead us not into temptation, but deliver us from the evil one

The testing of which this petition speaks are the 'birth-pains' of the new age rather than the ordinary testing of daily life. But the distinction should not be drawn too sharply, for the last days are upon us. The messianic woes have begun even if they may not yet have reached a crescendo. There are already wars, rumours of wars, false messiahs and persecution for God's people. This future-oriented prayer invites us to see our lives as part of a time of apocalyptic crisis. The last days have begun because the King has already come into the world. In Gethsemane Jesus urged his disciples to 'Watch and pray so that you will not fall into temptation' (Matt. 26:41). It is the word 'testing' again. Jesus said that his hearers would see the first birth-pains of the new age (Matt. 24:34). And we are already experiencing the tribulations of the last days. More people were killed in war in the twentieth century than in any other century of recorded history – an estimated 112 million deaths.[39] It is estimated that more Christians were martyred in the twentieth century than the rest of the church's history put together. Who of us is to say whether what we experience marks the climax of the signs of the end of the age? Who of us is to say whether Christ's return is imminent or whether we shall have to wait another two millennia? But what we can say is this: we should 'Watch and pray so that [we] will not fall into temptation.' We should pray that God will help us stand firm. We should pray for those Christians undergoing persecution. We should pray that the church will recognize false messiahs for who they are. We should pray for the 'gospel of the kingdom [to] be preached in the whole world as a testimony to all nations' (Matt. 24:14).

As we pray, we are to watch for Christ's return. That does not mean exploring the signs and trying to predict the date. In Matthew's Gospel to watch is to be ready (Matt. 25:1–13). If an important visitor were coming to your house you could spend the time at the garden gate watching for their car to come round the corner. Or you would tidy and clean the house, put flowers in their room and ensure the kitchen was well stocked. Jesus wants us to prepare for his coming not by looking to the horizon, but by doing his business: proclaiming the gospel and caring for the least of his brothers (Matt. 25:14–46).

The prayer Jesus taught his disciples to pray in the Sermon on the Mount, and which he urged Peter, James and John to pray in Gethsemane, was the prayer that he himself prayed in the garden. He asked God to spare him the time of testing and to deliver him from the evil one. But it was not to be. The Jews believed that the new age of liberation would come only after God's people had experienced intense pressure and anguish. Now Jesus takes that vocation upon himself. The disciples failed: they fled and abandoned him. In their time of testing they did not stay faithful. But Jesus was faithful to the very end. He was the faithful remnant of God's people (Zech. 13:7–9; Matt. 26:31). Jesus submitted to the will of the Father. The violent birth-pains of the eschatological age were felt by him as he hung on the cross. 'He would be the one who *was* led to the Testing, who was *not* delivered from Evil … This vocation is unique to Jesus: where he goes, the rest of us cannot follow. The rest of us are therefore commanded to pray that we may

[39] Kuzmič, 'Integral Mission', p. 151.

171

be delivered from the power of Evil. And we can pray that prayer with confidence precisely because Jesus has met that power and has defeated it once and for all.'[40]

The testings that precede the return of Christ are already around us, but we need not fear them for Christ has defeated the evil one.

5. Conclusion

We live in a world preoccupied with the present. The motto of our day, just as it was in Paul's day, is

> Let us eat and drink,
> for tomorrow we die.
>
> (1 Cor. 15:32)

This prayer reorients us to the true treasure – the treasure Jesus describes immediately after his discourse on prayer as *treasures in heaven* (Matt. 6:19–21).

To pray for the coming of God and his kingdom is not a request we should make lightly. 'This is a risky, crazy prayer of submission and conversion.'[41] Persecuted and oppressed Christians over the centuries have prayed this fervently. But for most of us life is comfortable. We want Jesus to come, but not yet. We do not long for the coming kingdom, because we look for pleasure in the things of this world. It is an attitude that springs from a deep malaise at the heart of our faith and our love for God. Tom Wright describes the Lord's Prayer as 'a marker, a reminder', of the church's status as 'the eschatological people of God'. But, he comments, 'all sorts of Christian traditions have been tempted in various ways to de-eschatologize themselves, and so to settle down into being simply a religion'.[42] Back in the second century Tertullian complained about those whose prayers are preoccupied with the present when our true hope lies in the consummation of God's kingdom: 'Even if it had not been prescribed in the Prayer that we should ask for the advent of the kingdom, we should, unbidden, have sent forth that cry, hastening toward the realization of our hope.'[43]

To pray this should be to be deeply challenged. Do we really want Christ to come today? Do we long to exchange the treasure of earth for the treasure of heaven? *For where your treasure is, there your heart will be also* (Matt. 6:21).

[40] N. T. Wright, *Lord and his Prayer*, pp. 68–69.
[41] Ibid., p. 32.
[42] Ibid., pp. 148–149.
[43] Tertullian, *De oratione* 5.

John 14 – 17
11. Praying with Jesus

Six times in his final discourse to his disciples, Jesus promises that whatever they ask in his name will be given to them. It is quite a promise – so much so that many of us find it embarrassing. We think of these verses as 'problem verses'. In John 16:23, for example, Jesus says, *In that day you will no longer ask me anything. I tell you the truth, my Father will give you whatever you ask in my name.* The day to which Jesus refers is the day when he will no longer be with the disciples. In that day they will be able to ask God directly just as Jesus has so far done on their behalf (16:26–27). They will pray in the place of Jesus as his representatives. When, then, does it mean to pray as representatives of Jesus *in his name*? John tells us by allowing us to listen in to Jesus at prayer. Here is a model for our praying and when we pray in this way God will give us *whatever we ask.*

John does not portray Jesus as a man of prayer in the way the Synoptic Gospels do. There is no reference to him withdrawing to pray, no Lord's Prayer, no prayer in Gethsemane. In John 11 Jesus prays outside the tomb of Lazarus not because he needs to pray but for the benefit of his hearers (11:42). The prayer of John 12:27–28 also appears to be for the benefit of the hearers rather than for Jesus, as is the answering voice from heaven (12:30). This is not to suggest there is no communication between Jesus and the Father. The emphasis falls instead on the unique relationship of Jesus to the Father (John 5:19–20, 30; 8:26–28, 38; 10:18; 12:49–50; 14:10; 15:15). Jesus hardly needs to petition the Father because both Father and Son are already intent on the same purposes.

In this wider context of 'prayer' that transcends the categories of human prayer, John provides the longest recorded prayer of Jesus in any of the four Gospels (17:1–26). It has been called his 'high priestly prayer', although such an allusion is not explicit in the text.

Here, too, 'the ordinary language of prayer breaks down because Jesus is speaking, as it were, within the Godhead'.[1] 'It becomes a prayer that is ultimately not for his own sake, but for the sake of his followers – including the Gospel's implied readers, who are enabled to listen in on Jesus' relationship to the Father and his perspective on God's purposes for the continuation of his ministry in their mission.'[2]

The prayer is immediately preceded by the confident exhortation *But take heart! I have overcome the world* (16:33). So Jesus does not pray because he needs to take heart, as is to be the case in Gethsemane. Nor does he pray because the outcome of his mission is in doubt. Instead he pulls back the veil on his relationship with the Father, just as he did in John 11:41–42 and 12:27–30, so that we can understand God's purposes in Jesus and for us. Indeed he says as much in 17:13: *I say these things while I am still in the world, so that they may have the full measure of my joy within them.*

Where does this leave our praying? John portrays Jesus' prayers as part of his unique relationship with the Father, and the prayer of John 17 is no exception. While Jesus offers the Lord's Prayer as a prayer for us to make our own, we cannot repeat John 17 as our own prayer. What we do find, however, is a summary of God's purposes in sending Jesus into the world. We discover what it means to pray in the name of Jesus with the priorities of Jesus. Indeed there are some significant similarities with the Lord's Prayer: both are addressed to the Father, both are concerned for the glory of his name, both ask for the keeping of disciples and their protection from the evil one, and both show a concern for the extension of God's kingdom albeit with different terminology.[3]

Elements of John 17 reflect its first setting in the hours before the crucifixion (e.g. 17:1), but other elements anticipate a post-resurrection context (e.g. 17:4), making it easier for the readers of John – past and present – to apply it to their situation. 'The prayer of John 17 summarizes what the Johannine Jesus stands for and shows what it means to pray in Jesus' name.'[4] And we need to know what it means to pray in Jesus' name, because the six promises – in three pairs – in the final discourse promise that whatever we ask in his name will be granted.

[1] Barrett, *John*, p. 514.
[2] Lincoln, 'God's Name, Jesus' Name', p. 161.
[3] See Carson, *Jesus and his Friends*, p. 171.
[4] Lincoln, 'God's Name, Jesus' Name', p. 172.

1. Whatever you ask (John 14 – 16)
a. Asking for the glory of God in salvation and judgment (John 14:12–14)

> *I tell you the truth, anyone who has faith in me will do what I have been doing. He will do even greater things than these, because I am going to the Father. And I will do whatever you ask in my name, so that the Son may bring glory to the Father. You may ask me for anything in my name, and I will do it.*

These two promises sound comprehensive. But the context suggests they should not be taken as blanket promises by Jesus to give us whatever we desire. In verse 12 Jesus says, *whoever believes in me will also do the works that I do; and greater works than these will he do* (ESV). Verse 10 tells us that the Father has done his work through the words of the Son. Soon, as believers proclaim the words of the Son, they will do those same works. Indeed they will do greater works. The nature of those 'greater works' has already been established in John's Gospel. Jesus says:

> For the Father loves the Son and shows him all he does. Yes, to your amazement he will show him even greater things than these. For just as the Father raises the dead and gives them life, even so the Son gives life to whom he is pleased to give it. Moreover, the Father judges no-one, but has entrusted all judgment to the Son, that all may honour the Son just as they honour the Father. He who does not honour the Son does not honour the Father, who sent him.
>   I tell you the truth, whoever hears my word and believes him who sent me has eternal life and will not be condemned; he has crossed over from death to life.
>
> (5:20–24)

The greater works occur when people receive eternal life or when, by rejecting Jesus, judgment is passed on them. This salvation or judgment event takes place as people respond to the words of Jesus. The miracles Jesus has done are to be surpassed by the greater miracle of conversion. The disciples will do greater works as they continue Christ's mission by proclaiming his word, so that people receive eternal life as they respond in faith or receive judgment when they fail to honour Jesus. In 6:29 Jesus says, 'The work of God is this: to believe in the one he has sent.' 'The disciples will go beyond what Jesus did in evangelizing the world and bringing about its salvation.'[5]

[5] Witherington, *John's Wisdom*, p. 250.

The disciples will do this work of salvation and judgment *because I am going to the Father* (14:12). These greater works are the works of the new age that Jesus inaugurates by his death and resurrection. Ascended to the Father, Jesus will send the Spirit (14:16) so that the absent Christ will be present by the Spirit as his disciples proclaim his word. Indeed the greater works done by the disciples are in reality done by the Risen Christ, who promises that *I will do it* in response to prayer.

To pray in Jesus' name, then, is to pray with this end in view: that the word of Jesus might be proclaimed and that people might respond with faith. In this way people receive eternal life and the name of God is glorified. The promise of 14:13–14 is that this greater work will be done in response to our prayers. Jesus will answer this prayer *so that the Son may bring glory to the Father* (14:13).

b. Asking for the glory of God in faithful and fruitful Christians (John 15:7–8, 16)

> *If you remain in me and my words remain in you, ask whatever you wish, and it will be given you. This is to my Father's glory, that you bear much fruit, showing yourselves to be my disciples ... You did not choose me, but I chose you and appointed you to go and bear fruit – fruit that will last. Then the Father will give you whatever you ask in my name.*

These two promises are set in the context of Jesus' discussion of himself as the true vine, and both are linked to bearing fruit. The promise of verses 7–8 is conditional on abiding in Christ and having his word abide in us, while verse 16 comes in the context of the intimate knowledge that justifies the term 'friends' for Jesus' disciples (15:13–15). So we are to pray as those who are intimate with God's purposes and who remain faithful to that revelation. 'Such a truly obedient believer proves effective in prayer, since all he or she asks for conforms to the word of God.'[6]

Abiding in Christ is developed in verses 9–13 as continuing to obey his command to love, and to love as Jesus loves. So we are to pray that we might continue to proclaim Christ's word and demonstrate his love, and to pray that as we do so we shall bear fruit. This fruit is to the Father's glory, glory that comes as people receive eternal life through faith in Jesus and as they continue to be faithful to him. It is this prayer that Jesus promises will be answered.

[6] Carson, *John*, p. 518.

c. Asking as the representatives of Jesus (John 16:23–24, 26–27)

In that day you will no longer ask me anything. I tell you the truth, my Father will give you whatever you ask in my name. Until now you have not asked for anything in my name. Ask and you will receive, and your joy will be complete ... In that day you will ask in my name. I am not saying that I will ask the Father on your behalf. No, the Father himself loves you because you have loved me and have believed that I came from God.

These two promises come in the context of a discussion of Jesus' departure (16:16–22). In a little while the disciples will no longer see Jesus – a reference to his death. This will be a time of sorrow for them, but their sorrow will turn to joy when they see him again after his resurrection and at his return. This is the *day* when they will no longer question Jesus, for they will be able to talk directly to the Father themselves. Jesus begins and ends the final discourse by proclaiming peace to the disciples (14:1; 16:33) – he is preparing them for a life of *trouble* without his immediate presence (16:33). In this time of trouble they can petition the Father just as Jesus has so far done on their behalf. Those who believe and love Jesus are loved by the Father (16:27) and so he hears their prayers. They share the trinitarian love that Jesus himself enjoys with his Father. The key idea is that where once Jesus prayed to the Father on their behalf, they will be able to pray as he did. When someone comes in the name of another, they come as a representative to enact that person's intentions with that person's authority. To pray in Jesus' name is to pray as Jesus prays. How do we know what it means to pray as Jesus prays? John is about to tell us in 17:1–26.

d. Whatever you ask in my name

In his book *Anything you Ask* Colin Urquhart says, 'There can be no doubt that it is God's purpose to give you whatever you ask in faith ... Jesus promises the answer to ALL your prayers of faith. Every one!'[7] He argues that the promises of 'whatever you ask' in the final discourse are unconditional. In fact Urquhart introduces a condition of his own to explain unanswered prayer, namely lack of faith or the wrong sort of faith.[8] Such a view, as we have seen, ignores the context and content of the promises in John. They are not a blank cheque but an invitation to pattern our prayers on the priorities of Jesus.

[7] Urquhart, *Anything you Ask*, p. 217.
[8] Ibid., pp. 78, 98, 104.

More seriously, such a view ignores the character of God. I was talking about fasting with a friend once and asked him if he had ever tried it. 'Oh yes,' he replied. 'I found God answering all my prayers and so I stopped.' I was confused. Maybe I had misheard. But no, he stopped fasting because he found God answering his prayers. 'It was too scary,' he explained. He knew that what he had said did not in fact add up. He knew that God would not just give him everything he wanted, but it was scary nevertheless. However muddled his thinking might have been, he was expressing a good instinct. Getting everything we want would be a disaster. We have neither the wisdom nor the purity to be given that much power. God is not some genie in the lamp. In the stories of Aladdin, whenever the magic lamp was rubbed a powerful genie would appear and grant the owner of the lamp anything wished for. Modern portrayals of the story often capture the irony of the situation. The genie is usually rather grumpy, affronted at having to use his vast power to please the whim of a mere mortal. How much more crazy for us, then, to treat God like a genie we control through prayer, to imagine that his great power can be harnessed to please our whims.

Yet the six promises of answered prayer in the final discourse remain. We cannot dismiss them. What links them all is that prayer is to be offered *in my name*. Praying in Jesus' name is not just the means by which we pray; it is a definition of the content of the prayers that Jesus promises to answer. 'If one is going to sign Jesus' name to a prayer to the Father, one had better be sure that it is the sort of prayer Jesus would himself endorse and sign his name to in the first place.'[9] When we pray in Jesus' name we pray as Jesus' representative in accordance with the revelation of Jesus' purposes.

In John 14 the invitation to pray in Jesus' name means to pray that, as we continue Jesus' mission by proclaiming his words, God's work will be done. It is to pray that we shall do the greater works that Jesus promises, namely that people will receive eternal life in response to our proclamation of Jesus' words. In this way God will be glorified. In John 15 the invitation to pray in Jesus' name means to pray that we shall continue to proclaim his words and demon-strate his love. It is to pray that by so doing we shall bear fruit to the Father's glory as people receive eternal life through faith in Jesus. In John 16 the invitation to pray in Jesus' name means to petition the Father as Jesus has done. To pray in Jesus' name is to pray in the light of his revelation of God's will or name, confident that whatever we ask that is aligned with his purposes in sending Jesus will be answered. Of such prayers Jesus can say, *I will do whatever*

[9] Witherington, *John's Wisdom*, p. 259.

you ask in my name, so that the Son may bring glory to the Father (14:13). 'This explanatory qualification is not intended to rationalize unanswered prayer but to encourage prayer that is in line with the will of God, as revealed in Christ, and that can therefore confidently expect to be answered … In this way believers become partners in Jesus' praying that the world may come to know the nature of his mission and his identity.'[10]

2. Praying with Jesus (John 17)

The prayer of John 17 divides into three sections: Jesus' prayer for himself, for the twelve and for all his disciples.

a. For God to be glorified through the word of Jesus (17:1–5)

Jesus begins his prayer by asking the Father to glorify the Son and he prays this because the time has come: *Father, the time has come. Glorify your Son* (17:1). In the first half of the Gospel of John Jesus repeatedly says that his hour has not yet come (2:4; 7:6, 8, 30; 8:20), but now his hour has come (12:23–33; 13:1, 31). His hour is the time when he will fall and die like a grain of wheat so that a harvest will follow (12:23–24). It is the hour when he will be 'lifted up from the earth' so that he may draw all men – a reference John tells us to his death (12:32–33). Jesus is praying that he will glorified as he is lifted up on the cross.

Glorification for Jesus in John's Gospel includes the cross. The hour of glory is the cross, resurrection and exaltation in one act. Picking up the story of the bronze serpent lifted up by Moses so that those who saw it would be saved from judgment, Jesus says, 'Just as Moses lifted up the snake in the desert, so the Son of Man must be lifted up, that everyone who believes in him may have eternal life' (3:14–15). Through the image of the serpent, the upward movement of crucifixion becomes a picture of exaltation. The symbol of shame becomes a symbol of glory. God's glory is seen in his grace to sinners (John 1:14). The reason the cross is a moment of glorification is that it brings eternal life to those who believe.

The Father and Son are glorified when eternal life comes to those who are Christ's (17:2–3). The word *for* (*kathōs*) or *just as* that begins verse 2 indicates a link between verses 1 and 2. The Son will be glorified when – crucified, risen and ascended – he receives the authority given to him in the Father's eternal plan (17:5; see also Matt. 28:18–20). He will use this authority to grant eternal life to

---

[10] Lincoln, 'God's Name, Jesus' Name', pp. 176–177.

those who believe, and so bring glory to the Father.[11] As we have seen, this fits the pattern established in the Gospel in which the Father is glorified as people receive eternal life through faith in the Son.

Jesus has glorified the Father *by completing the work you gave me to do* (17:4). Jesus has already said that he does the work of the Father as he proclaims the words given him by the Father. *The words I say to you are not just my own. Rather, it is the Father, living in me, who is doing his work* (14:10; see also 4:31–38). His work is to make the Father known. So the Father is glorified as the Son gives eternal life and as the Son makes him known. But these two activities are in reality one activity, as the explanation in verse 3 makes clear – eternal life is to know God. Jesus glorifies God by giving eternal life (17:2). Jesus glorifies God by making him known (17:4). But *this is eternal life: that they may know you, the only true God, and Jesus Christ, whom you have sent* (17:3). Eternal life comes through knowing God and knowing God leads to eternal life.

The pattern of these verses is clear:

A. May the Son be glorified by being lifted up on the cross
    B. May the Father be glorified as the Son gives eternal life
        C. Eternal life = knowing God
    B'. May the Father be glorified as the Son makes him known
A'. May the Son be glorified by being lifted up to heavenly glory

This analysis demonstrates that the key idea in these verses is that God is glorified when people receive eternal life through the words of Jesus. So to pray with Jesus is to pray for God to be glorified when people receive eternal life through the words of Jesus.

We can pray in this way because Jesus' prayer for himself has been answered: he was lifted up on the cross and later lifted up to heaven.

- Because Jesus was lifted up on the cross, he will draw all men to himself – 'I, when I am lifted up from the earth, will draw all men to myself' (John 12:32).
- Because Jesus was lifted up to heaven, the Father will do the greater work of granting eternal life – *I tell you the truth, anyone who has faith in me will do what I have been doing. He will do even greater things than these, because I am going to the Father* (14:12).

[11] Carson, *Jesus and his Friends*, pp. 174–177.

In 17:1–5 Jesus is practising what he invited us to do in 14:10–14. In 14:10–14 he invited us to pray that we shall do greater works than he did on earth so that the Father may be glorified. Those greater works are to bring salvation and judgment in response to the words of Jesus (5:20–24). He is going to the Father, inaugurating a new age in which, through his death, he will grant eternal life to those who are his. Jesus invites us to pray that the Father will be glorified as people receive eternal life in his name, and it is for this that he himself prays in 17:1–5.

b. For God's people to be kept in the word of Jesus (17:6–19)

In verse 9 Jesus says that he is now praying for his disciples, but the section begins at verse 6, with verses 6–8 providing the background to the requests Jesus makes for his disciples. Indeed all the main themes of the section are in verse 6 (ESV):

- the disciples no longer belong to the world
  I have manifested your name to the people whom you gave me out of the world
- the disciples now belong to Jesus and the Father
  Yours they were, and you gave them to me
- this transition has taken place through the word of Jesus
  I have manifested your name to the people whom you gave me … and they have kept your word

Verses 7–8 expand the third point: the disciples know that the words of Jesus are from the Father and thus that Jesus himself is from the Father (the *everything* given to Jesus in v. 7 are not the disciples of v. 6, but the words of v. 8). The words of Jesus reveal the identity of Jesus and the unity of the Father and Son. This background shapes the three requests Jesus makes in this section.

Because …	Jesus prays …
the disciples no longer belong to the world	→ for the disciples in a hostile world
the disciples now belong to Jesus and the Father	→ that the disciples will be kept
through the word of Jesus	→ in the word of Jesus

First, because the disciples no longer belong to the world, the world is now a hostile place. Jesus will soon leave this world, but the disciples will remain in the world (17:11). And now the world hates them because *they are not of the world* just as Jesus is not of the world (17:14). But Jesus does not ask for his disciples to be removed from the world (17:15), for he is sending them back into the world (17:18). Instead he asks that they might be kept in this hostile environment.

Thus, second, because the disciples now belong to Jesus and the Father, Jesus prays for those who have been given to him and asks that they might be kept (17:9–10). Jesus makes three petitions for his disciples: that they might be kept in God's name (17:11); that they might be kept from the evil one (17:15); and that they might be sanctified – kept distinctive – by the truth (17:17). Until now Jesus himself has kept them (17:12). With the exception of Judas, whose destruction was predicted in the Scriptures (17:12), Jesus has guarded them. But now Jesus is leaving them and so he prays that God will keep them. How will God keep them as Christ's? In the same way by which they came to belong to Christ – through the word of Jesus.

So, third, because the disciples now belong to Jesus through his word, Jesus prays that they might be kept in his word. The phrase translated in the NIV *I have revealed you* (17:6) is better translated *I have manifested your name* (ESV). And the phrase translated in the NIV as *by the power of your name* (17:11) and *by that name you gave me* (17:12) is better translated *in your name* (ESV).[12] Jesus is not praying that the disciples will be kept in some general sense by God's power. He is praying specifically that they will be kept in the revelation of God's name (17:11, 12), which they have received from him (17:6). This revelation of God's name is synonymous with God's word (17:6, 8) and the Son's revelation of the Father (17:7). He has given them the word of God so that they might share his joy (17:13–14) in being part of the divine unity (17:11). The disciples belong to Jesus through the truth and so Jesus prays that they will remain true to the revelation of God's name, which they have received from him (17:11, 12).

The disciples will face the pressure to retreat from that which makes them distinct and conform to the world around them. *Sanctify* in verses 17 and 19 means *set apart*. What set the disciples apart was the revelation of God's name that they received from Jesus. So now Jesus prays that this will continue: *Sanctify them in the truth; your word is truth* (17:17 ESV). Jesus addresses himself in this section to the *Holy Father* (17:11) or, we might say, the 'set-apart-Father'. The three petitions of this section are different expressions of the same concern. Jesus prays that, in the face of the hostility of the world and the evil one, the disciples might be kept

---

[12] See Carson, *John*, p. 562.

true to the revelation of God's holy name or word which they have received from him. It is this revelation of God's name that made them distinctive and which will keep them distinctive as they are sent back into the world in mission.

Jesus speaks of two purposes of this prayer. First, he prays that the disciples will be kept in God's name *so that they may be one as we are one* (17:11). The content of the truth is that Jesus is one with the Father (17:8). So the truth will make the disciples one, which will in turn demonstrate the truth that Jesus and the Father are one (17:23). Christian unity arises from a common commitment to the revelation of God in his word.

Second, Jesus says, *As you sent me into the world, I have sent them into the world* (17:18). They are not simply given to Jesus *out of the world* (17:6), but also sent back by Jesus *into the world* (17:18). Jesus prays that they might be *kept in the truth* so that they can *proclaim the truth* to a lost world. This qualifies the setting apart referred to in verses 17 and 19. 'They do not consecrate themselves to service for God *away from* the world, but rather in the act of entering *into* the world.'[13] Sanctification no longer has the sense of distance and takes on instead the idea of ethical distinctiveness so that the disciples can be both present in the world and separate from it. This is paralleled by the double sense in which the term 'world' is used in the Fourth Gospel: it is both human society in opposition to God (15:18–19) and the sphere of human life that is the object of God's missionary love (3:16). The disciples are to be separate from the former while present in the later.

In John 10:36 Jesus describes himself as 'the one whom the Father set apart [= sanctified] as his very own and sent into the world'. Jesus has completed his role of making God known (17:4, 6). Now he prays that the disciples might be sanctified in the truth as he sends them into the world. At the beginning of the final discourse Jesus says, *The words I say to you are not just my own. Rather, it is the Father, living in me, who is doing his work* (14:10). God does his work as Jesus speaks God's words. Now Jesus says, *I gave them the words you gave me* (17:8). Jesus is sending the disciples out on a lifelong mission in the same way the Father sent him (17:18). As the disciples proclaim the words of God given to them by Jesus, God will do his work. This is why the disciples must be kept in the revelation they have received, for this revelation is the means by which they will conduct their mission.

Once again Jesus is practising what he has said we should do. In 15:7–8 and 16 Jesus invited us to ask for the glory of God in faithful

---

[13] Ridderbos, *John*, p. 555.

and fruitful Christians. Now Jesus prays that his disciples might remain faithful to his word and so bear fruit as they are sent into the world.

In 17:20–26 Jesus turns his attention to his future disciples so that the focus of 17:6–19 is on the twelve apostles. But this does not make these verses irrelevant to us. It was to the Twelve especially that Jesus gave his words (17:7–8). They must be kept in this truth because it is through them that the revelation of God in Jesus will come to us. We *believe* because of *their word* (17:20 ESV). The truth given to them comes to us in the apostolic testimony recorded in the New Testament. The words of Jesus still do the work of God. So to pray with Jesus is to pray that we shall be kept in the truth in the face of the world's hostility. It is to pray that we shall faithfully proclaim that truth to the world into which Jesus has also sent us.

c. For God's people to share the life of God (17:20–26)

The work that God will do through the words of the disciples now becomes clear: others will believe through their word (17:20) – the very thing by which the Father and the Son are glorified (17:2–3). In this section Jesus makes two petitions. He prays for unity among his future disciples (17:20–23) and he prays that they might share his heavenly glory (17:24). The unity of the disciples is not just a unity with each other, but a participation in the trinitarian relationships (17:25) and the trinitarian love (17:26). This participation in the life of the Trinity will be complete when we share the trinitarian glory (17:24), but it begins on earth in the Christian community. In our congregations with all their faults and failings we are beginning to share the life of the Trinity!

In John 16:23–27 Jesus invites the disciples to pray to the Father, where once he had prayed on their behalf, because they now share in the trinitarian life. *The Father himself loves you because you have loved me and have believed that I came from God* (16:27). In verses 25–26 the unknown Father is known through the Son (see also 1:18; 14:8–10). One day we shall see the glory of the Trinitarian God, but even now we know God through the revelation of the Son, and through that revelation we already begin to share the trinitarian love.

The request in 17:24 that Christ's people might *see my glory* needs to be read in the light of the fact that the disciples are about to see Jesus' shame. Jesus wants those who see his shame – which is also his glory veiled – to see his glory unveiled. On the cross we see how much Jesus loves the Father (14:31) and in the glorification of Christ in heaven we shall see who much the Father loves the Son.

Again this prayer has a purpose. The unity of God's people has missionary consequences. It is through this unity that the world will know that Jesus was sent by the Father (17:21, 23). The link between Jesus and Yahweh has been a key issue throughout the Gospel and now the unity of believers will witness that they are one. Jesus prays that his followers might be one, participating in the trinitarian life, so that the world will believe.

verses 20–21 (ESV)	verses 22–23 (ESV)
for those who will believe in me through their word	*The glory that you have given me I have given to them [see 17:4],*
that they may all be one, just as you, Father, are in me, and I in you, that they also may be in us,	*that they may be one even as we are one, I in them and you in me, that they may become perfectly one,*
so that the world may believe that you have sent me.	*so that the world may know that you sent me and loved them even as you loved me.*

This unity is relational and observable rather than institutional. It is not found in pan-ecclesial bodies but in the relationships of the Christian community. Still less is it found by suppressing doctrinal difference, for this unity comes through the truth. We do not have to be perfect communities – we testify to grace, not to human achievement – but the mutual love of the believing community will demonstrate God's own love (17:23). 'Evangelism is a community act,' says Bruce Milne. 'It is the proclamation of the church's relationships as well as its convictions.' He continues:

> The biggest barriers to effective evangelism according to the prayer of Jesus are not so much outdated methods, or inadequate presentations of the gospel, as realities like gossip, insensitivity, negative criticism, jealousy, backbiting, an unforgiving spirit, a 'root of bitterness', failure to appreciate others, self-preoccupation, greed, selfishness and every other form of lovelessness. These are the squalid enemies of effective evangelism which render the gospel fruitless and send countless thousands into eternity without a Saviour.[14]

For many weeks I had been studying the Bible with two Muslims. On one occasion one of them said to me, 'I can accept that we cannot

[14] Milne, *John*, pp. 250–251.

be right with God through our own goodness. I can accept that Jesus came to die for our sin. But I struggle with the idea that Jesus is the Son of God. I think it is important, isn't it?' I had to agree! For many Muslims the Trinity is the key stumbling block in turning to Christ. Much of the literature on engaging with Muslims focuses on intellectual explanations and defences of the Trinity. How striking it is, then, to realize that Jesus says the life of the Christian community not only leads to belief, but to belief in the Trinity. People will see our lives together and acknowledge, in the words of Jesus, *you are in me and I am in you* (17:21).

Observing Christian community is not just important for Muslims. Time and again in church planting I have found that people are often attracted to the Christian community before they are attracted to the Christian message. Jesus said, 'all men will know that you are my disciples, if you love one another' (13:35). The challenge is to ensure that people *see* our love for one another. We need to introduce people to the network of believing relationships, which need mean nothing more complicated than inviting both believing and unbelieving friends round for a meal together. Lesslie Newbigin describes the congregation as 'the hermeneutic of the gospel' – in other words, there is a sense in which the Christian community explains the gospel message and provides the context in which the message is most readily understood.[15]

3. Conclusion

While it is appropriate to apply to John 17 in terms of mission, faithfulness and unity, it is first and foremost a model prayer. Its primary challenge is to make these concerns our priorities in prayer. When we pray in Jesus' name we pray as the representatives of Jesus. We are to pray with the priorities of Jesus.

In the first section of the prayer Jesus prayed for the glory of God, as eternal life comes through the gospel (17:1–5). It was a prayer for mission. Then he prayed for his people to be kept in the gospel, but this is so that they can take that gospel into the world (17:6–19). Once again this was a prayer for mission. And then in the final section he prayed that Christian believers might be one and share in the life of God (17:20–26). And again this is so that the world might see and believe. Again, it is a prayer for mission.

What we learn from the example of Jesus is that mission is to be at the heart of our praying:

---

[15] Newbigin, *Gospel in a Pluralist Society*, pp. 222–233.

- We pray for God to be glorified as people receive eternal life through the gospel of Jesus.
- We pray for Christians to remain faithful to the gospel as they go into the world with the gospel.
- We pray for Christian communities to reflect the life of the Trinity so that the world believes that Jesus was sent by the Father.

We should pray with passion when Christians do not proclaim the message of Jesus, when they are not faithful to his revelation and when Christian communities are fractious. We are to pray for the Father and Son to be glorified as people receive eternal life through the cross.

Our prayers reflect our lives, and our prayer meetings reflect our church lives. Charles Wesley wrote:

> His only righteousness I show,
> his saving grace proclaim;
> 'tis all my business here below
> to cry: Behold the Lamb![16]

As proclaiming Jesus becomes all our business it will feature prominently in our prayers. Jesus says in 17:4 that he has completed the work the Father gave – the work of making God known. This was his life's work, his constant priority. So it is no surprise to see this priority reflected in his prayer.

Yet this is not just a model prayer. It was a real prayer addressed by the Son to the Father. It was a prayer that is being answered day by day in the life, and through the prayers, of Christ's community. 'The gifts we exercise, the prayers we offer, the proclamation we share, the acts of compassion and mercy we endeavour, all flow from this primal moment in the shadow of Calvary as Jesus in prayer presents the mission of the church to the Father.'[17]

---

[16] Charles Wesley (1707–88), 'Jesus, the name high over all'.
[17] Milne, *John*, p. 237.

Ephesians 3, Philippians 1 and Colossians 1
12. Praying with Paul

Although in the book of Acts Luke portrays Paul as a man of prayer (Acts 9:11; 13:2–3; 14:23; 16:25; 20:36; 22:17; 28:8), it is in his letters that we get a fuller picture of Paul's practice of prayer. He not only reports *the fact* of his praying, but also *the content* of his prayers. He does so in part because this is how he wants the congregations to pray for themselves. Their praying – and ours – is to be shaped by his praying.

1. Ephesians 3: praying for unity

This prayer is in two sections, each of which follows a similar pattern. The word *that* (*hina*) is used three times, but it possibly 'has different meanings in the same long sentence',[1] and the last one appears to express the purpose of a request rather than a new request:

	I bow my knees ... [ESV]
	that
context:	*out of his glorious riches*
request:	*he may strengthen you with power*
means:	*through his Spirit in your inner being,*
purpose:	*so that Christ may dwell in your hearts through faith.*
	that *you,*
context:	*being rooted and established in love,*
request:	*may have power,*

[1] M. Barth, *Ephesians*, vol. 1, p. 368.

means: *together with all the saints,*
purpose: *to grasp how wide and long and high and deep*
                  is the love of Christ, and to know this love that
                  surpasses knowledge – that *you may be filled to*
                  the measure of all the fulness of God.

This analysis suggests that in both parts of the prayer the request is the same: a request for *power*. There is a lot of talk of power in the Christian life – 'power evangelism', 'kingdom power' and so on. People want spiritual power and others offer it to them in various forms. Paul, too, prays for power (see e.g. Eph. 1:19; Phil. 3:10–11; Col. 1:11), but power is not an end in itself for Paul. It has a specific purpose.

The goal of this prayer is that Christ might dwell in, or fill, his people and that they might grasp the extraordinary extent of his love. The oxymorons of the prayer give it rhetorical power: Paul prays that we might know what cannot be known and that the finite might be filled with the infinite. Already Paul has said that in Christ we have become 'a dwelling in which God lives by his Spirit' (2:22). Now he prays that, through the Spirit, the indwelling of Christ might be an experienced reality. But this is not some superspiritual experience or warm glow. The word *you* throughout is plural. This is a prayer that the congregation might know Christ's presence and his love in its communal life. The reference to *together with all the saints* (3:18) expands the horizon to include Christians elsewhere who are part of one family *in heaven and on earth* with one Father (3:14–15).

We live in a world marked by division and strife. It is not difficult to list countries experiencing conflict. We see it too in racism, class division and family break-up. But worse than all these, we are at enmity with God. We are by nature objects of God's wrath (2:3). The central theme of Ephesians is reconciliation and unity. This is the context in which this prayer comes. Verse 14 begins *For this reason*: having explained how God dwells in his reconciled people, Paul prays that this will be a lived reality.

Paul focuses upon the division between Jew and Gentile, but the reconciliation of Jew and Gentile is a pattern for all division because God's great purpose in election and salvation is to unite all things under the headship of Christ (1:9–10). In 2:12 Paul describes how the Gentiles were

- 'separate from Christ'
- 'excluded from … Israel'
- 'foreigners to … the promise'

He echoes these three descriptions in 3:6, but by now the situation has been transformed. Now Gentile believers are

- members together of one body
- heirs together with Israel
- sharers together in the promise

The two communities have been made one, as the dividing wall of hostility has been destroyed (2:14). This radical reconciling work is focused on Christ.

a. Christ is our peace (2:14–15)

Reconciliation is found *in Christ* and only in him: he is our peace. He has broken down the dividing wall of the law. The law defined the identity of the Jews, but it was an identity defined in distinction from everyone else. Now our identity is in Christ, so that our differences are no longer the primary things that define who we are.

b. Christ has made peace (2:15–16)

Christ has made peace through the cross. We were objects of God's wrath, but now Christ has borne God's wrath in our place. Now we stand before God in Christ's righteousness before God. And, accepted by Christ, we are to accept one another (Rom. 15:7).

c. Christ has preached peace (2:17–18)

In Christ the message of reconciliation goes to all without discrimination. This defined Paul's understanding of mission. Paul is in chains because he proclaims what was revealed to him: that God is reconciling Jew and Gentile to himself in Christ (3:1–9).

Having laid this theological foundation, Paul works out the practical implications of reconciliation in Christ. In chapter 4 he urges the Ephesians to 'be completely humble and gentle; be patient, bearing with one another in love. Make every effort to keep the unity of the Spirit through the bond of peace' (4:2–3). He appeals to the logic of there being one body, one Spirit, one Lord, one faith, one baptism, one God and one universal Father (4:4–6). He describes how the ascended Christ has given diverse gifts that we might be built up together in unity and maturity (4:7–16). The remainder of the letter describes life in the reconciled community. Repeatedly the logic underlying this practical exhortation is that we are to live as God's reconciled community, submitting to one another in love. 'Therefore each of you must put off falsehood and speak truthfully to his neighbour, for we are all members of one body ... Get rid of all bitterness, rage and anger, brawling and slander, along with every form of malice ... Submit to one another out of reverence for Christ' (4:25, 31; 5:21).

Through the reconciliation of Christ and the unity of the church God proclaims his eternal purposes to the spiritual rulers (3:10–11). What is happening in the church is the first sign that their plan to disrupt the order of God's beautiful world will be thwarted. This is the context in which our spiritual warfare is played out (6:10–18).

Unity and reconciliation are not happy by-products of salvation. They are central to the purposes of God. God did not save an ad hoc collection of individuals and then arrange for them to meet each Sunday morning. 'Christ loved the church and gave himself up for her to make her holy' (5:25–26). This is the wider context in which Paul prays that the Ephesians might have power to grasp the amazing extent of Christ's love, for it is by grasping this that they will love one another. 'Be kind and compassionate to one another, forgiving each other, just as in Christ God forgave you. Be imitators of God, therefore, as dearly loved children and live a life of love, just as Christ loved us and gave himself up for us as a fragrant offering and sacrifice to God' (4:32 – 5:2).

The requests of the prayer are made *out of [God's] glorious riches* (3:16), which are, in the context of Ephesians, the 'riches of his grace, expressed in his kindness to us in Christ Jesus' (2:7). It is in this gracious love that we have been established.

We grasp the extent of Christ's love *together with all the saints* (3:18), for there are some things we cannot learn on our own. The experience of Christian community teaches us about God's love. John says, 'No-one has ever seen God; but if we love one another, God lives in us and his love is made complete in us' (1 Jn. 4:12). We see God through the love of Christians for each other. This is how God 'lives in us', how *Christ dwell[s] in* our *hearts*.

In the film *The Mission*, set in eighteenth-century Latin America, the repentant slave trader Mendoza (played by Robert De Niro) climbs a waterfall as an act of penance with his armour – the symbol of his past life – roped to his back. The film powerfully portrays his struggle to reach the top. Release comes only when one of the indigenous people whom he had formerly terrorized cuts the rope so that his burden falls away. The objective reality of acceptance with God becomes a subjective and liberating experience through the acceptance of others.

Our unity is not only a testimony to one another of God's love.

It is a witness to the world. As Jesus said, 'By this all men will know that you are my disciples, if you love one another' (Jn. 13:35). We interpret the gospel to the world around us through our life together. This is why Paul moves from prayer to the doxology of verses 20–21. Once again he speaks of God's power within us. Once again the result is that God is glorified *in the church and in Christ Jesus* (3:21). When God does *immeasurably more than all we ask or imagine* (3:20) it does not mean we pray for ten converts and he gives us twenty. The great thing is that he is glorified. With power from God to love and live together, we bring glory to him as we display the wonders of his saving purposes to the world; and not only to the world, but to the spiritual powers (3:10–11).

At the heart of much evangelical piety is the individual soul before God. The *personal* relationship with God at the heart of evangelical experience has become the *individual* relationship with God. In this, evangelicalism is of its time. The autonomy of individual reason in Enlightenment thought became in Romanticism the autonomy of individual experience. With William Wordsworth, we are 'lonely as a cloud'.

But such a locus of piety is foreign to the Bible. The centre of biblical spiritual experience is corporate. *We* are told to pray, '*Our* Father.' God's purpose in salvation is to create a people who would be his people and for whom he would be their God. *I* have a relationship with God because *we* have a relationship with God. There are persons of God because there is a people of God. Too often, however, we reverse this. We say that an individual's contributions to corporate prayer depend on healthy private prayer. Corporate experience is predicated on individual encounters with God.

A Bible college lecturer described his time at a large mission conference as a period in which he had been spiritually low. The reason, he told me, was that he had been so busy teaching the Bible and praying with people that he had been unable to have his quiet time. It is a revealing explanation. First, it makes the quiet time the central measure of spiritual well-being when, to take just one example, a husband's care of his wife might be an equally valid measure according to 1 Peter 3:7. Tim Bradshaw speaks of 'a common evangelical spiritual heresy whereby the "prayer time" is regarded as the restoration of our link with God, as if outside this time the link is broken'.[2] Second, it is assumed that praying with others and teaching the Bible do not count, presumably because these are not done alone. Paul's prayer, in contrast, is that as a

[2] Bradshaw, *Praying as Believing*, p. 71.

congregation and together with all the saints, we might be filled with Christ and grasp the wonder of his unbounded love.

2. Philippians 1: praying for what is best

When in 1:9–11 Paul describes the *content* of his prayer for the Philippians, he is referring back to 1:3–4 where he has described the *practice* of his praying. Four times Paul says 'all'. To paraphrase: 'I thank my God on *all* the occasions I remember you, in *all* my prayers for *all* of you I pray with joy *all* the time.' You would feel like you were being prayed for if someone said that to you! As Paul moved around the Mediterranean he remained deeply committed to the churches he had planted. It is a challenge to us: when the focus of our ministry moves on, do we remain committed to the people among whom we have ministered in the past?

Every time Paul prays for the Philippians, he does so with joy. It would be great to know that every time someone prayed for you they did so with joy! Paul's words must have been a big encouragement to the Philippians. Paul is so positive. Joy is important to Paul. He commands the Philippians to be joyful (2:18; 3:1; 4:4). He says that the goal of his work among them is their progress *and joy* (1:25). But this is not a case of jollying people along. Paul gives two reasons why he always prays for the Philippians with joy.

a. Praying because we share together in gospel work (5)

Paul prays with joy for the Philippians because of their partnership with him in the gospel (5). Later he calls them his 'fellow-workers' (4:3). The letter to the Philippians is written to thank them for a gift they have sent Paul (4:10–19). They have been partners with Paul by supporting him financially. But gospel partnership goes much further than that – they are to pray for the gospel (1:19); to live for the gospel (1:27a); and to fight for the gospel (1:27b–28). However else we define ourselves (worker, student, parent, spouse), we are all gospel people. Paul is writing *to all the saints* (1). He is talking about his prayers for *all of you* (4). I give thanks for *all of you*, says Paul, because *all of you* have been partners with me in the gospel. Thus all Christians are gospel workers – not just leaders or people paid by the church.

Paul sees gospel work as a partnership. It is not done on our own. It is about working together and supporting one another in the face of a hostile world. Paul's affection for the Philippians comes because they have stood with him even when he was in chains (7–8). They have not backed off quietly to avoid getting caught up in Paul's suffering. Paul calls on them to be *contending as one man for the faith of the gospel* (1:27). We stand with one another in the gospel, supporting one another in the fight and working together.

b. Praying because we share together in gospel hope (6)

We are not just working together. God is working in us and he will complete the work he has begun (2:12–13). We all face challenging situations in which it is hard to stand for the gospel, but in those situations God is at work in us. Paul himself is writing from a prison cell. Yet he can view his imprisonment (12–14), the malicious activity of other Christians (15–18), the prospect of death and the labour of ministry (19–25), with joy because he sees God working through all these situations for the advance of the gospel (14, 18, 21, 25).

Paul prays with joy because the Philippians have worked for the gospel from the day they became Christians – *from the first day until now* (5). And Paul is confident that God will ensure they continue working for the gospel – from now until the final day. In verse 5 he looks back with joy because of their gospel partnership so far. In verse 6 he looks forward with joy to their gospel partnership to come.

It is easy for us to be discouraged, to start moaning or to be fearful. But Paul is full of joy, for he has his sights on *the day of Christ* (6, 10). There is a glorious future ahead of us. What Paul says in effect in verse 6 is that the worst-case scenario is that we all make it: *being confident of this, that he who began a good work in you will carry it on to completion until the day of Christ Jesus* (6). The road may get rough at times and we may not be as fruitful as we want to be, but we all make it. At the end of *The Fellowship of the Ring*, the first of J. R. R. Tolkien's *The Lord of the Rings* trilogy, the fellowship of the Ring breaks up. Frodo, the hero of the story, senses that he must go on alone to destroy the evil Ring. He thinks he will not make it, but there is no choice. And even if he succeeds in destroying the Ring, he will not make it back to safety. Paul's outlook is totally different. There may be difficult times ahead, but the worst-case scenario is that we all make it.

So Paul prays for the Philippians because they are partners with him in gospel work. He prays because he wants them to bear fruit in gospel work (11); to find joy in gospel work (26); and to stand firm in gospel work (27).

c. Praying that we might know how to live a gospel life (9)

It is difficult to divide up Paul's prayer in verses 9–11, for every clause expands or amplifies the one that precedes it. The word *and* in verse 10 is added by the NIV, incorrectly suggesting a prayer with two requests. This interprets the Greek word *hina* to mean *that* in the sense of introducing a second request, but *hina* can also mean *in order that* and this is the sense here.[3] This prayer is not a series of requests, but one expanding request. To paraphrase:

	I pray
request:	for love informed by the gospel
purpose:	so that you can discern what is best
	so that you may be pure and blameless = fruitful
	so that God may be glorified

The prayer starts by asking that knowledge will increasingly inform the love of the Philippians. We are not told the object of that love: is it love for God, one another or an unbelieving world? Probably the point is simply that love summarizes Christian discipleship and Christian moral conduct.[4] To live as a Christian is to live a life of love – for God, for one another and for the lost. So to pray that someone's love may abound is to pray that they might grow as a Christian.

But the key element is that this growth in love might be growth in *knowledge and depth of insight*. Paul does not pray for more love *and* more knowledge. Rather he prays for more love of a certain kind – love that is informed by both knowledge and insight. This is not love as mere sentiment or emotion. Their love must be both discerning and informed. Knowledge without love, the American Bible teacher Paul Rees used to say, is like an iceberg in the moonlight, while love without knowledge is like a forest fire in the noonday sun.

Perhaps in contrast to our own prayers, a request for knowledge is a characteristic of Paul's prayers (Eph. 1:17–19; 3:17–19; Col. 1:9). To understand the reason behind this recurring request for knowledge consider 1 Corinthians 1:18: 'For the message of the cross is foolishness to those who are perishing, but to us who are being saved it is the power of God.' The striking thing about this verse is that the power of God is not the cross per se, but the *message* of the cross. How else would we encounter the cross except through the message of the cross in the gospel? What brings the life-changing power of God into our lives is knowledge of the gospel. This is why Paul so often prays for knowledge. How are people going to be saved unless they know the gospel? How are Christians going to

---

[3] See Carson, *Spiritual Reformation*, p. 133; and O'Brien, *Philippians*, p. 78.
[4] See O'Brien, *Philippians*, pp. 75–76.

persevere unless they comprehend the gospel? How are Christians going to grow except they understand the gospel?

So Paul is not praying that the Philippians will discover something unknown. He is praying that their love will abound more and more in the knowledge of something they already know – the gospel. In Paul's writing, knowledge and insight are not abstract qualities. He is not interested in knowing many facts, possessing great analytical powers or even in exemplary moral reasoning. Knowledge, in Paul's thought, when it is viewed as a virtue, is knowledge of God through Jesus Christ. It is knowledge of the gospel.[5] 'Christian love will be accompanied by "knowledge" – that is, in Paul's use, that mature grasp of the meaning of the gospel that is the fruit of sound instruction and full experience.'[6] The gospel is the power of God for salvation and in it the righteousness of God is revealed (Rom. 1:16–17). So this is a prayer for gospel understanding. Paul is praying that they might know how to live a gospel life – a life of love that pleases God.

This gospel understanding needs to be contextualized. I need, for example, to be able to determine what to do with my time this evening. Will I spend it studying God's Word or with my family or visiting someone in need or planning a church activity or in prayer? Making these choices requires a clear sense of priorities and that priority is given to me in the gospel. But the application of gospel priorities to the myriad of choices we make in life requires love that abounds more and more in knowledge and depth of insight. The word *insight* (*aisthēsis*) here is unique in the New Testament, but occurs twenty-seven times in the LXX – twenty-two times in Proverbs where it conveys the sense of the ability to apply knowledge to specific situations.[7] So Paul is praying for love informed by the gospel that can be applied to the choices we make in life. Notice that this involves both a moral and an intellectual dimension: it involves both love and knowledge. True Christian moral reasoning depends on an intellect informed by the gospel *and* an inclination shaped by the gospel.

In summary, the gospel informs our love for God, for one another and for a lost world:

- *For God*: we understand in the gospel the character of God – his holiness, his love, his grace, his power. We discover what he has done for us in Christ – rescuing us from judgment through the gift of his own son.

[5] See ibid., p. 76.
[6] Carson, *Spiritual Reformation*, p. 126.
[7] See O'Brien, *Philippians*, pp. 76–77.

- *For one another*: we see one another as those for whom Christ died, those loved by God, those who are being sanctified. We see one another's faults in the light of our own sin. We are gracious and forgiving because God has been so gracious and forgiving to us. We think of other Christians with joy because they are partners with us in the gospel.
- *For a lost world*: we see our unbelieving friends as sinners in need of a saviour. We love them just as God loved the world and sent his own son. We recognize that the most loving thing we can do for them is to share the word of life with them.

When we pray for one another it is for this for which we should pray: that our love will be informed by the gospel.

d. Praying that we might want to live a gospel life (10–11)

Paul prays for a growing understanding of the gospel so that the Philippians might be able to discern what is best. The phrase in the NIV *discern what is best* (*to dokimazei hypas ta diapheronta*) could mean 'to test different options' or to 'approve what is excellent' (ESV). The difference need not be pressed, since in this context the goal of testing different options is to confirm which option is best.[8]

The important point is that when Paul prays that they might approve what is best he has something specific in mind. He is not talking about decision-making in general. He is not praying that the Philippians will be helped to make decisions which are currently unclear. The options are clear in Paul's mind and he prays that they might be clear in the minds of the Philippians as well. What is best is not waiting to be discovered through some decision-making process – it has already been made known in the gospel. It is to live a gospel life, to be *pure and blameless until the day of Christ* (10). There are two roads ahead of us all: living for the gospel and not living for the gospel. Paul prays that we might approve the right road; that we might *want* to live a gospel life.

The second half of the prayer expands what it means to approve what is best. What is best is to *be pure and blameless until the day of Christ*. Discerning what is best is defined by its intended outcome, so that what is best in any circumstance is that which leads to purity and blamelessness. Paul is praying that the Philippians might realize that the best thing is to prepare for Christ's coming. He is praying that their eyes will be focused on the future rather than on the present (see Col. 3:1–4). The best thing you can pray for someone is

---

[8] See Hawthorne, *Philippians*, pp. 27–28.

not that they will have a successful operation, gain promotion or find their ideal partner. It is that they will be pure and blameless in readiness for the coming of Christ.

If to be *pure and blameless* is the best thing you can pray for people, what does it mean? If *pure and blameless* means never doing anything wrong, then I have enough theology and enough self-knowledge to realize that no prayer on earth is going to make me pure and blameless until the day of Christ. I am not going to be pure and blameless until tomorrow, let alone until Christ comes. It is comforting, then, to see how Paul defines *pure and blameless* for verse 11a is an amplification of verse 10b. *Pure and blameless* means *filled with the fruit of righteousness. The fruit of righteousness* can mean righteous fruit or the fruit that flows from justification (the words *righteousness* and *justification* share the same Greek root). Many commentators assume the former, but the latter reading is better because the righteousness in question comes *through Jesus Christ* (recalling Rom. 3:24).[9]

Paul does not expect me never to put a foot wrong until the day of judgment. Rather Paul prays that my union with Christ will bear fruit in my life. The fruit of righteousness are the righteous acts consistent with a person made righteous by Christ. *Purity* is moral sincerity and integrity: it describes a transparent life in which what Christ has done in us is there to be seen. *Blameless* means not causing others to stumble (see 1 Cor. 10:32).

We shall be pure and blameless on that final day. I can be absolutely confident of this because my righteousness, my rightness-before-God, comes *from Jesus Christ* and not from me. Paul has already said that he is *confident of this, that he who began a good work in you will carry it on to completion until the day of Christ Jesus* (6). Paul's confidence that God will complete his work in the Philippians on the day of Christ does not preclude him praying that they will be pure and blameless for that day (see also 1 Thess. 5:23–24). This is what it means to pray in accordance with God's will. Paul prays for what God has promised to do. And, until that day, being pure and blameless means the righteousness of Christ bearing fruit in my life. Paul is praying that the Christians in Philippi will so understand the gospel that it bears fruit in their lives as they prepare for the return of Christ. It is that prayer, above all others, that we should be praying for one another.

But we are not done yet. It is easy to pass over verse 11b, thinking of it as a closing rhetorical flourish, as if Paul thought hard about the content of his prayer in verses 9–11a, but then simply threw in

---

[9] See O'Brien, *Philippians*, pp. 80–81.

to the glory and praise of God. I want to suggest, however, that the glory of God is the intended climax and goal of the prayer.

This is borne out if we look at other Pauline prayers (Rom. 15:5–6; Eph. 3:20–21; 2 Thess. 1:12). Paul's prayers repeatedly focus on God and his glory. We might even say that in the end this turns out not to be a prayer for the Philippians at all, but to be a prayer for the glory of God. We should perhaps invert our original analysis. This is not so much a request for love informed by the gospel from which certain results flow. Paul's central request is that God will be glorified, which occurs as the Philippians are pure and blameless, filled with the fruit of righteousness. And that in turn occurs as they grow in love and knowledge, able to approve what is best. And so it should be of all our praying. The Westminster Catechism begins by asserting that the chief end of man is to glorify God and enjoy him forever. In the same way, the chief end of our praying is the enjoyment of God and the glory of his name.

This prayer helps us define what is best in prayer:

1. *It defines what is important for Christian love and discipleship*: a growing understanding of the gospel and the ability to apply it to our lives.
2. *It defines what is best*: that we prepare for the coming of Christ by exhibiting the fruit of his work in us.
3. *It defines the goal and criterion of all our praying*: that God should be glorified.

3. Colossians 1: praying for other Christians

That the Spirit of God has recorded prayers for us in God's Word suggests that we should learn lessons for our praying from them. But there are other reasons, too, to suggest that this particular prayer should be a model for us. *For this reason*, says Paul in verse 9, we pray. It refers back to verses 3–8. The reason Paul gives thanks for the Colossians is that they responded with *faith* and *love* (3–5) to what they *heard* – the gospel of *hope* (5–6). The reason Paul prays for the Colossians is that they have become Christians. Colossians 1 is a model of how to pray for ourselves and other Christians.

The model nature of this prayer is reinforced when Paul says *we have not stopped praying for you and asking ...* (9). This is not a prayer occasioned by some specific crisis or opportunity, but it is what Paul goes on praying for the Colossians. There are issues at Colosse, but this has *always* been Paul's prayer for the Colossians since the very first time he heard of the establishment of a church in

Colosse. It is what Paul prays for as a matter of course, the normal stuff of his praying.

Not only that, but Paul is praying here for people he has *not met*. He has only heard about them (3–4, 9), as he did not plant the church at Colosse (7–8). Our prayers can often be parochial, but Paul has a big gospel vision (6). You can imagine Paul being eager to hear news from around the world – news that will fuel his prayers.

a. The request: knowledge of God's will

The heart of Paul's prayer is a request for knowledge of God's will. We can too easily read into this phrase rather individualistic views of guidance. But we need to appreciate something of what was going on in Colosse, where knowledge appears to have been a big issue. Some were suggesting the need for special, higher knowledge. They offered knowledge in addition to the 'simple' gospel of Jesus Christ – secret knowledge for the elite (2:8, 18). Paul, in contrast, says that he proclaims *the word of God in its fulness* – there is nothing lacking in the gospel (1:25). Although there is a mystery, it has been revealed – there is no secret message for the elite (1:26). It is now knowledge for everyone, including the Gentiles (1:27). This open secret is *Christ in you, the hope of glory* (1:27). Paul's purpose for the Colossians is 'that they may have the full riches of complete understanding, in order that they may know the mystery of God, namely, Christ, in whom are hidden all the treasures of wisdom and knowledge' (2:2–3). In Christ we already have 'all the treasures of wisdom and knowledge'. Paul's plea to the Colossians is 'just as you received Christ Jesus as Lord, continue to live in him' (2:6). They began with the gospel and they must continue with the gospel, not some 'advanced' knowledge. In 1:23 Paul urges the Colossians to *continue … not moved … from the gospel.* Paul emphasizes the supremacy of Christ, the fulness of revelation in Christ and the sufficiency of Christ for Christian living. In the gospel of Christ we have enough to keep going as Christians and to grow as Christians. There is no higher knowledge and no advanced level in the Christian life. Paul says, 'For in Christ all the fulness of the Deity lives in bodily form, and you have been given fulness in Christ, who is the Head over every power and authority' (2:9–10). The revelation we have in Christ is sufficient – he is not deficient in any way.

So the knowledge for which Paul prays is gospel knowledge. It is the knowledge of God's character and purposes revealed in Jesus Christ and the gospel. In the Bible the will of God is not a specific plan for my life – whom I should marry, what job I should do, where I should live. The will of God is the way of life that pleases

God. Indeed God's will describes not only how he wants us to live, but 'an understanding of God's whole saving purpose in Christ'.[10] It is knowledge of God himself, of his character and of his saving purposes (see Eph. 1:3–14). You may want to know who to marry, but God is more concerned that you be a good husband or wife. You may want to know where to work, but God is more concerned about the type of employee you are. In 1 Thessalonians 4:3 Paul tells what God's will is: 'It is God's will that you should be sanctified'.

Paul expands the knowledge of God's will by saying that it is *the knowledge of God's will in all spiritual wisdom and understanding* (Col. 1:9 NRSV). The knowledge of God's will involves, or is manifested in, spiritual wisdom and understanding. God does not make all our decisions for us, zapping them down as we go along. We are to apply our understanding of his ways. When asked what my wife's opinion on a subject is I often reply, 'I am fairly certain that she would want …' The more I know of her, the more I can predict her wishes. At times I am even brave enough to make decisions for her in her absence because I am confident of what she would want! It is this kind of knowledge for which Paul prays: that we might know God through the gospel so that we can discern his will in different situations. ' "Knowledge" is not something secret or esoteric but related to the practical business of knowing and doing God's will.'[11]

What does it mean to pray for the knowledge of God's character and purposes revealed in the gospel? We are praying that we might increasingly grasp the riches of God's grace towards us in Christ. We are praying that we might understand the character of God revealed in the gospel – his love, righteousness, justice and mercy. We are praying that we might understand what the gospel reveals about us – made in God's image yet deeply flawed by sin. We are praying that we might understand the person and work of Jesus Christ in whom all the law and prophets find fulfilment. We are praying that we might understand God's great plan of salvation. We are praying that we might understand the life of love and service for which we have been saved. Not only that; we are praying that we might be *full of it* and that we might be enabled to apply it to our lives with all spiritual wisdom and understanding.

A member of my church was talking to one of my friends. He was expressing his frustration with God. God was just not revealing his will clearly for this young man's life. So my friend asked him, 'What kind of communication would satisfy you? Would a fax message

[10] N. T. Wright, *Colossians and Philemon*, p. 57.
[11] Martin, *Ephesians, Colossians and Philemon*, p. 103.

from God be good enough?' 'That would be great,' he replied. So my friend said, 'Here you are,' and handed him a Bible.

b. The goal: a life worthy of the Lord

The knowledge for which Paul prays has a goal: a life worthy of the Lord. It is difficult for us to appreciate the import of what Paul is saying because we do not live in 'a shame culture'. With our strong individualism, we respect those who act differently and independently. But in Paul's culture, and in many cultures around the world still, there is a strong emphasis on acting in ways that preserve the honour of the family. People must be worthy of their family name and honour. In such cultures it is a terrible thing to step out of line or to bring shame to the family.

Paul wants us to act in the same way with regard to Christ. We must act in a way that brings honour to him. We are part of a new family and we must walk in a way worthy of that new identity. We must strive never to do anything that might bring discredit to Christ. Our lives must be beautiful, living testimonies to Christ. *A life worthy* (10) is literally *a walk worthy*. It is a typically Jewish expression. The picture is of walking alongside someone, going the same way as them. We are to act as if we were walking with Jesus, as indeed through the Spirit we are. In Galatians Paul says, 'let us keep in step with the Spirit' (Gal. 5:25), which means trying to *please him in every way* (10). It means acting in a way that brings honour to Christ's name. We should not underestimate the importance of prayer in this. P. T. Forsyth writes, 'The worst sin is prayerlessness. Overt sin, or crime, or the glaring inconsistencies which often surprise us in Christian people are the effect of this, or its punishment. We are left by God for lack of seeking Him. The history of the saints shows often that their lapses were the fruit and nemesis of slackness or neglect in prayer.'[12]

c. The goal expanded: good works, knowledge, endurance and thanksgiving

The goal of Paul's prayer is a life worthy of the Lord. Now Paul expands that goal by describing four characteristics of a life that pleases Jesus.[13] They are not intended to be a definitive list, but serve to flesh out what this life that pleases Jesus looks like. They are four things for which we can pray for ourselves and others. Often one

[12] Forsyth, *Soul of Prayer*, p. 11.
[13] O'Brien, *Colossians, Philemon*, pp. 19, 23.

will seem particularly pertinent in the life of someone for whom we are praying, but remember that these are Paul's constant prayer for the Christians in Colosse.

1. The first is *bearing fruit in every good work* (10). The natural reading of this verse is that the fruit *are* the good works. While we are not saved *by* our good works, we are saved *for* good works (see Eph. 2:8–10; Tit. 2:11–14). The Colossians once expressed their hostility to God in *evil deeds* (1:21 ESV). Now Paul prays that they will please him by doing *good* deeds – acts of witness, justice, kindness, self-denial and so on. He prays that the gospel will produce fruit through them just as it has been doing throughout the world (6).

2. The second characteristic is *growing in the knowledge of God* (10). Knowledge of God's will (9) leads to a worthy life (10a) which in turn leads to increasing knowledge of God (10b). It is a virtuous circle: gospel knowledge leads to gospel obedience and obedience leads to greater knowledge. This is because the impediment to knowledge of God is not ignorance, but sin. The problem with the fool who says in his heart there is no God is not that he lacks knowledge, but that

> They are corrupt, their deeds are vile;
> there is no-one who does good.
>
> (Ps. 14:1)

The reason people do not know God is not that he is hidden, but that they 'suppress the truth by their wickedness' (Rom. 1:18). We do not know God, because we refuse to submit to his will. But for the Colossians that has changed. They have turned to God in faith and love. As they now submit to God's will they come to know him more. And by knowing him more they know more of what pleases him, and the desire to do what pleases God grows.

3. The third characteristic of a life that pleases God is *being strengthened with all power according to his glorious might* (11). Paul prays that the Christians might be strengthened with *all* power, but Paul is also specific about the purpose of that power within us. We pray for power not to do mighty and miraculous works, but *so that you may have great endurance and patience*. In other words we pray for power to stick at the task of Christian service while we wait patiently for Christ's return. The world always looks for quick solutions and instant success. But we are called to endure. Through God's power we can be joyful in suffering, remain loving when rebuffed and trust God when things get rough.

4. The fourth characteristic for which Paul prays is *joyfully giving thanks* (11, 12). Thanksgiving is part of a life that pleases God, for

ingratitude represents a loss of perspective. A life worthy of Jesus is to overflow with joyful thanksgiving in the light of the salvation we have received at his hand. Some Christians easily start to moan about their problems, while others go through terrible times full of grace and joy. The difference is not what they endure, but whether their focus is on their problems or on the goodness and purposes of God. The point is not that we find some reason to give thanks *for* every circumstance. When bad things happen to us they are bad. We are not called to pretend that they are in some way good. The point is that in the middle of those bad things we do not lose our perspective. We can say, taking up the language of verses 12–14, 'What has happened has really caused us pain, but we continue to thank you, Father, because you have qualified us to share in the inheritance of the saints in the kingdom of light. For you have rescued us from the dominion of darkness and brought us into the kingdom of the Son you love, in whom we have redemption, the forgiveness of sins.'

Inheritance, rescue, redemption, forgiveness – it is knowledge of these things that enables us to live a life worthy of the Lord, even when life is hard.

When Christians are going through difficult times it is natural and right that we should plead with God to take away their problem. But at the same time we should pray that whether God takes away the problem or not they will not lose sight of their inheritance with the saints.

4. Conclusion

I want to end by comparing Paul's priorities in prayer with ours. Think through for yourself what your prayers for other Christians and yourself typically consist of. What are the requests you commonly make in prayer? If my experience is anything to go by, when we pray for other Christians we commonly pray for a return to good health, for guidance when making decisions and for success in forthcoming events like job interviews and exams. As one church leader put it to me, our prayer meetings sound too much like the description of a hospital waiting list. No doubt this is a caricature, but it does highlight the extent to which Paul's priorities in prayer often differ from our own.

What, then, about the ordinary cares of life – health, employment and parking spaces? Peter invites us to cast all our cares on God (1 Pet. 5:7) – to integrate God into the 'trivia' of life. We can pray for *anything*. But we should pray for such things with biblical priorities. Paul says, 'Do not be anxious about anything, but in everything, by prayer and petition, with thanksgiving, present your requests to God. And the peace of God, which transcends all understanding, will guard your hearts and your minds in Christ Jesus' (Phil. 4:6–7). We can present *everything* that makes us anxious to God. But notice how we are to do this. We pray with thanksgiving, for this reminds us of God's goodness. Even more importantly, notice the goal of this prayer. The reference to the peace of God is not the promise of a sense of peace – it is not that prayer will make us feel peaceful about anxieties. Peace is the *subject* of the sentence, not its object. Paul says peace will 'guard' or 'keep' us. This peace is the reconciliation that is ours through the cross. It is the gospel that will keep us faithful to God and his Word in the midst of problems. And this takes place through prayer. Prayer makes the difference between anxieties leading to bitterness or to maturity. It is for this we pray when we face troubles: that we might be kept *pure and blameless until the day of Christ* (Phil. 1:10).

You might like to work through Paul's prayers,[14] noting down the things for which he prays, and then compare them with the typical requests made in the prayer meeting of your church. Paul prays for the presence of Christ in the Christian community; for a growing appreciation of Christ's love; for a love informed by the gospel; that we might be pure and blameless until Christ comes; for knowledge of God's will; for lives worthy of Christ; and for the glory of God. There was a point in the life of our church when most of the learning went on not in our teaching meeting, but in our prayer meeting. People were learning biblical priorities as we discussed issues for prayer and then prayed for them. The gospel not only provides the foundation of prayer. It is to shape the content of prayer.

---

[14] The main examples of Paul's prayers are Rom. 15:13; 2 Cor. 13:14; Eph. 1:17–19; 3:16–21; Phil. 1:9–11; Col. 1:9–14; 1 Thess. 3:9–13; 2 Thess. 1:11–12; 2:16–17; 3:16; and Philem. 1:4–6.

1 Timothy 1 – 2
13. Praying together for the world

Imagine someone came to talk to your church about prayer. You had decided it was an important subject for you all to consider and you invite a well-known speaker. You look forward with great anticipation to what he is going to say. Finally the day comes. The speaker rises to his feet. He has spent many hours reflecting on the subject, he tells you. He has spent many hours in prayer. He feels he has a word from God laid on his heart. You wait with baited breath. He says, 'When you come together to pray ...' You are hanging on the edge of your seats. 'When you come together to pray, don't be angry.' There is a moment of silence as you wait for more, but it soon becomes clear that this is it: 'Don't be angry.'

In 1 Timothy 2:8 Paul writes, *I want men everywhere to lift up holy hands in prayer, without anger or disputing*. That is Paul's instruction on prayer to the church at Ephesus where Timothy is ministering. It is an odd statement that suggests that Paul is addressing a particular situation in Ephesus. But as we untangle that situation, we discover that what Paul has to say has a contemporary edge to it. It is a challenge to us not to be inward-looking, but to share God's concern for the world in outward-looking prayer.

The letter is written to Timothy, one of Paul's long-standing co-workers. Yet it is very much a public letter.[1] The closing benediction of the letter employs the plural form of *you*. The tone is much more that of a business letter to a 'fellow-worker' (Rom. 16:21) than a personal note to a close friend whom Paul elsewhere calls 'my son whom I love' (1 Cor. 4:17). Paul wants to strengthen Timothy's resolve to take decisive action (1:3) and he does so publicly in a letter all will hear so that all will understand Timothy's apostolic

[1] Fee, *1 and 2 Timothy, Titus*, p. 10.

mandate (1:1). Paul 'was writing through Timothy to the Ephesian church'.[2]

1. Knowledge for the few (1:3–11)

Paul launches straight into the concerns of the church at Ephesus. He wants Timothy to stop certain men teaching false doctrines (1:3). These men were probably people from within the church.[3] The teaching on identifying church leaders in chapter 3 and the instructions on handling failing leaders in chapter 5 suggest that these false teachers were the fulfilment of Paul's prediction that 'Even from your own number men will arise and distort the truth in order to draw away disciples after them' (Acts 20:30). Paul warned the Ephesian elders to guard not only the flock, but also *themselves*. He is saying, in effect, 'You, yes even you, could turn from the truth and harm God's flock.' We are not given a precise picture of their teaching. The use of the word *knowledge* (*gnōsis*) in 6:20 suggests a form of proto-Gnosticism, but true Gnosticism appeared later. The preoccupation with Jewish genealogies and the Mosaic law may indicate the influence of some form of Hellenistic Judaism. But we cannot clearly name the false teaching or its origins. Nevertheless we can trace its broad contours.

a. Speculative

We learn that it was speculative theology. The word *controversies* (NIV) in verse 4 is better translated *speculations* or *questionings*.[4] In contrast Paul's desire is to see a work of God that comes from faith; that is, from an acceptance of the *revealed* gospel of God. The wayward elders have chosen speculation rather than revelation. They have chosen genealogies and myths rather than gospel truth.

As Paul sums up his charge to Timothy in 6:20 he urges him to turn from *what is falsely called knowledge*. The false teachers offer *knowledge* – the knowledge of the initiated cognoscenti. This is the inside knowledge of the elite. With their help, their myths and genealogies, you can have greater knowledge and a higher spiritual life. It is knowledge for the few. Their successors, never far from the church, may be scholars who claim their historical or literary research will unlock the meaning of the Scriptures; or perhaps Spirit-endowed prophets who claim to reveal words of knowledge;

---

[2] Mounce, *Pastoral Epistles*, p. 28.
[3] Fee, *1 and 2 Timothy, Titus*, pp. 7–8, 40.
[4] Ibid., p. 42.

or even dynamic preachers whose interpretations take on an authority of their own.

This false teaching is impressive, finding new depths in the Bible and revealing unknown truths. It seems more exciting than the plain old gospel. But Paul says *they do not know what they are talking about* (1:7). They *understand nothing* (6:4). It is all *meaningless talk* (1:6). In 4:7 Paul describes such teaching as *godless myths and old wives' tales*. He says that rather than offering a higher spiritual life, these teachers are in fact *godless*. Rather than offering something new, they are simply peddling *old wives' tales*.

In contrast Paul describes the gospel as, literally, 'the gospel of the glory of the blessed God' (1:11). It is in the gospel that the glory of God is revealed – not in some higher knowledge or some advanced teaching. Knowledge of the glory of God is found not in the speculations of an elite, but in the public proclamation of the gospel. If you want to see the glory of God you will find it out in the world as Christ is preached, rather than among some exclusive elite.

b. Factious

But this *meaningless talk* is not harmless folly. All the urgency and passion of this letter testify to Paul's conviction that right thinking matters. This false teaching must be stopped because it leads to disputes and anger (2:8; 6:4–5). These divisions replace the work of God, which is *love* (1:5). Leaving the truth of God imperils the work of God (1:4) – it destroys the unity and nurture of the congregation. The word for *sound* doctrine is literally *healthy* doctrine (1:10). The gospel speaks health to the soul, but the false teaching spreads sickness in the congregation.

Paul exposes the roots of this false teaching. God's work of love arises from holding on to a pure heart, a good conscience and a sincere faith (1:5). But the myths and speculation arise from wandering away from *a pure heart and a good conscience and a sincere faith* (1:5). In 4:2 Paul says, *such teachings come through hypocritical liars, whose consciences have been seared as with a hot iron* (4:2). False teaching starts with moral failure that seeps into our understanding of the truth, so to maintain the truth you must maintain a *pure heart and a good conscience*. The idea resurfaces in 1:18–20 where Paul warns Timothy to guard his own heart and conscience. Timothy should not think himself immune. To reject *a good conscience* is to cause your faith to be shipwrecked (1:19) and destroy your ministry (1:20). With typical candour Friedrich Nietzsche recognized that all philosophies are in reality a justification of a person's morality:

It has gradually become clear to me what every great philosophy has hitherto been: a confession on the part of its author and a kind of involuntary and unconscious memoir; moreover that the moral (or immoral) intentions in every philosophy have every time constituted the real germ of life out of which the entire plant has grown. To explain how a philosopher's most remote metaphysical assertions have actually been arrived at, it is always well (and wise) to ask oneself first: what morality does this (does *he* –) aim at?[5]

The danger of a cauterized conscience is striking. Our hearts are deceitful. They begin to rationalize sin or make allowances. Gradually we become immune to conscience until it no longer guards our hearts. We need always to be attuning our conscience by the Word of God, by confession of sin and by meditating on the grace of Christ.

c. Introspective

Not only does the false teaching create division within the church; it also destroys the witness of the church. It ruins the reputation of the church – a repeated concern of Paul in 1 Timothy. Instead of co-operation in taking the gospel out to the world, there is strife and rivalry within the congregation. The energy of the church is directed inward instead of outward. The wayward elders have turned from gospel proclamation to arguments about law. Their preoccupation is with winning believers to their point of view. The extraordinary result is that *they are trying to convert believers instead of unbelievers*. In Acts 20 Paul had warned, 'Even from your own number men will arise and distort the truth *in order to draw away disciples after them*' (Acts 20:30; my emphasis).

Paul's reference to the law (1:9–11), which some have regarded as non-Pauline, must be seen in this context. Paul is saying, 'If you want to use the law, use it to convict the law-breakers of the pagan world in order to bring them to Christ. Don't use it for meaningless speculation.' There is no shortage of lawbreakers as Paul's list demonstrates (1:9–10) – it is not as if the Ephesian church can turn inward because it has finished its evangelistic task. The list is probably structured around the most extreme expressions of the sins prohibited in the second section of the Decalogue. The purpose of the law was to restrain such things rather than being a source of speculation and meaningless talk.[6]

---

[5] Friedrich Nietzsche, cited in S. N. Williams, *Revelation and Reconciliation*, p. 9.
[6] Fee, *1 and 2 Timothy, Titus*, pp. 46, 49.

These things, says Paul, are contrary to sound or healthy doctrine. The law should be addressed to outsiders to show them their spiritual sickness. Instead the false teachers are addressing it to insiders and so making them sick. The wayward elders are directing the law at the wrong target (1:9). The law is not for those made good by God's grace (those inside the church). They are now governed by the Spirit (Rom. 7:6; Gal. 5:18). Instead the law is for rebels (those outside the church). If they were using the law properly, the false teachers would be doing the same work as Paul. Law and gospel would *conform* to convict the ungodly and bring them to spiritual health in Christ (1:11).

2. Good news for all (1:11–20)

It appears from the way Paul continues that the wayward elders were rejecting his authority, although Paul's response is in fact a defence of *the gospel ... entrusted to me* (1:11). In defending the gospel, Paul once again challenges their introspection. In contrast to their knowledge for the few, the gospel is good news for all.

Paul's defence is almost certainly shaped by the accusations made against him. The false teachers were dragging up his past. 'This Paul,' they were saying, 'we know what he was like. He was a blasphemer and a persecutor of the church. Why should we listen to him?' Paul's response is to say, 'Yes, I was all those things and a lot more. I am the very worst of sinners. But that's the point. I am a living illustration of the gospel.' Paul is an example for others (1:16). God's grace to him is proof that no-one is beyond the mercy of God. 'In sheer wonder at the grace lavished upon him, Paul puts himself forward as "Exhibit A" of such grace for all sinners.'[7]

But not only has Paul received mercy; he has been entrusted with the gospel (1:11). Paul's claim that God *considered him faithful* is not a proud boast, but yet another demonstration of the grace of God (1:12). In the Greek original there is a lovely play on words: Paul was en*trusted* with the gospel and considered *trust*worthy despite being un*trusting* (1:11, 12, 13). Both Paul's conversion and his calling as a servant of the gospel demonstrate the grace of God (1:14).

A scene from Victor Hugo's novel *Les Miserables* (1862) is powerfully portrayed in the 1998 film directed by Bille August. Jean Valjean, recently released from a nineteen-year jail sentence for the theft of a loaf of bread, is stealing the silverware of

---

[7] Ibid., p. 50.

Monsignor Myriel, the bishop who has given him refuge. The bishop, investigating the noise, comes face to face with Valjean, before Valjean knocks him unconscious and escapes. The next day, as Myriel is telling his indignant housekeeper that they can use wooden spoons, Valjean is brought in irons to the bishop by a group of soldiers. But rather than welcoming the return of his cutlery, Myriel reprimands Valjean for not taking the candlesticks as well. The silverware, he tells the soldier, was a gift. As the soldiers leave, Myriel says to Valjean, 'Now don't forget. Don't ever forget. You've promised to become a new man.' 'Promise?' says the confused Valjean. 'Why are you doing this?' The bishop replies, 'Jean Valjean, my brother, you no longer belong to evil. With this silver I have bought your soul. I have ransomed you from fear and hatred. And now I give you back to God.' Myriel releases Valjean to a new life simply on the basis of an act of grace. In the same way, to Paul's continued amazement, God has set Paul on a new life on the basis of his grace. God is so confident in his grace that he 'lets us go free' and entrusts us with the task of taking the gospel to the world.

Here is a trustworthy saying that deserves full acceptance, says Paul, *Christ Jesus came into the world to save sinners – of whom I am the worst* (1:15). The point is that Christ came to save *sinners.* Paul may have been a blasphemer, a persecutor and a violent man, but it was for such people that Christ came. The thought echoes Mark 2 where Jesus eats with tax-collectors and 'sinners', and in so doing expresses his welcome and inclusion of them. The Pharisees are scandalized and so Jesus says, 'It is not the healthy who need a doctor, but the sick. I have not come to call the righteous, but sinners' (Mark 2:17).

And so we have returned to the concern for outsiders. The focus of the wayward elders is winning the 'righteous' to their cause. They are elitist and exclusive. But Jesus came to save sinners. His concern is for outsiders. He is welcoming and inclusive. Paul is the proof of this, for he once blasphemed against God and persecuted the church. Paul was a blasphemer, but has received faith and love (1:13–14). The false teachers in contrast started with faith and love, but now – and this is the astonishing climax to chapter 1 – they have become blasphemers (1:20). Their theology ends in disputes and strife. Paul's theology ends in doxology (1:17).

First Timothy 2:8, where we began, now starts to look like the remedy to the malady described in chapter 1. It is hard to remain bitter and divided when you are together in prayer. However, the remedy is not prayer per se, but outward-looking prayer for the evangelization of the world. In chapter 1 Paul has told Timothy to stop these inward-looking disputes. The opening of chapter 2, *I urge, then, first of all*, suggests what is to be put in their place.

3. From inward-looking disputes to outward-looking prayer (2:1–8)

Because 2:2 is the main verse we turn to in order to support prayer for those in authority, we can make the mistake of assuming that prayer for those in authority is the main thrust of this paragraph. It is not. The main thrust is 'prayer for everyone'.[8] The phrase *all men* (*pantes anthrōpoi*) is repeated in 2:1 and 2:4 (masked by the NIV's translation 'everyone ... all men'), and 2:6 continues the idea with the reference to *for all* (*pantes*). This is the thread that runs through this paragraph, holding it together. The focus is not on prayer per se, but on prayer for the evangelization of the world. When Paul says, *this is good, and pleases God our Saviour* (2:3), he is referring to the prayer for everyone in 2:1. Once this is recognized the logic of 2:1–4 becomes clear: God is pleased with prayer for everyone because he desires everyone to be saved. The link to the preceding chapter is also clear. The problem at Ephesus was a spiritual exclusivity and elitism. So Paul commands them to stop converting insiders to their point of view, and instead to pray for the conversion of everyone. The church is not only to replace their disputes with united prayer; they are also to replace their introspection with outward-looking prayer (2:8). The reference to *in every place* (ESV) may well be an allusion to Malachi 1:11 where offerings *in every place* are tied to God's name going to the nations. Prayer in every place is both the means and goal of mission: ' "My name will be great among the nations, from the rising to the setting of the sun. In *every place* incense and pure offerings will be brought to my name, because my name will be great among the nations," says the LORD Almighty' (my emphasis).

Prayer is one of those things that shape the identity of a group. Joel Green describes it as 'a boundary marker in group formation'.[9] The Pharisee in Luke 18:9–14 explicitly uses it in this way to distinguish himself from those outside his group. Green continues, 'What is fascinating, then, is that the book of Acts portrays prayer as a community-defining practice that invariably leads to the expansion of the community – that is, to the possibility of boundary dissolution rather than to boundary maintenance.'[10] In other words, a community that prays for the evangelization of the world will be a

[8] Ibid., p. 62.
[9] J. B. Green, 'Persevering Together', p. 200.
[10] Ibid.

community that is open to the world and inclusive of 'the other'. Evangelistic activity and evangelistic prayer are reciprocally related.

It is possible to distinguish between the four Greek words translated *requests, prayers, intercession and thanksgiving* (2:1), but Paul's intention is probably to express the richness of this prayer for everyone.[11] We should perhaps understand these words as intensifying one another. In every way possible, we might say, pray for the evangelization of the world. Even our thanksgiving, the most obviously distinguishable of the four words, should reflect this preoccupation.

Having said that prayer for those in authority is not the main thrust of this paragraph, those in authority are clearly singled out for special mention. This is because they have it within their power to create a context in which the gospel can be both proclaimed freely and demonstrated openly in godly and holy lives. When Paul himself was in Ephesus the civil authorities intervened to 'quiet' a riot that threatened to hinder the work of the gospel (Acts 19:23–41). Paul says we are to pray for those in authority so *that we may live peaceful and quiet lives in all godliness and holiness* (2:2). This is not a prayer for a peaceful life per se. That would indeed make it an indulgent, bourgeois prayer – something of which it has been accused. Paul's prayer is not that Christians avoid a life of trouble. In 2 Timothy he calls upon Timothy to *join with me in suffering for the gospel* (2 Tim. 1:8; see also 3:12). The goal of this prayer is *godliness and holiness*. It is a prayer that Christians might live in societies in which our godliness and holiness might be evident (1 Thess. 4:11–12; Titus 3:1–2). The erring elders are bringing the church into disrepute (see 1 Tim. 3:7; 5:15; 6:1; Titus 2:5, 8). This is one of the key concerns of Paul because the church's reputation is so crucial to its witness. Paul urges the Ephesians to pray that they will be able to live in such a way as to gain the respect of the outside world and adorn the gospel. First Timothy 2:2 is an extension of the prayer in 2:1 for all men. It fits into Paul's great concern to see an outward-looking church committed to world evangelization.

The statements *God wants all men to be saved* and *Christ Jesus… gave himself as a ransom for all men* (2:4, 5–6) recall theological debates about election and universalism. Did Christ's death make possible the atonement of all or did it achieve the atonement of the elect alone? If God wants everyone to be saved does this mean everyone is saved, or is God's intention unrealized? But these questions, important as they are, are not the concerns of the text.

---

[11] Fee, *1 and 2 Timothy, Titus*, p. 62; Mounce, *Pastoral Epistles*, pp. 79–80; Guthrie, *Pastoral Epistles*, p. 69.

Paul's concern is to show that the gospel is not just for those inside the church but for the world outside. God's intention is to save *all men* as opposed to Jews alone or just an elite with special knowledge. We cannot be content to revel in Christ's sacrifice for us. It must drive us to pray for the whole world (1 John 2:2). What we have in Christ is not for us only, but for the whole world. God's mercy is exercised without distinction of race or status. The wayward elders at Ephesus championed knowledge for the few. Paul wants us to pray for the spread of the gospel that is good news for all.

In 1:1 and 2:3–4 Paul talks of *God our Saviour* – an expression he uses only in the pastoral epistles (see 1 Tim. 4:10; Titus 1:3; 2:10; 3:4). The concern of God is for the salvation of all men (2:4; 4:10). Jesus Christ came into the world to save sinners (1:15). That Christ is preached among the nations and believed on in the world is part of the mystery of godliness (3:16). So Paul's concern throughout 1 Timothy is for the outsider. The church at Ephesus is being introspective; it has lost its evangelistic zeal; its vision is too narrow. Instead it should share God's vision for all men.

So it is that in 2:5–7 we get a great rationale for world mission. Verse 5 begins with *For*, indicating that we are about to be given an explanation. This is the reason why God delights in prayer for mission and why he himself is a missionary God.

a. One God

The first reason for prayer for world mission is that there is one God (2:5). This was the great affirmation of faith in the Old Testament: 'Hear, O Israel: The LORD our God, the LORD is one' (Deut. 6:4). Because there is one God we must worship him alone – God will not share the worship of his people with another. But God is also the one God over the nations. Just as God will not share the worship of his people with another, neither will he share the worship of the nations with another. 'Our *exclusive* faith (*there is one God*, and no other) leads necessarily to our *inclusive* mission (the one God *wants all men to be saved*).'[12] God desires that all people from every nation turn to him and be saved. In Isaiah 43 God calls upon his people to be his witness because

> Before me no god was formed,
> nor will there be one after me.
>
> (Is. 43:10)

---

[12] Stott, *1 Timothy and Titus*, p. 67.

God himself says to the nations:

> Turn to me and be saved,
>   all you ends of the earth;
>   for I am God, and there is no other.
>
> (Is. 45:22)

The concern of the Ephesian elders for genealogies may have been a concern for racial purity. But God is not the God of a Jewish elite alone. He is the one God over all the world (Rom. 3:29–30). God's choice of Abraham and Israel was not a choice against other nations – it was not a choice to exclude. It was a choice made *for* the nations. God's promise was that through Abraham 'all people on earth will be blessed' (Gen. 12:3).

It may seem a truism for Christians to say that there is one God. But, as Lesslie Newbigin has pointed out, Christians in the West have been shaped by the split in modern thinking between the public and private.[13] In the public discourse of politics, science and economics there is no place for the language of God. Politicians do not consider the relevance of God's will to public policy. Scientists do not discuss the purposes of God in the phenomena they investigate. God-talk is relegated to the world of private values and beliefs. The church, argues Newbigin, has largely accepted this private and public split, addressing its message to the private world. It has done little to help people see the relevance of the gospel to their involvement in the public spheres of work, politics and economics. It is all too easy for us to live in two worlds with one set of values operating in church and another at work. Yet there is one God. The God of Sunday mornings is the God of Monday mornings too. For us to pray for evangelization of the world in the light of the one God must include praying that the gospel will find a place in public discourse. It must include praying for one another that we shall live both our public and private lives *in all godliness and holiness* (2:2).

In postmodernity private truth becomes individual truth with each person shaping his or her own private values and beliefs – 'what is true for you need not be true for me'. The only absolute truth is pluralism and the absolute value is tolerance. To claim to know *the* truth or to regard other beliefs as wrong is dismissed as arrogance. But *there is one God* (2:5) and if there is one God then there is one truth. The claim to know the truth is not an arrogant claim to superior knowledge. It is to point to the God who has

[13] See e.g. Newbigin, *Gospel in a Pluralistic Society*.

revealed himself. Paul describes conversion as *to come to a know-ledge of the truth* (2:4; see also 2 Tim. 2:25; 3:7; Titus 1:1–2) and he describes himself as *a teacher of the true faith to the Gentiles* (2:7). Why should we pray for world mission? Because there is one God over all nations to whom all peoples must submit. He is the God over all of life and the God who has revealed *the* truth.

b. One Saviour

The second reason Paul gives here for prayer for world mission is that there is one mediator (2:5–6). Many agree there is one God, but add that there are many roads to that one God. 'Christian, Jew, Muslim – we all worship the one God, but in our different ways,' we are told. Even the world faiths that are not monotheistic are somehow supposed to be different expressions of one reality. But Paul will have none of it. There is only one way to God, only one way of knowing him, only one mediator – the man Christ Jesus (see also John 14:6; Acts 4:12). John Stott speaks of a 'double unique-ness': 'First there is the uniqueness of his divine-human person, and secondly the uniqueness of his substitutionary, redeeming death.'[14] When we present Christ to people we are presenting their only hope. Why should we pray for the evangelization of the world through the message of Christ? Because it is the only hope of the world.

If 2:5 expresses the idea that there is only *one* mediator, 2:6 expresses the idea that this one mediator is the mediator for *all*. His work of salvation embraces people from every nation, tribe, people and language (Rev. 7:9). The ransom price he paid to set us free was sufficient for all people. The basis of prayer for the world is the inclusiveness of the gospel. In chapter 1 Paul argued that if God could show mercy to him, then he can show mercy to *lawbreakers and rebels, the ungodly and sinful, the unholy and irreligious; for those who kill their fathers or mothers, for murderers, for adulterers and perverts, for slave traders and liars and perjurers* (1:9–10). Sometimes we pray without conviction for the conversion of certain people because we lack the imagination to see them saved. Because we lack the imagination, we suspect that God lacks the power. In Acts 18 the Lord speaks to a despondent Paul in a vision: 'Do not be afraid; keep on speaking, do not be silent. For I am with you, and no-one is going to attack and harm you, because I have many people in this city' (Acts 18:9–10). Jesus has his people in every city, in every tribe, among every type of person. No matter for whom we

---

[14] Stott, *1 Timothy and Titus*, p. 71.

are praying, we can be confident that Jesus has his people among them – people who will respond to the gospel in faith and repentance. Not everyone for whom we pray will be saved. But prayer for mission will be answered, for *Christ ... gave himself as a ransom for all men* (2:5–6).

The phrase *the testimony given in its proper time* (2:6) is a difficult one. It is not clear from the text who gives the testimony or to what. The context, however, suggests that the testimony is to the concern of the one God for the salvation of all people. As we have noted, the word *For* at the beginning of 2:5 suggests that 2:5–7 is an explanation of the statement that prayer for everyone pleases the God who wants everyone to be saved (2:1–4). Paul's description of his role as a herald and apostle might indicate that the testimony is the apostolic testimony. But, while the phrase *the testimony given in its proper time* may provide the bridge between Christ's mediatorial work and Paul's apostolic ministry, to read it as the apostolic testimony still raises the question: the testimony to what? It seems best, then, to see the testimony as the death of Christ. The ultimate proof that God desires the salvation of all people is the cross. God was so concerned for the salvation of the nations that he gave his Son as a ransom for all men. As a result, 'not to pray for all people is to run counter to the purpose for which Christ died'.[15]

c. One task

Paul's third reason why we should pray for mission is tied up with his own ministry. His appointment by God as an apostle to the Gentiles (or *nations*) is another evidence of God's concern for *all men* (2:6). The dramatic expostulation *I am telling the truth, I am not lying* (2:7) coming immediately before *a teacher ... to the Gentiles* emphatically highlights the focus of this verse. The gospel is not just for the Jews, since Paul has been sent by God to take the gospel to the nations (see Rom. 11:3; Gal. 2:7). The argument recalls that of 1:11–20. Paul is living proof of God's grace to those apparently furthest from the truth. Paul has been *entrusted* with the gospel despite having acted in unbelief ('untrust'). He is the display board of Christ's unlimited patience (1:16). Now he has been sent to the Gentiles – to those far from Christ, but for whom Christ came (1:15). Why should we pray for world mission? Because the risen Christ sends us out into the world with the gospel. Because the risen Christ has commanded us to make disciples of all nations.

[15] Mounce, *Pastoral Epistles*, p. 94.

One God, one Saviour and one task – because of these three great missionary truths Paul wants *men everywhere to lift up holy hands in prayer* (2:8). The NIV makes *lift up* the main verb of the sentence, but this is misleading. Paul says, 'I want men everywhere *to pray*, lifting up holy hands.' The emphasis is on prayer, not on posture. Indeed the key thing about the hands is that they are *holy*. In the Old Testament *holy hands* are a symbol of the purity of heart required to approach God in prayer (Exod. 30:17–21; Ps. 24:3–4; Is. 1:15). Instead of using their hands in *anger or disputing* the men of the church are to use them in prayer.

These verses are often described as a manual for church order. They are, however, nothing of the sort.[16] Paul's concern is not public worship, but the centrality of the gospel in the life of the church. They are not a look inward at our conduct inside the church, but a passionate plea to be outward-looking. The word *men* in 2:8 is not the generic word for people used in 2:5 – it means male persons. Paul is not forbidding women to pray – elsewhere Paul assumes that women will pray in public (1 Cor. 11:5). Rather Paul is calling upon a particular group of men to do what they are not currently doing. Instead of *anger or disputing* the men in Ephesus are to be united in prayer (2:8). In the same way we are to stop disputing, to end our introspection and pray instead for the evangelization of the world.

The challenge of 1 Timothy 1 and 2 is to prevent our churches becoming holy huddles – cliquey and inward-looking. 'Prayer', says S. D. Gordon, 'opens a whole planet to man's activities. I can as really be touching hearts for God in far away India or China through prayer, as though I were there.'[17] This challenge is an urgent one for us today. A survey of the prayer habits of over 6,000 church members, mainly from the UK, showed that two-thirds pray regularly for health and healing, but only one-third pray regularly for the conversion of the lost.[18] Commenting on 1 Timothy 2, John Stott says:

> I sometimes wonder whether the comparatively slow progress towards peace and justice in the world, and towards world evangelization, is due more than anything else to the prayerlessness of the people of God. When President Marcos was toppled in 1986, Filipino Christians attributed his downfall 'not to people power but to prayer power'. What might not happen if God's

---

[16] Fee, *1 and 2 Timothy, Titus*, pp. 7, 21.
[17] S. D. Gordon, *Quiet Talks*, p. 9.
[18] Teal, *On our Knees?*

people throughout the world learned to wait upon him in believing, persevering prayer?[19]

In the UK the traditional midweek church meeting often provided a focus for missionary prayer. But the house groups that have in many cases replaced it can all too easily become insular and self-regarding. Paul's call is for our churches and small groups to become hotbeds of missionary activity – outward-looking and inclusive with a vision for the nations. Paul expects that vision to be reflected in prayer for the evangelization of all people. Such prayer is both the cause and effect of a gospel vision for the nations. Such prayer is what churches should engage in when they meet together, for *this is good, and pleases God our Saviour, who wants all men to be saved and to come to a knowledge of the truth* (2:3–4).

[19] Stott, *1 Timothy and Titus*, p. 62.

Ephesians 6
14. Praying in the battle

Asked if financial markets are as powerful as they are thought to be, George Soros – the well-known currency speculator – replied, 'Yes, but you mustn't think of them as human: they follow the herd instinct.' Just as a mob generates its own momentum, so companies, organizations, governments, the media – even whole societies – seem at times to function in a way greater than the sum of the individuals within them. A company, for example, can have a dynamic that appears to control the decisions made by individuals within it. The drive for profits or the nature of the decision-making process can allow a company to trade unethically or pollute the environment in a way that individuals in isolation would not countenance.

How should we understand such phenomena? Some would argue that corporate evil is an illusion that undermines individual responsibility before God. Whatever the appearances may be, the actions of a company are the cumulative result of the decisions made by its individual managers, employees and shareholders. Others argue that sin affects all levels of human existence, including social structures and cultural pressures. These can coalesce into different forms of corporate evil, whether state tyranny, unethical company policies or corrupt cultural norms. Others identify this aggregate power with spiritual forces that take control of companies, societies and regions. They should be challenged in Jesus' name through 'warfare prayer' and symbolic action.

Perhaps the most prominent New Testament passage on spiritual warfare is Ephesians 6:10–20. Paul calls on the Ephesians to *pray in the Spirit on all occasions with all kinds of prayers and requests* (18). But this call to prayer is set in the context of a spiritual battle: *our struggle is not against flesh and blood, but against the rulers, against the authorities, against the powers of this dark world and against the spiritual forces of evil in the heavenly realms* (12). In the light of this struggle we are to equip ourselves with the armour of God (13–17).

1. Naming the powers

What does Paul mean here by *the powers*? The terminology used in the New Testament for what are often referred to as 'the Principalities and Powers'[1] covers a range of meanings including both earthly powers and spiritual beings.

a. Power

The Greek word *dynamis* is used of power, might, strength, ability, and sometimes of the one who exercises power. In the New Testament it is used of God who is described as 'the Mighty One' (Luke 1:49; see also Mark 12:24). It is used of Christ (Luke 24:19) whose miracles are literally 'mighty acts' (Luke 19:37). *Dynamis* is also used of the Holy Spirit (Luke 4:14; Acts 1:8), Christians (Eph. 1:19), the gospel (Rom. 1:16; 1 Cor. 1:18), and the coming of Christ (Matt. 24:30; Mark 9:1). The term *dynastēs* is used of a human official (Acts 8:27). In the Magnificat Mary sings of how God has brought down 'rulers' from their thrones (Luke 1:52). The New Testament also speaks of 'the power of the enemy' (Luke 10:19) who can do counterfeit 'works of power' (2 Thess. 2:9), while in Revelation 17:12–13 the ten kings give their *power* to the Beast. Romans 8:38–39; 1 Corinthians 15:24; Ephesians 1:21 and 1 Peter 3:22 also refer to 'powers', but whether these are human rulers or spiritual forces is disputed. Mark 13:25, however, speaks explicitly of 'the powers in the heavens' (ESV; 'the heavenly bodies' in the NIV).

b. Authority

The term *exousia* means authority or ruling power. In a similar way to *dynamis*, it is used both of authority and the bearer of authority. It is used for the authority of God, of Jesus and of believers, but also of secular authority or jurisdiction (Matt 8:9; Luke 12:11; 19:17; 20:20; 23:7; Titus 3:1). Its use in Romans 13:1–3 is generally held to refer to human authorities, although some have argued that this refers to angelic powers.[2] Elsewhere *exousia* is clearly used of spiritual forces: 'His intent was that now, through the church, the

---

[1] From the AV translation of Eph. 3:10; 6:12; Col. 1:15; 2:15; and Titus 3:1.
[2] See e.g. Morrison, *Powers that Be.*

manifold wisdom of God should be made known to the rulers and authorities in the heavenly realms' (Eph. 3:10).

c. Ruler

The word *archē* can mean 'beginning' or 'first' (Mark 1:1; John 1:1), but is also used of 'ruling power' or 'authority', while *archōn* is used to mean 'ruler' or 'prince'. It is often used of human powers or rulers (including religious leaders: Matt. 9:18; Luke 23:13; Acts 23:5). 'Remind the people to be subject to rulers and authorities' (Titus 3:1; see also Matt. 20:25; Luke 12:11; 20:20; Acts 4:26). But like *dynamis* and *exousia*, *archē* is also for spiritual forces. Ephesians 3:10 talks about 'the rulers ... in the heavenly realms', and the devil is referred to as 'the prince of demons', 'the ruler of demons', 'the prince of this world' and 'the ruler of the kingdom of the air' (Matt. 9:34; 12:24; John 12:31; 14:30; 16:11; Eph. 2:2).

d. Names and thrones

Names (*onoma*) and thrones (*thronos*) are metonyms – words where part of a concept or an associated object is used to represent a concept as a whole. *Name* implies the power and authority of the person named. In the New Testament it is usually used in this way of God or Christ, although sometimes in contrast to other 'names' including angelic names (Heb. 1:4; see also Acts 4:12; Eph. 1:21; Phil. 2:9–11). The term *throne* refers to the authority of the one who sits on the throne. The plural is used of the thrones of the twelve disciples (Matt. 19:28) and the twenty-four elders (Rev. 4:4) as well as human rulers (Luke 1:52).

In the New Testament words for power are frequently used together in groups. 'For by him all things were created: things in heaven and on earth, visible and invisible, whether thrones or powers or rulers or authorities' to give just one example (Col. 1:16; see also 1 Cor. 15:24; Eph. 1:21; 3:10; 6:12; Col. 2:10, 15; 1 Pet. 3:22). Combined together in this way, they add breadth and depth. A strong differentiation between the terms is probably not intended.

Reviewing the use of these words reveals that the language of power is common throughout the New Testament. Most of the terms are used in the New Testament of (1) divine power, (2) human power and structures, *and* (3) spiritual forces. Their use for spiritual powers can refer to both the good angelic forces of God and the evil spirits of Satan. That a term can be used of either human or spiritual forces does not mean that *both* senses are implied in any given text.

As is the case so often in exegesis the context must be decisive in determining the meaning of a term for 'power' in the New Testament.[3]

2. Interpreting the powers

The following are the main contrasting understandings of the powers, their relation to personal sin and social evil, and what Christians should do in response.

1. Hierarchies of demons can control organizations, towns and regions, affecting the receptiveness of people to the gospel and the level of sinfulness.[4] Their power should be challenged through 'warfare prayer', symbolic action and claiming areas in Jesus' name. Naming spirits and spiritual mapping are sometimes seen as an important part of this approach. A variation on this view maintains that all organizations, structures and geographic areas have a spiritual being over them. In Daniel 10 the messenger who comes in response to Daniel's prayer is resisted by the prince of Persia until help comes from the angel Michael. The impact of these spirits can be both good and evil.

2. The powers are social structures, cultural traditions, human rulers and the forces that maintain or legitimize their power.[5] Paul borrows the language of contemporary Jewish mythology, but he himself demythologizes or reinterprets it to mean human powers. Where these social structures and cultural forces usurp the life-giving rule of Christ, they should be challenged in his name – what Richard Mouw calls 'political evangelism'. Walter Wink argues that the powers have both an external manifestation and an inner spirituality or ethos.[6] The 'demonic' and 'angelic' in the New Testament are not personal spiritual beings but metaphors for the inner ethos of the powers. We need to address both in Christ's name, countering the prevailing culture of violence with his shalom.

3. Traditionally spiritual warfare has been seen in terms of the individual's struggle against the world, the flesh and the devil. Demonic powers tempt individuals into sin and error. Spiritual

[3] The key references to 'principalities and powers' are Rom. 13:1–3; 1 Cor. 2:6–8; 15:24–27; Eph. 1:20–23; 3:8–11; 6:10–20; Col. 1:15–20; 2:9–10, 13–15; and 1 Pet. 3:21.
[4] See e.g. Wagner, 'Territorial Spirits', pp. 83–102.
[5] See Caird, *Principalities and Powers*; Berkhof, *Christ and the Powers*; and Yoder, *Politics of Jesus*, pp. 135–162.
[6] Wink, *Engaging the Powers*; *Naming the Powers*; and *Unmasking the Powers*; see also Goldingay, *Daniel*, pp. 313–314.

warfare involves resisting temptation, maintaining the truth in the face of heresy and intercession to God.

What are we to make of these different approaches? Too much of the first approach, I would suggest, is speculative – some of it is even dependent on occult sources. Paul Hiebert further argues that such an approach tends towards dualism[7] – the belief that the world is an uncertain struggle between the forces of good and evil so that, instead of confidently praying to the sovereign God, we have to do battle with demonic forces to allow God to act or 'release' his power. It may be true that there are hierarchies of demons controlling territories, but the fact that we are not told about such things in the Bible (except for a few elusive references in the Old Testament, such as Dan. 10:12–14) suggests that 'warfare prayer' does not play the central role in mission that is often claimed for it.

The second approach takes seriously the corporate nature of evil, but it uses the wrong biblical categories. Despite claims to take 'myth' seriously, it still sees talk of spiritual forces as mythological language. As we have seen, the language of power is used in the New Testament for earthly power structures, but in a number of key passages on spiritual warfare the reference is to invisible spiritual forces. Without reinterpreting Paul it is hard to see a phrase like 'rulers and authorities in the heavenly realms' (3:10) as a reference to the inner ethos of an organization or society. John Stott says that those who want to make the powers political or social structures do not provide an 'adequate account [of] the fact that all three references to the principalities and powers in Ephesians also contain a reference to the heavenly realms, that is, the unseen world of spiritual reality'.[8] The second approach, one suspects, is adopted by people who want to take the New Testament language of principalities and powers seriously, but who find belief in personal spiritual forces fitting uneasily with their modern scientific rationalism.

It is better, I think, to maintain the third approach to individual spiritual warfare *and* to recognize – as Christians throughout the ages have done – that evil manifests itself in corporate and social structures. The biblical category for this is the 'world'. This is used in the Bible for creation as an object of God's love (John 3:16), but it is also used of human society and culture in opposition to God's will (1 John 2:15–17). This is a better framework within which to look at social evil than territorial spirits or demythologized powers. Satan tempts individuals into sin and error, but the lies of Satan also

[7] Hiebert, 'Spiritual Warfare'.
[8] Stott, *Ephesians*, p. 273.

affect whole cultures and, as a result, social structures. Idolatry is as much a social phenomenon as an individual act.

3. Battling with the powers

This review of the language of the powers in the New Testament provides the context in which we understand Ephesians 6. Paul says, *our struggle is not against flesh and blood, but against the rulers, against the authorities, against the powers of this dark world and against the spiritual forces of evil in the heavenly realms* (12). The word *and* before the phrase *against the spiritual forces of evil in the heavenly realms* is added in the NIV. It creates a misleading impression that *the powers of this dark world* (a phrase used only here in the New Testament and which literally is *world-rulers of this darkness*) and *the spiritual forces of evil in the heavenly realms* are different entities. In reality Paul is piling up different phrases to express one opponent: the spiritual forces of evil. They are deliberately contrasted with *flesh and blood*. They are the agents of *the devil's schemes* (11).

Ephesus was a prominent centre of occult activity. Paul's first visit there had precipitated an encounter with the demonic in which the name of Jesus had proved the more powerful (Acts 19:11–20). Many of the believers in Ephesus had come from an occult background. 'Many of those who believed now came and openly confessed their evil deeds. A number who had practised sorcery brought their scrolls together and burned them publicly. When they calculated the value of the scrolls, the total came to fifty thousand drachmas' (Acts 19:18–19).

In Ephesians 5:22 – 6:9 Paul addressed specific groups within the church (wives, husbands, children, fathers and slaves). But in 6:10 he once again addresses the whole congregation. Spiritual warfare is a reality for all believers whether we perceive it to be or not. Although Christians are no longer under the authority of 'the ruler of the kingdom of the air, the spirit who is now at work in those who are disobedient' (2:2) we are still vulnerable to Satan's attacks, as is clear from Paul warning not to 'give the devil a foothold' (4:27).

a. Spiritual warfare is to stand

Ephesians 6:10–13 can be analysed as follows (my emphasis):

> *Finally, be strong in the Lord and in his mighty power.*

Command: Put on the full armour of God

Reason: *so that you can take your* stand *against the devil's schemes.*

Explanation: *For our struggle is not against flesh and blood, but against the rulers, against the authorities, against the powers of this dark world and against the spiritual forces of evil in the heavenly realms.*

Command: *Therefore* put on the full armour of God,

Reason: *so that when the day of evil comes, you may be able to* stand *your ground, and after you have done everything, to* stand.

This reveals that Paul twice commands us to *put on* the full armour of God, and the reason is *so that* we can *stand*. In verses 14–17 he simply reverses this, telling us to *stand* by the means of putting on the armour of God. We are commanded to put on the armour of God so that we can stand (11, 13). We are commanded to stand by putting on the armour of God (14).

To stand is to resist temptation. It is to resist the world, the flesh and the devil (2:1–3). It is to avoid falling into the ways of darkness (5:3–20). With the exception of the sword of the Spirit, the armour is essentially defensive – belt, breastplate, shoes, shield and helmet. With *truth* (14) we refute the lies of Satan and the deceptions of a culture under his influence. *The breastplate of righteousness* (14) is the righteousness that is ours in Christ through which we counter the accusations of Satan (Zech. 3:1–5). *The gospel of peace* (15) is the message of reconciliation with God and with one another that enables us to stand together (2:14–18). Through *faith* (16) we overcome the *flaming arrows* of doubt that Satan directs at us. When Satan points to our sin, we remain confident in the sufficiency of Christ's atonement. When Satan appears to triumph, we remain confident in the ultimate victory of Christ. The *salvation* (17) that is ours in Christ protects us in the battle. In *the word of God* (17) we have the enduring source of truth which powerfully builds up God's people. *Truth* could refer to *our* sincerity and *righteousness* to *our* godly living (14). But the other weapons refer to what God has done (gospel, salvation and word) and our confidence in what God has done (faith). So, although the distinction need not be pressed, we should probably read *truth* and *righteousness* in this way as referring to God's provision on our behalf. We stand firm in what God has done for us in Christ. Paul draws his imagery from Isaiah and in so doing suggests that the Christian is to put on the armour with which God himself and his Messiah are clothed (Is. 11:5; 59:17).

It is clear that the armour of God is the gospel. Commentators delight in describing the intricacies of Roman military hardware, but Paul's focus is on what the armour represents: the gospel. The gospel is the revelation of truth, the gift of righteousness, the means of peace, the provision of salvation, the Word of God. To put on this armour is to remind ourselves of the gospel. The temptation is to turn from the gospel to a message that will be more acceptable to our culture. To stand is to remain true to gospel truth in the face of a hostile world and to remain true to gospel living in the face of a beguiling enemy. We have all the military kit we need. All we need is the confidence to stand firm in the gospel and not leave the battlefield.

To *stand* in this way is essentially a corporate act. The word *you* throughout Ephesians 6:10–20 is plural. We are called to stand *together*. The image is of a Roman battalion, standing with their shields together to form an impenetrable wall of defence. While they remain disciplined and united they can resist the onslaught of the enemy. The central theme of Ephesians is that through our reconciliation to God those who are in Christ have been reconciled to one another. When Paul asks for prayer at the end of this section, he describes his message as *the mystery of the gospel* (19). He has already defined this in terms of the reconciliation of Jew and Gentile in Christ (3:6). To pray *in the Spirit* (18) is for Jew and Gentile to pray together, for Paul has already said *we both have access to the Father by one Spirit* (2:18) or *in one Spirit* (it is the same Greek preposition in both verses). The power of God in which we stand (10) is the power through which Christ dwells in his people and which 'enables believers to love in the way that Christ did'.[9] Having been reconciled to one another in Christ, we are to *make every effort to keep the unity of the Spirit through the bond of peace* (4:3). The call to *not give the devil a foothold* (4:27) comes in the context of a warning against speech that divides. We prevent the devil getting a foothold when we avoid *falsehood* (4:25), *anger* (4:26) and *unwholesome talk* (4:29), and instead say only what is *helpful for building others up* (4:29). In Ephesians 3 Paul says, *[God's] intent was that now, through the church, the manifold wisdom of God should be made known to the rulers and authorities in the heavenly realms* (3:10). What God has done in Christ 'has been set against a cosmic backdrop'. Now as the letter closes, 'the cosmos dimension of the drama of salvation comes to the fore'.[10] The spiritual battle in which we are engaged is advanced through our unity. The reconciled

---

[9] O'Brien, *Gospel and Mission*, p. 121.
[10] Lincoln, *Ephesians*, p. 459.

Christian community is God's demonstration to the powers that their work of cosmic disruption and disharmony will soon be over. The church is the sign and foretaste of God's plan *to bring all things in heaven and on earth together under one head, even Christ* (1:10).

b. Spiritual warfare is to proclaim

Not all the armour is defensive. The final piece is *the sword of the Spirit, which is the word of God* (17). The movement of the section is from standing to proclaiming (19). Advance is implied, too, in verse 15. The NIV's *firm* footing is a possible translation, but the NRSV is probably to be preferred: *As shoes for your feet put on whatever will make you ready to proclaim the gospel of peace* (15 NRSV).[11] The Christian soldier is to be ready at all times to proclaim the gospel. The nation of Israel in the Old Testament was not only the custodian of God's revelation, but also of the seed of promise. From this nation would come the Saviour. So God protected Israel physically in the face of constant threat from the nations – a threat orchestrated by Satan (Rev. 12:9). Israel fought in holy wars to defend herself with God's help. Now, however, the promised Saviour has come. The battle continues, but at a spiritual level. Our weapons are no longer the 'weapons of the world' (2 Cor. 10:4) but the sword of the Spirit – the Word of God.

Spiritual warfare is to proclaim the gospel. The power of Satan lies in the credence we give to his lies, and it is through the truth of the gospel that the lies of Satan are countered. It is through the power of the gospel that people are released from the grip of Satan. It is through the reconciliation of the gospel that we are united in Christ. The gospel we proclaim is the gospel of peace. We make war by making peace. We, as it were, declare peace on the world.

Peter O'Brien describes Ephesians 6 as 'the Pauline Great Commission':

> We are involved in the same spiritual warfare as the apostle, we have the same injunction laid upon us to stand firm, the same divine weapons available for us to use (especially the essential spiritual weapon of prayer), and the same defensive and offensive postures to adopt. We are to resist temptation and to devote our lives energetically to spreading the gospel. These are not optional extras. They are musts and this is why the apostle's words about sharing the gospel effectively in the power of the

[11] See Lincoln, *Ephesians*, pp. 448–449; and Stott, *Ephesians*, p. 280. See also Rom. 10:15.

Spirit wherever we find ourselves may be styled 'The Pauline Great Commission'.[12]

Satan has been in the business of deception since the Garden of Eden (John 8:44). His lies run deep in human cultures, creating social evil and injustice. The lie that this world is all there is and that fulfilment is found through material possessions, for example, is foundational to the economism and consumerism that create social injustice. It is the gospel that liberates people from these lies and enables them to live justly. Just as lying is Satan's basic *modus operandi*, so gospel proclamation is the *modus operandi* of spiritual warfare, for it is through the proclamation of the truth that we undermine Satan's lies.

In 2 Corinthians 4 Paul says that people reject the gospel because 'The god of this age has blinded the minds of unbelievers, so that they cannot see the light of the gospel of the glory of Christ, who is the image of God' (2 Cor. 4:4). Spiritual warfare is to do battle with *the god of this age* who blinds people to the glory of Christ. But only God can open blind eyes, which he does through an act equivalent to the first act of creation. Just as God said, 'Let light shine out of darkness,' so he makes 'his light shine in our hearts to give us the light of the knowledge of the glory of God in the face of Christ' (2 Cor. 4:6). The word we proclaim is called *the sword of the Spirit* because the Spirit of God 'gives it its effectiveness, its cutting edge'.[13] Since it is God who opens blind eyes, we do not use deception (2 Cor. 4:2). Instead our role is to proclaim Christ *plainly* (2 Cor. 4:2, 5), and, as we do so, to pray that God will open people's eyes. Conversion is God's work, and so proclamation and prayer must go hand in hand:

> Unless the LORD builds the house,
> its builders labour in vain.
>
> (Ps. 127:1)

c. Spiritual warfare is to pray

In the Greek, verses 14–20 are all one sentence, so that the imagery of the armour is tied together with Paul's request for prayer. The call to prayer is further linked to the armour by the reference to the role of the Spirit in both activities (17, 18). To pray is part of what it means to engage in spiritual warfare. The essence of verses 14–20 is:

[12] O'Brien, *Gospel and Mission*, p. 125.
[13] Lincoln, *Ephesians*, p. 451.

put on the armour and pray. We are to pray *at all times ... with all prayer and supplication ... with all perseverance ... for all the saints* (18 ESV). This fourfold emphasis on *all* suggests that prayer is to be woven into the fabric of life. We are never out of the battle and so we should never be long without prayer. 'Most Christians', suggests Stott, 'pray sometimes, with some prayers and some degree of perseverance, for some of God's people. But to replace "some" by "all" in each of these expressions would be to introduce us to a new dimension of prayer.'[14] P. T. Forsyth puts it this way: 'The note of prayer becomes the habit of the heart, the tone and tension of its new nature; in such a way that when we are released from the grasp of our occupations the soul rebounds to its true bent, quest, and even pleasure upon God. It is the soul's habitual appetite and habitual food.'[15]

This requires us to *be alert* (18) (see Mark 14:34–38). It is part of Satan's strategy to keep us from prayer, and so we need consciously to remind ourselves and one another to make prayer a priority. 'The greatest thing any one can do for God and for man is to pray ... There are people that put prayer first, and group the other items in life's schedule around and after prayer.'[16] People always find time for what they consider to be important. When people have no time for prayer it is not because they have no time, but because they have not made prayer a priority. Andrew Murray quotes a Dutch proverb to the same end: 'What is heaviest must weigh heaviest.'[17] When we complain that we do not have time to pray in the morning or to come to a church prayer meeting it is not because we have less time than people who do. There are twenty-four hours in their day just as there are in ours. It is rather that we have made choices about our priorities that make it difficult for us to give time to prayer. But those choices can be remade. A concert violinist was once asked the secret of her skill, to which she replied 'planned neglect'. She had found that if she did all the things that needed doing she never had time to practice. Now she started with violin practice even if that meant the neglect of other things. The problem is never lack of time – it is competing priorities.

Paul tells the Ephesians to pray *for all the saints, and also for me* (18–19 ESV – there is no new sentence as there is in the NIV). What we are to pray for one another is informed by what Paul requests for himself: that he, and we, may proclaim the gospel boldly. Paul is in a spiritual battle and he wants the Ephesians to join him in it through

---

14 Stott, *Ephesians*, pp. 283–284.
15 Forsyth, *Soul of Prayer*, p. 60.
16 S. D. Gordon, *Quiet Talks*, p. 7.
17 A. Murray, *Ministry of Intercession*, p. 14.

their prayers. Twice he asks that he may declare the gospel *fearlessly* (19, 20), the word (*parrēsia*) used for freedom of speech.[18] Sitting in prison Paul longs for freedom, but 'not freedom from confinement, but freedom to preach the gospel'.[19] He describes himself as *an ambassador in chains* (20). On festive occasions officials wore decorative chains 'to reveal the riches, power and dignity of the government they represent'.[20] Paul, however, is a representative of the crucified King and his chains are of a different sort. Despite this, his desire is that he might *declare [the gospel] fearlessly, as I should* (20). Spiritual warfare is to proclaim *and* to pray for proclamation.

4. Conclusion

Spiritual warfare is not about naming territorial spirits, claiming ground or binding demons. It is all about the gospel. It is to live a gospel life, to preserve gospel unity and to proclaim gospel truth. It is to do this in the face of a hostile world, a deceptive enemy and our own sinful natures. And it is to pray to a sovereign God for gospel opportunities. Advance comes through godliness, unity, proclamation and prayer.

---

[18] Lincoln, *Ephesians*, p. 454.
[19] Stott, *Ephesians*, p. 285.
[20] M. Barth, *Ephesians*, vol. 2, p. 782.

Mark 15
15. Praying when God is silent

Responding to the death of his wife from cancer, C. S. Lewis expresses forcefully an experience common to many – the silence of God.

> Meanwhile, where is God? This is one of the most disquieting symptoms. When you are happy, so happy that you have no sense of needing Him, so happy that you are tempted to feel His claims upon you as an interruption, if you remember yourself and turn to Him in gratitude and praise, you will be – or so it feels – welcomed with open arms. But go to Him when your need is desperate, when all other help is vain, and what do you find? A door slammed in your face, a sound of bolting and double bolting on the inside. After that, silence. You may as well turn away. The longer you wait, the more emphatic the silence will become. There are no lights in the windows. It might be an empty house. Was it ever inhabited? It seemed so once. And that seeming was as strong as this. What can this mean? Why is He so present a commander in our time of prosperity and so very absent a help in time of trouble?[1]

The question of why God does not answer prayer is often not simply an intellectual inquiry, but a question born of personal pain and frustration. There are times when it seems we address only a void.

The problem of unanswered prayer is experienced most acutely when those prayers arise from suffering. It is part of the wider issue of theodicy – how we reconcile the love and power of God with the

[1] Lewis, *Grief Observed*, pp. 7–8.

reality of suffering. Hearing only the silence of God, we feel forsaken by him.

In *The Brothers Karamazov*, by the nineteenth-century Russian novelist Fyodor Dostoyevsky, Ivan Karamazov describes to his pious brother, Alyosha, a series of stories he has collected about the suffering of children. In one story a five-year-old child is tortured by her parents. When she wets the bed she is locked in the outside privy all night and forced to eat her own excrement, while her tears to 'dear, kind God' go unheeded. Ivan comments:

> Do you realize what it means when a little creature like that, who's quite unable to understand what is happening to her, beats her little aching chest in that vile place, in the dark and cold, with her tiny fist and weeps searing, unresentful and gentle tears to 'dear, kind God' to protect her? Can you understand all this absurd and horrible business, my friend and brother, you meek and humble novice? ... They tell me that without it man could not ever have existed on earth, for he would not have known good and evil. But why must we know that confounded good and evil when it costs so much? Why, the whole world of knowledge isn't worth that child's tears to her 'dear and kind God'.[2]

Even if it could be shown that such suffering serves a higher purpose, Ivan argues, it would be a price too high to pay. Even if at the end of history it is shown that suffering has led to eternal harmony Ivan will not accept it. He collects these stories to prepare himself for that day – so that he will not get carried away by the moment and fail to protest.

> I understand, of course, what a cataclysm of the universe it will be when everything in heaven and on earth blends in one hymn of praise and everything that lives and has lived cries aloud: 'Thou art just, O Lord, for thy ways are revealed!' ... But there's the rub: for it is that I cannot accept ... While there's still time, I make haste to arm myself against it, and that is why I renounce higher harmony altogether. It is not worth one little tear of that tortured little girl who beat herself on the breast and prayed to her 'dear, kind Lord' in the stinking privy with her unexpiated tears! ... Too high a price has been placed on harmony. We cannot afford to pay so much for admission. And therefore I hasten to return my ticket of admission ...

[2] Dostoyevsky, *Brothers Karamazov*, p. 283.

Tell me frankly, I appeal to you – answer me: imagine that it is you yourself who are erecting the edifice of human destiny with the aim of making men happy in the end, of giving them peace and contentment at last, but that to do that it is absolutely necessary, and indeed quite inevitable, to torture to death only one tiny creature, the little girl who beat her breast with her little fist, and to found the edifice on her unavenged tears – would you consent to be the architect on those conditions? Tell me and do not lie!

'No, I wouldn't,' Alyosha said softly.[3]

Ivan Karamazov's argument is an argument against any theodicy that justifies suffering as a price worth paying. The price is too high. This includes both attempts to explain suffering as the result of human free will or as that which is necessary for human maturity. The question of suffering eludes our neat explanations and theories. They work in the classroom, but shatter too easily when on our knees we hear only the echo of our own voice. The question remains.

Job cries out to God for an answer to the question of his suffering. Job's friends explain suffering by arguing that there is always a direct link between suffering and specific sin (Job 4:7–8; 22:4–11), but this perspective is rejected by God (Job 42:7). For the purposes of the book, Job is innocent (Job 1:8). Elihu argues that the purpose of suffering is not retribution but education (Job 33:13–17). But whatever truth there may be in this it does not satisfy Job. Elihu says God is too great and too distant to bother with Job's complaint (Job 35:4–9, 13–14). But God does meet with Job. Job has been demanding answers from God and God does respond. However, he does not come to answer Job, but to question him:

> Who is this that darkens my counsel
>   with words without knowledge?
> Brace yourself like a man;
>   I will question you,
>   and you shall answer me.
>
> (38:2–3)

God's rhetorical questions highlight the fact that Job did not make the world, nor does he govern it. Furthermore, Job has no idea what 'behemoth' and 'leviathan' are for. Behemoth may be a hippopotamus, leading David Clines to say that the message of Job is that

---

[3] Ibid., pp. 286–288.

'suffering is a hippopotamus'.[4] The only sense a hippo makes, it makes to God. The purpose of its existence is not known to human beings. It is not *for* human beings. We cannot domesticate it. And the moral order is like the natural order. In both are things incomprehensible to us, even threatening, but which are nevertheless the work of a wise God and which fulfil his purposes. What Job must realize is that God is inscrutable. The important thing is knowing God. Job does not receive answers to his questions but he does receive a new experience of God. When asked for a theoretical theodicy, God does not give one. Instead God calls on us to trust him. The quote of C. S. Lewis with which I started this chapter is from his book *A Grief Observed*. Towards the end of the book Lewis writes:

> When I lay these questions before God I get no answer. But a rather special sort of 'No answer'. It is not the locked door. It is more like a silent, certainly not uncompassionate, gaze. As though He shook His head not in refusal but waiving the question. Like, 'Peace, child; you don't understand.' Can a mortal ask questions which God finds unanswerable? Quite easily, I should think. All nonsense questions are unanswerable. How many hours are there in a mile? Is yellow square or round? Probably half the questions we ask – half our great theological and metaphysical problems – are like that.[5]

But this does not mean the Bible offers us only blind trust in omnipotence. Henri Blocher says that theories that offer an explanation of evil 'run into the Rock of Divine Revelation and so capsize'.[6] Blocher says that three great truths are consistently affirmed in Scripture: (1) The evil of evil – we cannot justify evil and suffering; (2) the lordship of the Lord – God even wills acts of sin and evil; and (3) the goodness of God and his works. Most theodicies, says Blocher, sacrifice one of these truths. What brings them together is the cross. On the cross the evilness of evil is demonstrated. On the cross the complete sovereignty of God is demonstrated (see e.g. Acts 4:28). And on the cross the unadulterated goodness of God is demonstrated. 'No reason of man can justify God in a world like this,' says P. T. Forsyth. 'He must justify Himself, and He did so in the Cross of His Son.'[7]

---

[4] Clines, *Job 1 – 20*, p. xlvi.
[5] Lewis, *Grief Observed*, pp. 58–59.
[6] Blocher, *Evil and the Cross*, p. 84.
[7] P. T. Forsyth, cited in Surin, *Problem of Evil*, p. 133.

1. Forsaken by God, Jesus reveals God to us

Throughout his Gospel, Mark has portrayed Jesus as the rejected and suffering Messiah. In his last hours all of this opposition comes to a climax as he is betrayed, condemned, disowned, mocked, tortured and crucified. The cross is the climax of our rejection of God. When God is among us we drive him from the world on to the cross. From the Garden of Eden onwards we have rejected the rule of God. And now he sends his own son and we say, 'Come, let's kill him, and the inheritance will be ours' (12:7). When we get the chance we murder our Creator.

But then Mark takes the story to another level altogether: *And at the ninth hour Jesus cried out in a loud voice, 'Eloi, Eloi, lama sabachthani?' – which means, 'My God, my God, why have you forsaken me?'* (15:34). Here is a person crying out to God in the hour of need and receiving no answer. The prayer is unheeded. God is absent. But this prayer comes from the lips of Jesus. This is God – God present in the godforsaken one. We shall never grasp the full meaning of these words. Some have attempted to soften their offence, suggesting that Jesus was recalling the whole of Psalm 22, from which he quotes, and therefore implying its more affirmative ending. But, as C. E. B. Cranfield suggests, 'The burden of the world's sin, his complete self-identification with sinners, involved not merely a felt, but a real, abandonment by his Father.'[8] There cannot be a more desolate, poignant and terrible moment in all of history and eternity. At this point Jesus is forsaken by God. The horror from which he recoiled in Gethsemane is experienced in full (14:33–36). He is abandoned by his Father to death. In every other recorded prayer of Jesus, he calls God 'Father' – this is the only exception.

Welling up from his lifetime of biblically based prayer there came, as though by a reflex, a cry not of rebellion, but of despair and sorrow, yet still a despair that, having lost contact with God, still asks God why this should be. The son, rejected by the tenants, looks in vain for this father and asks why. The question of Job – why do the innocent suffer? – mingles with the question not only of the psalmists but of millions in the ancient and the modern world, and becomes the question ... that God himself uses when forsaken by God, that God the Son uses when forsaken, unthinkably, by God the Father. Unless we wrestle with this question we not only cut ourselves off from

[8] Cranfield, *Mark*, p. 458; see also Hooker, *St Mark*, p. 376; *Message of Mark*, p. 102; and Lane, *Mark*, pp. 572–573.

understanding the central Christian mystery and glory; we trivialize the gospel which meets the world at its point of deepest need.[9]

All the cries of those who feel forsaken by God, the cries of those who rail in anger against God, find an echo in Jesus' words. And yet this is God. God forsaken by God. God questioning God. God himself experiences the full effects of human sinfulness. And there is no reply, no voice saying, *You are my beloved son* (1:11 ESV). No dove descending. No explanation. At his baptism the heavens were *torn open* (1:10), but now heaven is shut up to Jesus. Jesus experiences the full extent of godforsakenness.

Father and Son united in perfect love throughout all eternity are torn apart on the cross. The Father loses his own Son, his only Son, his beloved Son. The Father directs his wrath against that which he loves the most. And the Son dies in agony, abandoned by his Father, further from God than anyone has ever been. In every sense this is a moment of utter darkness: *At the sixth hour darkness came over the whole land until the ninth hour* (33). The darkness of the land mirrors the darkness of heaven. The light is snuffed out. Father and Son are torn apart. *With a loud cry, Jesus breathed his last* (37). In the other Gospels this is a cry of triumph: 'It is finished!' But in Mark it is just a loud cry – a last cry. Jesus dies – forsaken by mankind and forsaken by God. He is alone and abandoned.

And then in verse 39 we read, *And when the centurion, who stood there in front of Jesus, heard his cry and saw how he died, he said, 'Surely this man was the Son of God!'* This is an extraordinary statement. What is it that the centurion hears? He hears Jesus cry, *My God, why have you forsaken me?* What does he see? He sees Jesus suffering alone and forsaken. He sees Jesus die in shame and he says, *Surely this man was the Son of God.* How much the centurion himself understood of what was happening we cannot be sure, but 'for Mark they are a proclamation of the truth about Jesus'.[10] What has been confessed from heaven (1:11) is now confessed on earth and Mark 'invites his readers to make his words their own'.[11] At the moment at which God is most absent, we see the presence of the living God. It is so extraordinary. This godforsaken moment is the very point at which the centurion recognizes God – God is revealed by the absence of God.

Yet this is the climax of Mark's Gospel. This is where Mark's message has been heading all along. This verse is the key verse for

[9] N. T. Wright, *Mark*, p. 217.
[10] Hooker, *St Mark*, p. 378.
[11] Ferguson, *Mark*, p. 264.

Mark's overall message. The opening verse of Mark's Gospel sets out the structure of the book: *The beginning of the gospel about Jesus Christ, the Son of God* (1:1). Mark's story is the account of how Jesus is the Christ and the Son of God. The confession by Peter that Jesus is Christ in 8:29 is the climax of the first part of the Gospel. This confession by the centurion – a Gentile at that – is the climax of the Gospel as a whole. This final declaration, which ties the gospel together, is the punchline – the Christ of God is the Christ who suffers and dies.

Throughout Mark there is a theme of seeing. In chapter 4 we read:

He told them, 'The secret of the kingdom of God has been given to you. But to those on the outside everything is said in parables so that,

> "they may be ever seeing but never perceiving,
> and ever hearing but never understanding;
> otherwise they might turn and be forgiven!" '
>
> (4:11–12)

In chapter 8 Jesus says, 'Why are you talking about having no bread? Do you still not see or understand? Are your hearts hardened?' (8:17). He then heals a blind man at Bethsaida – showing that when the disciples 'see' and 'recognize' that he is the Christ in 8:27–30 it is through the work of God. At this point Jesus begins to teach them that the Christ must suffer and die (8:31). But like the blind man at Bethsaida, who at first does not see properly (8:24), the disciples do not see properly what kind of a Christ Jesus is – one who will suffer and die (8:32–33).

In verses 29–32 and 35–36 the bystanders expect the sign of the Christ to be that he will come down from the cross. Even at the last they do not understand what sort of a Christ the Christ of God is to be. Jesus is the Christ, but for Jesus this means dying. They say, *Let this Christ, this King of Israel, come down now from the cross, that we may see and believe.* They want to *see* something that will make them believe. But they are blind. They think the Christ will be revealed if he comes down from the cross. But it is by staying *on* the cross that Jesus reveals God. It is as the centurion *saw how he died* that he recognizes in Jesus the Son of God. This is the centrepiece of God's revelation of himself. The heart of God's revelation is a man dying on a cross. It is not the firestorm of Sinai, nor a glimpse of glory from inside a rock, nor the fire on Mount Carmel, nor Isaiah's vision of the throne, nor even the glory of Jesus on the mountain (9:2–8). It is a man crying out, *My God, my God, why have you forsaken me?* In his poem 'Jesus of the scars', written after the First World War, Edward Shillito writes:

> The other gods were strong; but thou wast weak;
> They rode, but thou didst stumble to a throne;
> But to our wounds only God's wounds can speak,
> And not a god has wounds, but thou alone.[12]

The theologian who is most noted for applying the cross to our knowledge of God is Martin Luther. In his contribution to *The Heidelberg Disputation* (1518),[13] Luther addresses the question of how we can know God. There are some visible things mankind could look at: creation, spiritual experiences, miracles. But Luther says they do not reveal God, or rather they reveal something of God, but it is the kind of knowledge that puffs us up. People like this think they have knowledge, but are fools.

Is God, then, unknowable? If he cannot be known through what is visible, how can he be known at all? Luther's answer is that God is known through what is *contrary*. He is *absconditus Deus* – the hidden God. God is revealed in suffering and the cross: glory in shame; wisdom in folly; power in weakness; victory in defeat. God is known through the message of the cross. 'It could never be enough for a man, nor could it benefit him, to know God in his glory and majesty unless he knows him at the same time in the humility and shame of the cross. In this way he destroys the wisdom of the wise and brings to nought the understanding of the prudent. As Isaiah says, "Verily thou art a hidden God" (Isaiah 45:15).'[14]

What Luther calls 'the theology of the cross' stems from his understanding of righteousness and justification. Luther's great realization was that God justified sinners. God declares to be just those who are unjust. Luther realized that if that were so, human notions of justice could never lead us to understand God's justice. God's justice is revealed in the opposite of justice: in the justification of sinners.

God determined to be known through suffering so that he would be hidden from all those who exalt themselves. Only someone who has had 'all the spirit [taken] out of him and [been] broken' can know God. It is not just that God can be known through suffering, but that God uses suffering to make himself known. For Luther this encompasses both the sufferings of Christ, but also the sufferings of

[12] Cited in Carson, *John*, p. 647.
[13] Luther, *Early Theological Works*, pp. 274–307.
[14] Martin Luther, *The Heidelberg Disputation*, Thesis 20, in *Early Theological Works*, p. 291.

the individual. God humiliates us so that we might know him. Luther talks about God's alien work (*opus alienum*) – his actions which are alien to his nature, but by which he achieves his proper work (*opus proprium*). God assaults us in order to break us so that suffering is a 'precious treasure'.

What Luther calls 'theologians of glory' pursue wisdom, experience and miracles and they say that suffering is bad. But the 'theologian of the cross' values suffering as that through which God is revealed. We want God to answer our prayers through powerful interventions, but in the cross we recognize by faith the presence of God in weakness. By faith we recognize in the cross the presence of the God who has hidden himself from the proud. The silence remains silent, but we see in the cross the hidden God who is with us in our suffering. John Stott writes:

> I could never myself believe in God, if it were not for the cross. The only God I believe in is the One Nietzsche ridiculed as 'God on the cross'. In the real world of pain, how could one worship a God who was immune to it? I have entered many Buddhist temples in different Asian countries and stood respectfully before the statue of the Buddha, his legs crossed, arms folded, eyes closed, the ghost of a smile playing round his mouth, a remote look on his face, detached from the agonies of the world. But each time after a while I have had to turn away. And in imagination I have turned instead to that lonely, twisted, tortured figure on the cross, nails through hands and feet, back lacerated, limbs wrenched, brow bleeding from thorn-pricks, mouth dry and intolerably thirsty, plunged in God-forsaken darkness. That is the God for me! He laid aside his immunity to pain. He entered our world of flesh and blood, tears and death. He suffered for us. Our sufferings become more manageable in the light of this. There is still a question mark against human suffering, but over it we boldly stamp another mark, the cross which symbolizes divine suffering.[15]

2. Forsaken by God, Jesus unites us to God

On the cross Jesus participates in a universal experience of god-forsakenness. We live in a godforsaken world that bears the mark of Good Friday still. But Jesus' sufferings are also unique. He experienced our godforsakenness *on our behalf*. He experiences the judgment of God and the absence of God that should be ours

[15] John Stott, *The Cross of Christ* in *The Essential John Stott* (IVP, 1999), p. 312.

240

in order to unite us to God. As Jesus is divided from his Father, he reconciles us to God. *With a loud cry, Jesus breathed his last. The curtain of the temple was torn in two from top to bottom* (37–38).

The temple was one great lesson in the inaccessibility of God. Its purpose was to demonstrate that God was so holy and so glorious that we could not come to him. There was a court of women and Gentiles beyond which they could go. Then a court beyond which the men could not go. Then an area in which only the priests were allowed. Beyond that, behind a great curtain, was the Holy of Holies – the ultimate symbol of God's presence. Only the High Priest could enter the Holy of Holies; he could do so only once a year and only through the shedding of sacrificial blood (Heb. 9:7). Even then he entered with terror, for God is holy and glorious. God dwells in unapproachable light and is a consuming fire.

But as Christ makes his last cry, the curtain is torn from top to bottom. It was a thick curtain – too thick to tear by hand. And it is torn from the top. Both symbolically and literally, this is an act of God. The God who is inaccessible is suddenly accessible. God who is a consuming fire is now knowable, welcoming and accepting. The way to God is open. According to the writer to the Hebrews the temple was only a shadow of the real thing (Heb. 9:1–10). Jesus entered 'the greater and more perfect tabernacle' (Heb. 9:11). He did not enter something that symbolized the presence of God – he entered the very presence of God. He did not enter through the blood of sacrificed animals – he entered through his own blood shed on the cross: 'through the eternal Spirit [he] offered himself unblemished to God'. His blood can 'cleanse our consciences from acts that lead to death, so that we may serve the living God' (Heb. 9:14).

At the very point at which our hatred and rebellion reaches its climax, God flings open his arms to embrace us in his love. At the point at which Jesus is left abandoned and alone, he makes us family. Forsaken by God, Jesus unites us to God. Jesus bears the judgment we deserve. He absorbs the holy wrath of God. His blood cleanses us. Through Jesus the way to God is open as the curtain is torn in two. We can know God and be near him.

There is a terrible ironic clue to what is going on in the mockery of 15:31. *In the same way the chief priests and the teachers of the law mocked him among themselves. 'He saved others,' they said, 'but he can't save himself!'* What they did not realize was that Jesus does indeed save others, but he does so by *refusing* to save himself. *His* death is *our* life and our salvation. *His* forsakenness by God makes possible *our* acceptance by God.

The One who experienced the full extent of godforsakenness has risen. Mark highlights the fact that it is the crucified One who was risen (16:6). The absence of God is not the last word. The silence of prayer will be broken. Christ has risen as the first fruits of a new age in which suffering will be overcome and God will be among his people.

In the meantime this world still bears the mark of Good Friday. Mark ends his Gospel with people who are 'trembling and bewildered' (16:8). The experience of godforsakenness remains a reality in our world. We do feel sometimes that our prayers are unheard. The resurrection functions as a promise to which we cling in the silence. 'Trembling and bewildered' we trust God and believe his promise. But we must not suppress this experience. David Smith warns us, 'Vast tracts of biblical witness in which people of God pour out their hearts in lament because of the hiddenness of God are rendered obsolete by the optimistic revivalism of much contemporary evangelicalism. We need prayer for these times ... There is a triumphalism that says the only experience of the church is success. And then you have to invent success.'[16]

In the book of Revelation the prayers of the saints are pictured as incense rising up to God, just as incense had been offered up in the temple (Exod. 30:7–9; Ps. 141:2). They are first mentioned in Revelation 5 in which the reign of the Lamb is represented in his authority to open the scroll of history. 'The four living creatures and the twenty-four elders fell down before the Lamb. Each one had a harp and they were holding golden bowls full of incense, which are the prayers of the saints' (Rev. 5:8). God holds the scroll – the record of his purposes in salvation and judgment. And who can unlock it? Only the Lamb who was slain. But in the midst of this picture of God's sovereignty and Christ's authority we read of bowls of incense, which are the prayers of the saints. Before the throne of history and in the presence of the One who unlocks the purposes of God are our prayers. Our prayers are integrated into the reign of the Lamb over history.

The prayers of the saints reappear in the narrative in Revelation 8. Revelation has three 'sevens' of judgment: seven seals, seven trumpets and seven bowls. Revelation 8:1–5 is the climax of the seven seals and at this moment of climax our prayers are again integral. God consummates the kingdom of the Lamb, the judgment of the wicked and the vindication of his people in response to the prayers of all the saints. The prayers stored, as it were, in the bowls of incense in 5:8 are now offered to God. The time has come for

---

[16] David Smith, Tyndale Fellowship Conference 2000.

their fulfilment. 'For what all the people of God have for so long asked in their prayers is now at last to be done. The prayer for the coming of the kingdom will now, at the opening of the seventh seal, be answered. Here, in fact, we can see the key significance that the prayers of the saints are given in Revelation's portrayal of the outworking of God's purpose for the world.'[17]

More of our prayers than we realize will find their fulfilment in the consummation of history. Prayers we think of as directed to the present are in fact being stored up to be answered on the final day. When we pray for those suffering ill health we are expressing our longing for the day when there will be no more sickness (Rev. 21:4). When we pray for God to end wars and oppression we are expressing our longing for the day when the kingdoms of this world will become the kingdom of our God and of his Christ (Rev. 11:15). When we pray for mercy on those suffering natural disasters we are expressing our longing for the day when creation itself will be remade (Rev. 21:1). The prayers of the persecuted will be answered on the day when God vindicates his people (Rev. 16:5–6). The prayers we think have gone unanswered may in fact be stored up in the bowls of incense held by the twenty-four elders, waiting for a greater fulfilment than ever we anticipated. On the day the seventh seal is opened God will answer them in the consummation of history. Many of your prayers are lodged there and one day they will determine the ultimate course of history.

The Jewish writer Elie Wiesel describes the following incident from his time in Auschwitz:

> One day when we came back from work, we saw three gallows rearing up in the assembly place, three black crows. Roll call. SS all round us, machine guns trained: the traditional ceremony. Three victims in chains – one of them, the little servant, the sad-eyed angel ... All eyes were on the child. He was lividly pale, almost calm, biting his lips. The gallows threw its shadow over him ... The three victims mounted together onto the chairs.
>
> The three necks were placed at the same moment within the nooses.
>
> 'Long live liberty!' cried the two adults.
>
> But the child was silent.
>
> 'Where is God? Where is He?' someone behind me asked.
>
> At a sign from the head of the camp, the three chairs tipped over ...

[17] Bauckham, 'Prayer in the Book of Revelation', p. 257.

Then the march past began. The two adults were no longer alive. Their tongues hung swollen, blue-tinged. But the third rope was still moving; being so light, the child was still alive ...

For more than half an hour he stayed there, struggling between life and death, dying in slow agony under our eyes. And we had to look him full in the face. He was still alive when I passed in front of him. His tongue was still red, his eyes were not yet glazed.

Behind me, I heard the same man asking:

'Where is God now?'

And I heard a voice within me answer him:

'Where is He? Here He is – He is hanging here on this gallows ...'[18]

For Wiesel the hanging of God upon the gallows of the child represents the death of his faith. He can longer believe in God, so that it is as if God is now dead. The message of the cross is that the experience of godforsakenness is real. 'God lets himself be pushed out of the world onto the cross,' said Bonhoeffer.[19] 'God is dead,' said Friedrich Nietzsche. For Nietzsche this meant that mankind had outgrown its need for notions of a God. We must now choose to live, argues Nietzsche, without God. There is a sense in which the cross anticipates Nietzsche. The cross is the climax of mankind's decision to live without God. But the cross is not the end. The world was godless and godforsaken. God was dead. But on the third day he rose again. God has made the one we crucified both Lord and Christ (Acts 2:36). Suffering and silence and godforsakenness are not the last word.

3. Conclusion

In the midst of our problems, our hurts, in bereavement or pain, we cry out to God: Why me? Why Lord? Do you care? Why are you letting this happen? What reason is there in this? My God, why have you forsaken me? In the cross we find that these cries of confusion, pain and even rage are part of the story of Jesus. God himself identifies with the godforsaken. He places himself with sinners and feels the full effects of sin on the cross. This is the amazing thing: when we feel forsaken by God and cry out to him we echo the words of God himself. This does not mean the experience of godforsakenness is illusory, but that it has a counterpart in the

---

[18] Wiesel, *Night*, pp. 76–77.
[19] Bonhoeffer, *Letters and Papers from Prison*, p. 360.

experience of God himself. Forsaken by God, Jesus reveals the presence of God. Forsaken by God, Jesus reveals God in all his love, compassion and mercy. When we feel that God is absent we can at least say this: God himself has experienced this before us and in greater measure. Jürgen Moltmann says:

> Anyone who suffers without cause first thinks that he has been forsaken by God. God seems to him to be mysterious, incomprehensible God who destroys the good fortune that he gave. But anyone who cries out to God in this suffering echoes the death-cry of the dying Christ, the Son of God. In that case God is not just a hidden someone set over against him, to whom he cries, but in a profound sense the human God, who cries with him and intercedes for him with his cross where man in his torment is dumb.[20]

But we can say more. Forsaken by God, Jesus also unites us to God. In the midst of our darkness the way to God is open. In the midst of the mess that is life in this world the curtain is torn and God beckons us forward to his heaven. The 'answer' to unanswered prayer is the cross and the promise of a new creation. This is the peace that will guard our hearts even when our anxious requests go seemingly unheeded (Phil. 4:6–7).

The chapter from *The Brothers Karamazov* referred to above continues with Ivan saying:

> Alyosha said suddenly with flashing eyes, 'you said just now, is there a being in the whole world who could or had the right to forgive? But there is such a being, and he can forgive everything, everyone and everything and *for everything*, because he gave his innocent blood for all and for everything. You've forgotten him, but it is on him that the edifice is founded, and it is to him that they will cry aloud, 'Thou art just, O Lord, for thy ways are revealed!'[21]

[20] Moltmann, *Crucified God*, p. 252.
[21] Dostoyevsky, *Brothers Karamazov*, p. 288.

Ephesians 1
16. Praying in eternal perspective

If God knows all things, even the thoughts of our hearts, what do we hope to communicate in prayer? If God ordains all events as part of an eternal plan, what do we hope to achieve through prayer? If God is sovereign why pray at all? Peter Baelz poses the question like this:

> Suppose I were to ask my friends to pray for David Smith, who was undergoing an operation in a hospital at the other end of the land; or for Charles Brown, who was going out as a Christian missionary to Polynesia. What would they do? No doubt many of them would utter, aloud or to themselves, some such words as, 'God, help David Smith', or 'God, be with Charles Brown'. But what account of their actions would they give to an inquirer who asked them what, exactly, they thought they were doing? Were they informing an all-knowing God of their desires and needs? Were they persuading an unchanging God to change the course of nature and history? Were they prompting an all-loving God to an act of mercy and loving-kindness? Or if they said they were laying bare the depths of their own being to the pervasive love of God and in silent communion holding within this healing presence the one for whom they prayed, could this be anything more than a movement of the individual soul towards the divine, a flight of the alone to the Alone? When intercession is made, can God be said to *act*?[1]

Paul's prayer for the Ephesian believers in Ephesians 1:15–19 is set in the context of his great exposition of God's sovereignty in 1:3–14. God's purposes for Christians began before the foundation

[1] Baelz, *Prayer and Providence*, pp. 13–14.

of the earth (4) and will extend into the eternal future (14, 18). This is the context of Paul's prayer and this shapes its content.

Paul begins his prayer for the Ephesians with thankfulness: *For this reason, ever since I heard about your faith in the Lord Jesus and your love for all the saints, I have not stopped giving thanks for you, remembering you in my prayers* (15–16). The faith and love of the Ephesians prompt his prayer. He has just described their faith in verse 13. God has chosen those in Christ from before the creation of the world and is fulfilling his purpose in their lives according to his good pleasure (4, 11). The evidence of this is that when people hear the gospel they respond with faith: *you also were included in Christ when you heard the word of truth, the gospel of your salvation* (13). Paul has also spoken of their love – or at least of their unity in Christ. In verse 12 he speaks of the Jews – those *who were the first to hope in Christ* – and in verse 13 he says that his Gentile readers *also were included in Christ.* The unity of Jew and Gentile in the reconciled community of Christ is the central theme of the letter. Paul says this unity is for the praise of God's glory (12, 14). So Paul prays with thankfulness. Verse 15 begins, *For this reason.* This is the reason why Paul prays. He prays because God is fulfilling his purposes in the reconciled Ephesian community. He joins the praise of God's glory as he remembers how God has united Jew and Gentile in Christ. He praises God because he sees in this a foretaste of God's eternal plan for the cosmic unity that God will bring about in Christ (9–10).

1. Praying for knowledge of the sovereign God

In this prayer Paul prays for wisdom, revelation, knowledge and enlightenment, which come through the work of *the Spirit* within us (17–18). This is a prayer for knowledge and it begins with a request that the believers *may know [God] better* (17). The prayer follows, and reflects the language of, Paul's hymn to the sovereign love of God in 1:3–14. Paul prays for *wisdom and revelation* (17), which he has already defined as knowledge of God's sovereign will (8–9). Paul wants the Christians in Ephesus to appreciate the glorious, gracious sovereignty of God and to join the praise of God's electing love and eternal purposes.

a. God changes reality in response to prayer

Some people answer the question of the efficacy of prayer in the light of God's sovereignty by saying that prayer changes only us – it does not change the world. It creates a change within the heart of the praying person, but does not change reality. As I pray for peace I become a more peaceable person. Even some who would not articulate this as a theological position, in practice emphasize subjective change almost exclusively.

It is certainly true that prayer effects change in the praying person and that this is an important part of biblical prayer. Paul himself prays that the Ephesian believers may *know* [God] better ... be *enlightened* in order that [they] may *know* the hope to which God has called [them] ... and his *incomparably great power* (17–19). He is not praying for hope or power per se, but for a greater awareness of hope and power. Prayer involves bowing before the will of our heavenly Father who knows what is best. We pray with Christ, 'your will be done' (Matt. 26:42).

This is the truth of prayer, and it is an important truth; yet it is not the whole truth, for prayer does effect change in the world. God acts in response to our prayers. For example, he declares his intention to destroy the people of Israel, but refrains from doing so because of the prayers of Moses (Exod. 33:12–17; Num. 14:11–20). James suggests there are things God does not do because we do not pray: 'You do not have, because you do not ask God' (Jas. 4:2). Although Paul prays for changed hearts in Ephesians 1, it is a change in the hearts of other people. Paul is not just opening himself up to change through the process of prayer. He is asking God to effect change in the world beyond the praying person.

Indeed the Bible even speaks of God himself changing in response to prayer. Amos saw God preparing locusts and fire in judgment, but in response to Amos's prayer 'the LORD relented' (Amos 7:1–6). This language involves an element of accommodation to our limited understanding. Elsewhere the Bible says that God does not change his mind: 'He who is the Glory of Israel does not lie or change his mind; for he is not a man, that he should change his mind' (1 Sam. 15:29; see also Num 23:19). But in recognizing the anthropomorphic nature of this language we must not lose the meaning intended. God is open to the requests of his people. God responds to human activity (see Jer. 18:8; 26:3, 13, 19; Joel 2:13–14; Jonah 3:10; 4:2) – especially the prayers of his people.

The Puritan Thomas Goodwin in his book *The Return of Prayers* encourages Christians to look for answers to prayer. He says, 'when a man hath put up prayers to God, he is to rest assured, that God will in mercy answer his prayers; and to listen diligently, and observe how his prayers are answered'.[2] His book sets out how to discern God's answers to prayer. Goodwin laments those who fail

---

[2] Goodwin, *Return of Prayers*, p. 3.

to acknowledge that their prayers have been returned by God 'richly laden', because they do not recognize the sometimes unexpected ways in which God answers prayer.[3]

b. God is sovereign

Others make sense of the agency of human prayers by denying that God is sovereign or by suggesting that his sovereignty is limited. From within evangelicalism the so-called openness of God theology or open theism represents a revision of the classical doctrine of God's sovereignty along these lines. Clark Pinnock argues that God has limited his omnipotence to give his creatures genuine freedom. 'God is not viewed as being completely in control and exercising exhaustive sovereignty. Though no other power can match God's power, each has a degree of influence that it can exercise. The situation is pluralistic: there is no single and all-determining divine will that calls all the shots. God controls some things, but not everything.'[4] This involves risk: God can neither guarantee nor know the future since it is affected by our free decisions. 'God freely enters into give and take relations with us which are genuine and which entail risk-taking on his part ... According to open theism the future is partly settled and partly unsettled, partly determined and partly undetermined and, therefore, partly unknown even to God and it holds that God himself has a temporal aspect.'[5]

Prayer according to this view is ordered by God as an expression of human freedom in the sense that there are blessings that God will give only if people freely choose to pray.[6] Even outside open theism, we find statements of popular theology such as 'God has been hindered in His purposes by our lack of willingness. When we learn His purposes and make them our prayers we are giving Him the opportunity to act.'[7] Such language suggests that prayer is about giving God permission to act.

The Bible, however, suggests that God is completely sovereign:

> Many are the plans in a man's heart,
>   but it is the LORD's purpose that prevails.
>   (Prov. 19:21; see also Ps. 33:11)

[3] Ibid., p. xx.
[4] Pinnock, *Most Moved Mover*, p. 53.
[5] Ibid., pp. 5, 13.
[6] For a response to open theism see Bray, *Personal God*; Gray and Sinkinson, *Reconstructing Theology*; and Tiessen, *Providence and Prayer.*
[7] S. D. Gordon, *Quiet Talks*, p. 36.

Paul says God *works out everything in conformity with the purpose of his will* (11). Simon Gathercole points out that, while *his will* in this verse is (with Pinnock) defined as God's will for salvation in Christ (9–10), it is hard to avoid the claim that (contra Pinnock) God *works out everything* – that God causes all things to pass.[8] Markus Barth reminds us that the purpose of the passage is to demonstrate that 'this will was motivated by no factors outside God'[9] – it was determined *before the creation of the world* (4) solely because of *the riches of God's grace* (7; 2:4, 7) and *in accordance with his pleasure and will* (5, 9). He comments, 'not even human need or anxiety appears as motivation of God's work ... what determines the course of God's action is exclusively God's good pleasure to love us'.[10]

God is sovereign not only over the general course of history, but also over the human heart (Exod. 4:21; 9:12; 10:1; Deut. 2:30; Josh. 11:20; 1 Kgs. 8:58; 1 Chr. 29:18; Ps. 105:25):

> The king's heart is in the hand of the LORD;
>   he directs it like a watercourse wherever he pleases.
>
> (Prov. 21:1)

His grace is not dependent on human actions (Exod. 33:19; Rom. 9:9–21). God is portrayed as knowing the future not just in general terms but in quite specific terms (Job 14:5; Ps. 22:1, 6–8, 14–18; John 21:18–19). 'Before a word is on my tongue', says the psalmist, 'you know it completely, O LORD' (Ps. 139:4). He continues:

> All the days ordained for me
>   were written in your book
>   before one of them came to be.
>
> (Ps. 139:16)

Both Joseph and Daniel interpret dreams that provide a detailed picture of the future God has planned (Gen. 37:5–11; 40 – 41; Dan. 4; 7–12). This knowledge of the future makes God superior to other so-called gods (Is. 41:21–23; 43:9; 44:7; 45:21). As the Book of Common Prayer says, God's 'never-failing providence ordereth all things both in heaven and earth'.[11]

Indeed some prayers – such as the request that a particular person might be converted – make no sense if God is *not* sovereign over

[8] Gathercole, 'New Testament and Openness Theism', pp. 53–54.
[9] M. Barth, *Broken Wall*, p. 65.
[10] Ibid.
[11] Collect for the Eighth Sunday after Trinity, *Book of Common Prayer*.

human hearts. It is because the God to whom we pray *works out everything in conformity with the purpose of his will* (11) that our prayers have such potency. The irony of open theism is that, because God is not seen as fully sovereign, their treatment of prayer focuses not on objective change in the world but on the process of 'conversational love'[12] – a position similar to those who maintain God's sovereignty by limiting the efficacy of prayer to the praying person. We express our belief in God's sovereignty most when we pray in the expectation that he can intervene in human lives and human history to bring about the things for which we pray. Instead of thinking of God's sovereignty as that which impedes prayer we should think of it as the space in which prayer is efficacious.

c. The sovereignty of God and the efficacy of prayer

The Bible, then, claims both that God changes reality in response to our prayers and that he is sovereign. God is sovereign, but not in a way that compromises human responsibility; and we are responsible, but not in a way that compromises God's sovereignty (e.g. Gen 50:20; Acts 4:27–28). We are free and God is freer.

Beyond these explicit biblical affirmations we should move cautiously. Yet we can say that the claim that God changes reality in response to prayer need not be incompatible with his sovereignty if his response to prayer is part of his sovereign will. Just as when God sends rain he also sends clouds as the cause of that rain, when he ordains events he can also ordain prayers as the cause of those events. This is not a limit to his sovereignty, but the ultimate expression of it. God is able to achieve his will in response to our prayers. 'We do not pray in order to change the decree of divine providence,' writes Thomas Aquinas; 'rather we pray in order to acquire by petitionary prayer what God has determined would be obtained by our prayers.'[13] C. S. Lewis and P. T. Forsyth put it like this:

> If our prayers are granted at all they are granted from the foundation of the world ... If there is – as the very concept of prayer presupposes – an adaptation between the free actions of men in prayer and the course of events, this adaptation is from the beginning inherent in the great single creative act.[14]

[12] Pinnock and Brow, *Unbounded Love*, pp. 141–150; and Pinnock, *Most Moved Mover*, p. 46.
[13] Thomas Aquinas, *Summa theologiae* 2a2ae.
[14] Lewis, *Letters to Malcolm*, p. 69.

If our prayers reach or move Him it is because He first reached and moved us to pray ... The world was made by a freedom which not only left room for the kindred freedom of prayer, but which so ordered all things in its own interest that in their deepest depths they conspire to produce prayer ... Our prayer is the momentary function of the Eternal Son's communion and intercession with the Eternal Father ... Our prayer is more than the acceptance by us of God's will; it is its assertion in us ... Prayer is that will of God's making itself good ... So when God yields to prayer in the name of Christ, to the prayer of faith and love, He yields to Himself who inspired it.[15]

When we ask why we should pray, we should not neglect the obvious answer: because God tells us to pray. God offers us prayer as a possibility and commands us to pray because he is a relational God who purposes to have a relationship with his people. It is not that God receives new data through our prayers but that through our prayers information is clothed in love, making it communication. God has ordained that he will be affected by our loving communication to him. This is a mystery – if God's ways could be grasped by us, then he would be less than God. From eternity he has woven our prayers into the cause and effect of the universe. It is prayer that makes the difference between biblical predestination and fatalism. God wants us to pray because he does not want to move us around like chess pieces on a cosmic chessboard. He wants a relationship with us. Amazingly God wants our cooperation. As Emil Brunner says, 'Through God's self-communication man becomes a "labourer together with God" (1 Cor. 3:9) – a thought of such audacity that a man whose heart is rooted and grounded in the sovereignty of God as the foundation of all his faith scarcely dares to give it expression.'[16]

So in the light of God's sovereign will Paul prays. This means we cannot manipulate God in prayer. We cannot twist his arm by praying for a long time – God is sovereign and his will is unchanging. Yet God sovereignly chooses to use our passionate, persistent prayers as an appointed means by which things happen. In 2 Corinthians Paul writes, 'On him we have set our hope that he will continue to deliver us, as you help us by your prayers' (2 Cor. 1:10b–11a). What he says, literally, is 'as you cooperate on our behalf'. In prayer we cooperate with God in his great plans of

[15] Forsyth, *Soul of Prayer*, pp. 14, 57–58, 87.
[16] Brunner, *Dogmatics*, vol. 3, p. 334.

deliverance. Augustine said, 'Without God we cannot; without us he will not.'[17]

[Prayer] is a genuine and actual sharing in the universal lordship of God. The will of God is not to preserve and accompany and rule the world … in such a way that He is not affected and moved by it, that He does not allow Himself to converse with it … God wills to converse with the creature, and to allow Himself to be determined by it in this relationship. His sovereignty is so great that it embraces both the possibility, and, as it is exercised the actuality, that the creature can actively be present and co-operate in His over-ruling … Permitted by God, and indeed willed and created by Him, there is the freedom of the friends of God concerning whom He has determined that without abandoning the helm for one moment He will still allow Himself to be determined by them.[18]

2. Praying for knowledge of our hope

Having prayed for a better knowledge of the sovereign God, Paul then prays for knowledge of our hope: *I pray also that the eyes of your heart may be enlightened in order that you may know the hope to which he has called you, the riches of his glorious inheritance in the saints* (18). Why pray that someone will be more aware of their hope? Is this just escapism? Why does this matter?

Consider Helen. Helen has a long-term illness. She has prayed that God will cure her. Other Christians have said that God always heals those who ask with faith, and so now she cannot understand why God has not healed her. Is it because she does not have enough faith? Or is it that God does not love her? Maybe she is not a child of God at all. So not only does she have to cope with her physical problems; now she has a crisis of faith. But suppose you prayed that her eyes would be enlightened to know the hope to which she was called. Helen would realize that God does not put everything right in this life. She would realize, as Paul says, that 'our present sufferings are not worth comparing with the glory that will be revealed in us' (Rom. 8:18).

Consider Oliver. Oliver is trying to read his Bible and make sense of it. He has read about Abraham receiving a promise from God about the future. He has read about the Israelites waiting for the fulfilment of that promise. He has read about the prophets looking

[17] Cited in Bewes, *Talking about Prayer*, p. 43.
[18] K. Barth, *CD* III/3, p. 285.

ahead to a new day. He has read about Jesus proclaiming the coming of God's kingdom. Only when he understands Christian hope will he make sense of the Bible. Only when he sees how it is all moving towards a new humanity in a new creation will he see how it all fits together.

Consider Peter. Peter is a student. Leaving home, growing up and starting his studies have forced him to think hard about life for the first time. And what he sees is a crazy, mixed-up world – a world of suffering and pain, of frustration and disappointment. At best he might hope to get a good career – working hard, climbing the corporate ladder, but for what? What would it all add up to? Like the writer of Ecclesiastes he looks out on the world and concludes that all is meaningless. But what if you prayed that Peter would see beyond this material world? The final verse of Ecclesiastes says that one day *God will bring every deed into judgment* (Eccles. 12:14). One day God will bring meaning to this world, and realizing that would bring meaning to Peter's life.

Or consider Emma. Emma has been a Christian for a few years now. She knows all the right things: she reads her Bible most days and goes to church regularly. But pursuing her career, doing up her house, going out at the weekend – these are the things that are important to her. She lives for the things of this world. Suppose you prayed that her eyes might be enlightened in order that she might know the hope to which she was called. Suppose you prayed that she would value treasure in heaven above treasure on earth. Suppose she starting putting the kingdom of God first in her life instead of all the things the pagans run after (Luke 12:29–31). It would change her life, and not only her life, but the lives of many others as she become sold out in the service of God.

We had some friends who emigrated to Australia. During the months leading up to their move it dominated every aspect of their life. They could not ignore it as they made decisions. They could hardly go on living as if it were not happening. They had to be sure they were ready. The day is coming when we shall enjoy rest and blessing in God's presence forever. This should radically affect our plans, the use of our money and time, the way we face problems and so on. Yet we so easily forget our eternal hope. We get preoccupied with the trivia of our lives. Our eyes drop from the horizon and we lose sight of our glorious inheritance. So Paul prays that the eyes of their heart may be enlightened. He prays that they will know the hope to which they are called. We get preoccupied with the blessing of this world and so Paul prays that they will know the riches of God's glorious inheritance in the saints. Praying this for people could drastically change their lives!

Imagine you are on the threshold of eternity. Imagine you are a thousand, million, billion, trillion years into eternity – if indeed eternity can be counted in years. Now look at the requests on your typical prayer list. How important do they seem now? We should let the future return of Christ determine the priorities of our prayers.

Paul elaborates the awareness of hope for which he prays in two ways: in terms of a rich inheritance and great power. The ESV captures the structure of his thought well: *that you may know what is the hope to which he has called you,* [1] *what are the riches of his glorious inheritance in the saints, and* [2] *what is the immeasurable greatness of his power towards us who believe ...*

The thought here could be of the inheritance God has for us (as in 14), but it could also be that we are *his* inheritance. God brought Israel 'out of Egypt, to be the people of his inheritance' (Deut. 4:20; see also 9:26, 29; 2 Sam. 21:3; 1 Kgs. 8:51; Pss. 28:9; 33:12; 94:14; 106:5; Is. 19:25; 47:6; 63:17). Now Jew and Gentile have been united in Christ as God's inheritance. Together we are God's possession (14). Our hope is not just for heaven, but for God himself. His eternal purpose is to have a people who are his people (Rev. 21:3).

Power was a big thing in Ephesus, which was an occult centre. The Ephesians would have felt surrounded by alien powers. They would have felt weak and vulnerable. So Paul prays that they will realize the power we have as Christians: *I pray also that the eyes of your heart may be enlightened in order that you may know ... his incomparably great power for us who believe* (18–19). It is this power that makes our hope certain and it is this power that will keep us. We are those, in Peter's words, 'who through faith are shielded by God's power until the coming of the salvation that is ready to be revealed in the last time' (1 Pet. 1:5). And it is power beyond compare, for it is resurrection power: *That power is like the working of his mighty strength, which he exerted in Christ when he raised him from the dead and seated him at his right hand in the heavenly realms* (19–20). It is not just that the resurrection reveals the amazing extent of God's power, but that the resurrection was the first act of the power that will recreate the world. Christ's resurrection is the first fruits of our resurrection hope.

On Easter morning Jesus' body lay lifeless, just flesh, which would eventually have rotted into dust. But God reached down and wrenched Jesus from the grave. God did what he did at creation: he brought life when there was no life. Death is the one force that no person can escape and no person can overcome. But on that first Easter day God took on death and won. He overcame the power of death. And that same power is at work within us. We often feel like the Ephesians must have done – surrounded by alien powers with all sorts of social pressures to conform with the world's way of thinking, to keep quiet about our Christian beliefs, to fit in with what is going on. The power of the world seems so strong. But a much greater power is at work within us if we would only realize it.

As Paul describes this resurrection power he continues with another assertion of God's sovereignty. This sovereignty is not blind fatalism, nor is it an impersonal law or faceless force. This sovereignty has a face: the face of Jesus Christ. In verses 3–5 God's sovereignty is the loving choice of a Father. The sovereign One is the *Father* who has *adopted [us] as his sons through Jesus Christ* (3, 5). Now it is the rule of the Crucified One.

> *That power is like the working of his mighty strength, which he exerted in Christ when he raised him from the dead and seated him at his right hand in the heavenly realms, far above all rule and authority, power and dominion, and every title that can be given, not only in the present age but also in the one to come. And God placed all things under his feet and appointed him to be head over everything for the church, which is his body, the fulness of him who fills everything in every way.*
>
> (19–23)

Paul says that Christ now reigns over all things *for the church*. Verse 22 is literally *and gave him as head over all things to the church* (ESV). Christ is twice given to the church: first in his humiliation and second in his exaltation. The One on the throne of heaven is the Lamb who was slain (Rev. 5:6). 'O! it is excellent to have a giant's strength,' wrote William Shakespeare, 'but it is tyrannous to use it like a giant.'[19] But God's sovereignty is loving rather than tyrannous. The One who has all authority is the One who gave his life for us. The Puritan Elisha Coles said, 'Never look on the great attribute of sovereignty without your mediator.'[20] God has placed the crucified One *above* everything (21) and appointed him *head over everything* (22). And not only that, God has given him authority for a purpose. He has all authority for the church – for us! He has been given power so that he can care for us, nurture us, guide us and rescue us. Paul 'does not simply set Christ's rule and authority over the cosmos in parallel to his relation to the church but subordinates the former to the latter'.[21] All the powers arrayed against us – and Paul is at pains in verse 21 to emphasize that

---

[19] *Measure for Measure*, II.ii.107.
[20] Horn, *Puritan Remembrancer*, p. 176.
[21] Lincoln, *Ephesians*, p. 79.

it is *all* the powers – are subject now to Christ. This means that the small group of Christians in Ephesus are not just some new and insignificant cult but participants in the heavenly reign of God. Christ is *head over everything* but only the church is *his body* (22–23). Christ fills *everything in every way* (see Ps. 72:19; Is. 6:3; Jer. 23:23–24) but only the church is his *fulness* (23) (see Col. 2:9–10).

This is what God's sovereignty means: it means Jesus, the Crucified One, reigning from heaven on our behalf. This is our great incentive to pray, for we can participate in the reign of Christ through prayer: 'In [Christ] we are set at God's side and lifted up to Him and therefore to the place where decisions are made in the affairs of His government. And this is what takes place in ... Christian prayer ... We then find ourselves at the very seat of government, at the very heart of the mystery and purpose of all occurrence.'[22]

[22] K. Barth, *CD* III/3, p. 287.

Study guide

The aim of this study guide is to help you get to the heart of what Tim has written and challenge you to apply what you learn to your own life. The questions have been designed for use by individuals or by small groups of Christians meeting, perhaps for an hour or two each week, to study, discuss and pray together.

The guide provides material for each of the sections in the book. When used by a group with limited time, the leader should decide beforehand which questions are most appropriate for the group to discuss during the meeting and which should perhaps be left for group members to work through by themselves or in smaller groups during the week.

In order to be able to contribute fully and learn from the group meetings, each member of the group needs to read through the section or sections under discussion, together with the Bible passages to which they refer.

It's important not to let these studies become merely academic exercises. Guard against this by making time to think through and discuss how what you discover *works out in practice* for you. Make sure you begin and end each study by focusing on God in praise and prayer. Ask the Holy Spirit to speak to you through your discussion together.

PART 1. THE FOUNDATIONS OF PRAYER

Genesis 1 to Revelation 22
1. The conversation of friends (pp. 27–38)

1 'Prayer is that for which we were made' (p. 27). Is this how you see the reason for your existence?
2 What features in the creation story underline the importance of relationships?
3 How would you answer someone who suggested that God set about the work of creation because he was somehow incomplete without us?
4 What is 'the riddle of creation' (p. 29)? How does the answer to this shape our understanding of prayer?

'Creation is an act of grace in which God invites us to share the love of the trinitarian life' (p. 29).

5 In thinking about the effect of human sin, why is it important to stress that 'the root problem is not that mankind now shuns the presence of God, but that God excludes us from his presence' (p. 30)?

6 What is 'the foundation for the Bible's understanding of prayer' (p. 31)?

7 What differences are there between the way God's presence was experienced in Eden and from Sinai onwards? How is this significant?

8 What truth is underlined by the contrast between Psalms 48 and 137? Can you think of ways in which we mistake the signs of God's presence for the reality?

9 With the coming of Jesus, 'the signs of tabernacle and temple have given way to reality' (p. 35). How does the New Testament draw this out?

'All that the temple represented is now true of the community of believers. The church is the place where God dwells on earth' (pp. 35–36).

10 How does Jesus emphasize the invitation to friendship with God in what he says to his disciples?

11 'But even prayer is not the reality – not ultimately' (p. 38). Why not? What more is there?

Luke 11:1–13
2. Praying to the Father (pp. 39–49)

1 Where do the roots of calling God 'Father' lie? How does this help us to understand what the fatherhood of God means?

'... it is no cosy thing to call upon God as Father: it is a subversive act' (p. 41).

2 '... for the most part in the Bible the language of fatherhood is associated with salvation rather than creation' (p. 42). Why is this so important?

3 What is so significant about the fact that the Lord's Prayer begins '*Our* Father'?

4 On which one occasion is Jesus recorded as addressing God as *Abba*? How does this clarify its meaning for us?
5 Given that the Jews already thought of God as Father, what fresh perspective did Jesus bring to the subject?
6 How would you respond to someone who wanted to address God as 'Mother'? Why?
7 What truths about God and prayer does Jesus teach in Luke 11:5–13?

'[God] delights to answer our prayers and give us good things even if those good things are not always the good things we want or think we need' (p. 47).

---

8 How are we to explain the differences between Luke and Matthew at the end of this passage?
9 What is the 'heart of prayer'? Why is it so important to keep hold of this?
10 What attitude does the author now 'repent' of? What do you think about this?

Hebrews 4 – 5
3. Praying through the Son (pp. 50–61)

1 What is it about the 'radical simplicity of the gospel' that 'continues to trouble people'? How is this expressed in relation to prayer? How about you?
2 Why does our eternal High Priest have to be human? How do we know that Jesus genuinely fulfils this requirement?
3 What 'second condition for being a priest' (p. 53) does the writer to the Hebrews highlight? How does Jesus fulfil this?
4 Jesus was descended from the tribe of Judah – but priests have to be from the tribe of Levi. How is this problem overcome?
5 Why is Jesus a 'better' priest? What consequences of this fact does the writer draw out?

'Jesus saves completely. There is nothing we can do to jeopardize what he has done. There is no sin we can commit that will put us outside his salvation. His perfect sacrifice means every sin is covered' (p. 55).

---

6 What is so significant about the fact that Hebrews 4:16 comes in the wake of 4:12–13?

7 Do you feel confident in coming to God in prayer? What three reasons for confidence does the author highlight?

8 'The basis of prayer is the gospel' (p. 58). What practical implications of this truth can you think of?

9 What does it mean to pray 'in the name of Jesus' (p. 59)?

10 How might you be in danger of returning to 'paganism' (p. 59)?

'God does not hear our prayers because our motives are pure, but because of the blood of Jesus Christ' (p. 60).

Romans 8 and Jude
4. Praying by the Spirit (pp. 62–73)

1 What 'sad irony' (p. 62) does the author highlight? What do you feel about this?

2 Why is it significant that 'both men and women are adopted as "sons"' (p. 63)?

3 How does knowing that Paul 'uses the language of exodus' (p. 63) in Romans 8 help us to understand what he is saying?

4 'If some Christians err in basing their assurance of salvation on feelings alone, many others err in basing it on facts and arguments alone' (p. 64, quoting Moo). Which error do you tend to fall into? Why? How does what the author says help?

'The relationship between God and mankind only works because God is at work on both sides of the relationship: both to accept prayer and to inspire prayer' (p. 64).

---

5 'The Spirit of God has been given so that the routine is filled with God's presence' (p. 67). How does this affect the way you think about prayer?

6 How are we to reconcile God's promises of freedom from sin and death with our experience of these things?

7 What is 'wonderful and surprising' (p. 67) about the fact that the Spirit prays for us?

8 What does the author mean by 'justification by quiet times' (p. 68, quoting Bradshaw)? To what extent does this apply to you? What is the antidote to this way of thinking?

9 We do not necessarily know God's will for the situations we bring to him in prayer. Why doesn't this matter?

10 According to Jude, what does it mean to 'pray in the Spirit'? In what ways is this surprising?

James 1 and 5
5. Praying with faith (pp. 74–86)

1 What do you understand by 'the providence of God' (p. 74). What is its relationship to prayer?
2 What do we know of the background of James's first readers? How does James deal with this?
3 How can James encourage us to face trials with 'pure joy'? What experience have you had of this?
4 What is wisdom? What is its relationships with the trials of life?
5 'Faith is not convincing ourselves that God will necessarily relieve our problems in the present' (p. 79). Why not? What is it, then?

'Trials become temptations when we blame God rather than rejoicing in his good purposes for us' (p. 80).

---

6 How can bad things happen and an all-powerful God still be good?
7 How does the author interpret James 5:13–20? Do you agree? Why?
8 How does the story of Peter's release from prison in Acts 12 illustrate what the author has been saying in this chapter?

PART 2. THE PRACTICE OF PRAYER

Genesis 18 and 32
6. Praying with the Patriarchs (pp. 89–102)

1 In relation to their experience of prayer, in what ways are we so much better off than Abraham, Isaac and Jacob?
2 Why should we be 'wary of making Abraham's "prayer" a model for our own' (p. 90)? What value is there in studying it, then?
3 'Election is not about the moves of a cosmic chess master ...' (p. 91). What is it about? How is this relevant to prayer?
4 What do you think of 'prayer that takes the form of questioning God' (p. 93)? How does Abraham's story help?
5 Why and how should 'the nations be part of our daily prayer routine' (p. 95)?
6 In what way is Jacob's struggle with God in Genesis 32 'formative for all God's people' (p. 96)?

7 What 'dimension to our relationship with God that our sentimental age often misses' (p. 97) does this story reveal? Have you
found this to be true?

8 In what ways do you find prayer to be a struggle? To what
extent do you think prayer is *supposed* to be a struggle?

'*Who knows what problems we avoid because of our prayers – or
what problems are left when we do not pray!*' (p. 100).

Isaiah 37, Nehemiah 9 and Daniel 9
7. Praying with the Old Testament saints (pp. 103–119)

1 'The Bible invites us, as it were, to argue with God' (p. 103).
What do you make of this?

2 How does Hezekiah's story 'reassure us that God can fulfil his
promises' (p. 107)?

3 What is the 'key issue' (p. 107) in this story? How does this
apply to you?

'*There is no better way to pray for the glory of God than to pray
for mission*' (p. 108).

---

4 What significance is there in the fact that Nehemiah's prayer in
Nehemiah 9 is a story?

5 What arguments does the prayer use in inviting God to answer?
How does this apply to us today?

6 Turning to Daniel 9, if Daniel knew that God had promised to
do what he was praying for, why did he bother to pray at all?

7 How do the points Daniel makes in his prayer help us in ours
today?

8 What are 'the only arguments used by Bible prayers and the
only arguments we can use before God' (p. 114)?

9 In relation to God's Word, what 'important principle' (p. 115) is
set out here?

10 Do you find the discernment of God's will to be a 'mysterious
process' (p. 116)? Why is this not the case?

'*The promises of God are like moulds into which we pour our
prayers like liquid metal*' (p. 116).

---

11 Why does 'prayer as a conversation' (p. 116) often cause con-
    fusion and frustration? What expectations do you have in this
    area? How does what the author says about this help?
12 What is wrong with assuming that 'stating our needs is reason
    enough for God to answer' (p. 117)? What attitude should we
    adopt instead?
13 What should be 'the chief end of our prayers' (p. 119)? How can
    we put this into practice?

1 Samuel 1 – 2
8. Praying with Hannah (pp. 120–137)

1 Do you find the quotation from Richard Foster to be 'intimidat-
    ing' (p. 121)? What light does Hannah's experience shed on this?
2 In what way is Hannah's response to her situation 'a model of
    true piety' (p. 122)?

---

*'Prayer is not the quietening of the soul. It is an expression in faith
of the passions of the heart' (p. 123).*

---

3 Which do you lean towards – mystical prayer or prophetic/
    responsive prayer? What dangers are associated with the former
    approach?
4 What 'important note' (p. 125) is there for us to remember in
    Hannah's prayer as recorded in 1 Samuel 2? Why is this so
    important?
5 What is significant for us about the fact that Hannah 'is picking
    up the language of Moses' (p. 126)?
6 What is 'the key idea' (p. 129) in Hannah's song?

---

*'If we only sing of our happiness on earth we shall not have the
resources to cope in times of anguish' (p. 129).*

---

7 In what way is Hannah's story 'a picture of what is to come for
    all who trust in God' (p. 129)?
8 What would you say to someone who suggested this story
    teaches us that 'God will provide children to childless women
    who earnestly pray to him' (p. 131)? What does it teach us, then?
9 'The story of Hannah is a reminder that God works his purposes
    out through …' (p. 134). What is it that the author points out
    here?
10 What connections are there between Hannah and Mary the
    mother of Jesus?

'If we think we can prevail by our strength, then we shall pour our energy into activity. If we grasp the fact that we can prevail only through God's strength, then we shall pour energy into prayer as well' (p. 136).

---

11 In what ways is Hannah's prayer a model for ours as well?

Psalm 2 and Acts 4
9. Praying with the psalmist (pp. 138–151)

1 'Praying with the psalmist is not straightforward' (p. 139). Why not?
2 Why is Psalm 2 a good place to begin exploring what it means to pray with the psalmist?
3 What is the basic message of Psalm 2? How is this brought out by its structure?
4 How does Psalm 2 shape the prayer of the church in Acts 4?
5 What is the 'one unifying factor in human behaviour' (p. 143)? How does God respond to this?
6 '… celebrating the kingdom of God helps us put the din of the nations in perspective …' (p. 145). What does this mean in practice?
7 In what way does Psalm 2 speak of 'the proclamation of the gospel' (p. 145)?

'[God] is a gracious enemy who does not come by stealth, but announces his coming through his people so that men and women have the opportunity to escape his judgment' (p. 146).

---

8 What scope is there for more boldness in the way you communicate the gospel? How do Psalm 2 and Acts 4 help?
9 In what ways is the psalter 'the prayer book of Jesus Christ' (p. 147)? What difference does this make to the way we read the psalms?
10 What do you make of Walter Brueggemann's suggested categorization of the psalms?
11 Why is it important not to 'divorce the psalms from the Christian gospel' (p. 149)? How does this help when facing some of the difficulties raised by the psalms?
12 Does your spirituality 'allow you to express indignation before God' (p. 150)? Why is this important?

Matthew 6
10. Praying as Jesus taught us (pp. 152–172)

1 Does the teaching of Jesus in Matthew 6:5–6 mean that Christians should avoid prayer meetings? Why not? What does he mean, then?

2 In verse 7 is Jesus discouraging us from praying for sustained periods of time? What is he saying?

3 Do you see prayer as 'a mechanism to make things happen' (p. 156)? What is the problem with this view?

4 'True prayer arises as we ...' (p. 157). How does the author complete this statement? What distorts true prayer?

5 What is the best way of using the Lord's Prayer? What does it mean to describe it as 'the "true Exodus" prayer of God's people' (p. 158)?

6 What exactly are we asking for in the request 'Hallowed be your name'?

7 What does the author mean by describing the Lord's Prayer as 'an eschatological prayer – even an apocalyptic prayer' (p. 162)?

8 How might 'Give us today our daily bread' be more accurately translated? What difference does this make to the meaning of the phrase?

9 What does the author mean when he describes the focus of the Lord's Prayer as being 'eschatological'? How does this apply in relation to debts and testing?

'As we pray the Lord's Prayer in the present, we reorient ourselves to God's promised future and live afresh in the light of Christ's coming' (p. 166).

---

10 'The Lord's Prayer gives us a window on to the priorities of Jesus ...' (p. 166). What do these turn out to be? How far do they match your priorities in life?

11 How is the kingdom of God advanced? What part do you play in this?

12 What is the 'best commentary' (p. 168) on the phrase 'Forgive us our debts, as we also have forgiven our debtors'? Why?

13 '... prayer to God cannot ignore my relationships with my neighbours' (p. 170). Why not? How might this be relevant to you?

14 What 'unique' (p. 175) aspect of Jesus' vocation does the Lord's Prayer highlight?

15 How would you answer the questions with which this chapter closes – 'Do we really want Christ to come today? Do we long to exchange the treasure of earth for the treasure of heaven?' (p. 172)

John 14 – 17
11. Praying with Jesus (pp. 173–187)

1 What promise is made six times in Jesus' final discourse to his disciples? Do you find this 'embarrassing' (p. 173)? Why?
2 'John does not portray Jesus as a man of prayer in the way the Synoptic Gospels do' (p. 173). Why not? What does he emphasize, then?
3 Given that 'we cannot repeat John 17 as our own prayer' (p. 174), how can this chapter help us in our thinking about prayer?
4 What are the 'greater things' that those who have faith in Jesus will do? How do John 14:12–14, John 15:7–8, 16 and John 16:23–24, 26–27 shape your view of what it means to pray in Jesus' name?
5 How would you answer someone who wanted to use Jesus' promises to give us whatever we ask in his name as a 'blank cheque' (p. 177)?

'How … crazy for us … to treat God like a genie we control through prayer, to imagine that his great power can be harnessed to please our whims' (p. 178).

---

6 How can we pray John 17:1–5 'with Jesus' (p. 180)?
7 What can we learn from what Jesus asks for his disciples in John 17:6–19, and in John 17:20–26 for those who believe as a result of their message?
8 If we follow the example of Jesus in this chapter, what will be 'at the heart of our praying' (p. 186)? In what ways do you put this into practice?

Ephesians 3, Philippians 1 and Colossians 1
12. Praying with Paul (pp. 188–205)

Ephesians 3
1 In praying for power, what specific purpose does Paul have in mind?

2 What is the 'central theme of Ephesians' (p. 189)? How does this find its focus in Christ?

3 'God did not save an ad hoc collection of individuals and then arrange for them to meet each Sunday morning' (p. 191). What did he do, then? What was God's purpose in establishing the church?

4 'At the heart of much evangelical piety is the individual soul before God' (p. 192). In what way can this be a problem? To what extent do you identify with what the author describes here?

Philippians 1

5 What enables Paul to pray with joy?

6 Why is Paul so keen to pray that his friends will 'grow in knowledge'?

'*True Christian moral reasoning depends on an intellect informed by the gospel* and *an inclination shaped by the gospel*' (p. 196).

---

7 What is the important point to note about Paul's request that his friends 'might be able to discern what is best'?

8 What exactly does Paul mean when he asks for lives to be 'pure and blameless'?

Colossians 1

9 What factors make this prayer a particular model for us?

10 What lies at the heart of Paul's prayer here? Why was this such an issue at Colosse?

11 How enthusiastic are you to lead 'a life worthy of the Lord'? What do you think this means?

'*The worst sin is prayerlessness ... The history of the saints shows often that their lapses were the fruit and nemesis of slackness or neglect in prayer*' (p. 202, quoting P. T. Forsyth).

---

12 What 'four characteristics of a life that pleases Jesus' (p. 202) does Paul set out here?

13 How do your priorities in prayer match those of the apostle Paul?

1 Timothy 1 – 2
13. Praying together for the world (pp. 206–219)

1 What is superficially 'odd' (p. 206) about 1 Timothy 2:8? How does what Paul says have 'a contemporary edge'?

2 What concerns for the church at Ephesus does Paul express through his letter to Timothy?
3 What characteristics of false teaching does Paul highlight here?

'It is hard to remain bitter and divided when you are together in prayer' (p. 211).

---

4 What is the main thrust of Paul's instruction about prayer in 1 Timothy 2:1–8? How does this link with what he has been saying in chapter 1?
5 'Evangelistic activity and evangelistic prayer are reciprocally related' (p. 213). Why is this? How does it work out in practice?
6 Referring to 1 Timothy 2:2, 'Paul's prayer is not that Christians avoid a life of trouble' (p. 213). What is it, then?
7 In what ways do these verses present 'a great rationale for world mission' (p. 214)?
8 'It is all too easy for us to live in two worlds with one set of values operating in church and another at work' (p. 215). How true is this of you?
9 'The basis of prayer for the world is ...' (p. 216). What? Why is this so important?
10 What is 'the challenge of 1 Timothy 1 and 2' (p. 218)? To what extent does this apply to you?
11 What scope is there for the groups to which you belong to become more like 'hotbeds of missionary activity' (p. 219)?

Ephesians 6
14. Praying in the battle (pp. 220–231)

1 In Ephesians 6 what does Paul mean by 'the powers'?
2 What are the different ways of understanding them in today's world? Which do you think is correct?
3 How does Paul describe the nature of effective spiritual warfare?
4 'It is clear that the armour of God is ...' (p. 227) What? How do we put this armour on?

'To stand is to remain true to gospel truth in the face of a hostile world and to remain true to gospel living in the face of a beguiling enemy' (p. 227).

---

5 Why is it important to stress that spiritual warfare is a corporate act?

6 If it is true that 'spiritual warfare is to proclaim the gospel' (p. 228), how effective a soldier are you?

7 In the light of this passage, why is prayer often a struggle? What distracts you from making it a priority?

Mark 15
15. Praying when God is silent (pp. 232–245)

1 What experience have you had of 'hearing only the silence of God' (p. 233)?

2 How does the story of Job help us to come to terms with the problem of suffering?

3 What perspective does the cross of Jesus bring into this discussion?

'There cannot be a more desolate, poignant and terrible moment in all of history and eternity' (p. 236).

---

4 What is 'so extraordinary' (p. 237) about the centurion's statement that Jesus was the Son of God? How is this seen as 'the climax of Mark's Gospel'?

5 What did Martin Luther mean by *absconditus Deus*? How does this help with the problem of suffering?

6 In what ways is it the case that this 'world bears the mark of Good Friday still' (p. 242)? How do you experience this?

7 'There is a triumphalism that says the only experience of the church is success' (p. 242). In what ways does this echo your experience? What is the answer to it?

8 What truths are underlined by the references to 'the prayers of the saints' in Revelation?

'In the midst of the mess that is life in this world the curtain is torn and God beckons us forward to his heaven' (p. 245).

Ephesians 1
16. Praying in eternal perspective (pp. 246–257)

1 How would you answer someone who suggested that prayer is more about changing us than about changing the situations for which we pray?

2 Does God ever change his mind? What evidence is there on each side of the question?

3 What do you think of the idea that 'God has limited his omnipotence to give his creatures genuine freedom' (p. 253)?

'We express our belief in God's sovereignty most when we pray in the expectation that God can intervene in human lives and human history to bring about the things for which we pray' (p. 251).

---

4 How is it possible to hold together the ideas that God changes reality in response to our prayers and also that he is sovereign?

5 Why does praying that 'someone will be more aware of their hope' (p. 253) matter so much? What examples can you add to those the author suggests?

6 'We should let the future return of Christ determine the priorities of our prayers' (p. 255). What would this do to how you pray?

7 What is 'the great incentive to prayer' (p. 257) with which the author concludes?

The Bible Speaks Today series

Genesis 1—11
David Atkinson

Genesis 12—50
Joyce G. Baldwin

Numbers
Raymond Brown

Deuteronomy
Raymond Brown

Judges
Michael Wilcock

Ruth
David Atkinson

Chronicles
Michael Wilcock

Nehemiah
Raymond Brown

Job
David Atkinson

Psalms 1—72
Michael Wilcock

Psalms 73—150
Michael Wilcock

Proverbs
David Atkinson

Ecclesiastes
Derek Kidner

Song of Songs
Tom Gledhill

Isaiah
Barry Webb

Jeremiah
Derek Kidner

Ezekiel
Christopher J. H. Wright

Daniel
Ronald S. Wallace

Hosea
Derek Kidner

Joel, Micah & Habakkuk
David Prior

Amos
J. A. Motyer

Jonah
Rosemary A. Nixon

Matthew
Michael Green

Sermon on the Mount (Matthew 5—7)
John R. W. Stott

Mark
Donald English

Luke
Michael Wilcock

John
Bruce Milne

Acts
John R. W. Stott

Romans
John R. W. Stott

1 Corinthians
David Prior

2 Corinthians
Paul Barnett

Galatians
John R. W. Stott

Ephesians
John R. W. Stott

Philippians
J. A. Motyer

Colossians & Philemon
R. C. Lucas

1 & 2 Thessalonians
John R. W. Stott

1 Timothy & Titus
John R. W. Stott

2 Timothy
John R. W. Stott

Hebrews
Raymond Brown

James
J. A. Motyer

1 Peter
Edmund P. Clowney

2 Peter & Jude
Dick Lucas & Christopher Green

John's Letters
David Jackman

Revelation
Michael Wilcock